Paddling
AMERICA

Paddling
AMERICA

Discover and Explore Our 50 Greatest Wild and Scenic Rivers

SUSAN AND ADAM ELLIOTT

FALCON®

Guilford, Connecticut

FALCONGUIDES®

An imprint of The Rowman & Littlefield Publishing Group, Inc.
4501 Forbes Blvd., Ste. 200
Lanham, MD 20706
www.rowman.com

Falcon and FalconGuides are registered trademarks and Make Adventure Your Story
is a trademark of The Rowman & Littlefield Publishing Group, Inc.

Distributed by NATIONAL BOOK NETWORK

British Library Cataloguing-in-Publication Information available

Library of Congress Cataloging-in-Publication Data available

ISBN 978-1-4930-3368-3 (paperback)
ISBN 978-1-4930-3369-0 (e-book)

∞™ The paper used in this publication meets the minimum requirements of American National Standard for Information Sciences—Permanence of Paper for Printed
Library Materials, ANSI/NISO Z39.48-1992.

Printed in the United States of America

For Juniper Alma
May you get to experience more wild places than us.

The Skagit River has many great
emerald pools. ADAM ELLIOTT

Contents

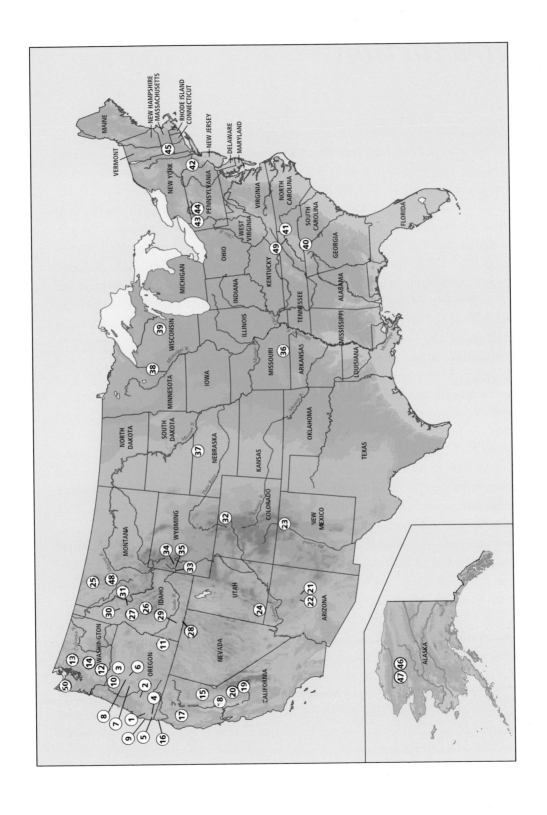

Introduction

Our home-on-wheels, a 24-foot Coachman Catalina RV we call Gilly, rolled up to the Casa Loma store near the Tuolumne River in California. We stopped in the cafe, ordered burritos, and waited for our friends to meet us at the corner. That day, we would cross off the Tuolumne from our list of national Wild and Scenic rivers. We repeated this day over fifty times on our Wild River Life tour, a road trip aimed at paddling fifty of the most beautiful, most wild, most scenic, and most beloved rivers across our country.

We started this tour with very little understanding of what it meant for a river to be designated as Wild and Scenic. With the fiftieth anniversary of the Wild & Scenic Rivers Act approaching in 2018, our desire to know more about these rivers grew. We had an itch to live simply while traveling across America, and so we sold everything, moved into an RV, and hit the road as the Wild River Life. In addition to floating these rivers, we also hoped to increase awareness about this form of river protection. This guidebook is part of that effort: to share what we learned along the way and encourage more people to know these spectacular rivers.

Our river exploration aspirations began long before Wild River Life. Adam learned to kayak and raft at a young age on the big, muddy waters of the Southwest. As soon as he could, he began guiding multiday river trips on Utah's San Juan River, then on the Colorado River through the Grand Canyon. He traveled to China to guide Chinese citizens on their iconic home rivers, manage a rafting company, and slip away for first descents on the edge of the Tibetan plateau when he could. His boat and camera further propelled him around the world, to the Brazilian jungle with National Geographic TV's *Monster Fish* and to Mexico's waterfalls with River Roots's *Chasing Niagara*.

Susan jumped in her own boat soon after her first trip as a commercial whitewater rafting guest while in high school in Pennsylvania. As a raft guide, kayak instructor, and traveling high school teacher, she devoted years to exploring rivers from New York to South Carolina, Montana to California, and internationally in Ecuador, Mexico, Peru, and China. Today, with a graduate degree in hand, she's on her way to helping repair and enhance river systems as a river restoration engineer and scientist. And as a member of the board of directors for American Whitewater, she is helping this non-profit organization improve access to, and the health of, rivers nationwide.

As we explored, we increasingly recognized a scarcity of healthy river systems. The Great Bend of the Yangtze, the section of river where we first met, was transformed by massive dams and disappeared under a series of mammoth, stairstep reservoirs. Towns and cities sent their raw sewage and smoldering landfills into rivers, where

The Wild River Life family now totals four! ADAM ELLIOTT

these problems would move downstream. Rampant and unplanned development pushed natural rivers into concrete ditches or underneath growing urban sprawl. With each trip we found ourselves even more grateful to return home to our own nation's healthy ecosystems, pristine watersheds, and protected rivers. We soon came to realize that the United States is the only country in the world with a national protected system of rivers.

And so, with our gear trailer loaded with kayaks, packrafts, stand-up paddleboards, and a complete multiday raft kit, we set out from our home in White Salmon, Washington, to not only paddle America's Wild and Scenic rivers but also to inspire others to do the same.

As the road trip rolled on, we learned that we would give birth to our daughter halfway through the project. We began imagining the rivers through the eyes of a child. We dreamt of her first Wild and Scenic float trip. We wondered what these rivers would look like to a one-year-old, to a five-year-old, to a ten-year-old. Would the river still feel pristine for her? Would more rivers be protected? We realized that our work promoting these rivers may mean our daughter will be able to experience them in their wild states. Perhaps our work would even help protect new Wild and Scenic rivers for her to enjoy. We certainly hope she will learn that none of us can take a protected, free-flowing river for granted. Rather, we must celebrate these rivers frequently, preferably with a paddle in hand.

See you on the river.

The Wild & Scenic Rivers Act

WILD AND SCENIC ORIGINS

Damage to our rivers in the decades leading up to the 1960s became the primary impetus for the Wild & Scenic Rivers Act. Our nation went dam crazy. Rivers became reservoirs, water quality plummeted, fish stocks disappeared, and both upstream and downstream ecosystems suffered greatly. The Clean Water Act helped the pollution problem, but our nation continued to erase, plug up, and relocate entire rivers to satisfy development and population growth.

It took several specific and fortuitous events to spawn the Wild & Scenic Rivers Act. Coincidental meetings between wilderness advocates and congressional staff fostered unlikely legislative champions. Scientific literature began to publish research that pointed to the essential role of free-flowing rivers in the health and integrity of broader landscapes. Conservation organizations became empowered to take action.

Of course, without key outspoken proponents, the Wild & Scenic Rivers Act would never have passed. Frank and John Craighead, a pair of candid brothers, zealously committed themselves to preventing the West's pristine rivers from suffering a similar ruin as their favorite childhood streams on the East Coast. Pollution and development had pushed the waterways of their youth to extinction, and the brothers fought hard to stave off such misfortune in other regions.

Most importantly, local advocates everywhere began to speak up for their backyard rivers. In his book *Wild and Scenic Rivers: An American Legacy,* Tim Palmer reminds us that "every stream in the Wild and Scenic system was added because people were motivated to save their waterway, if not from the explicit threat of a dam that would completely bury their place under a reservoir, then from strip mining, clear-cutting or overdevelopment." It took this collection of figures, moments, and ideas to catalyze the Wild & Scenic Rivers Act.

NATIONAL RIVER PROTECTION BEGINS

On October 2, 1968, President Lyndon Johnson signed the Wild & Scenic Rivers Act. The original eight designations actually included twelve separate rivers. For instance, the Saint Croix River designation also covered over 100 miles of the Namekagon River, a major tributary, in addition to about 100 miles on the St. Croix.

Today, the official count of designated rivers is at 208, as listed in the sections of the public law identifying the rivers. However, in his extensive research, Wild and Scenic expert Tim Palmer has determined an alternate method of counting that considers cases where a designated river also includes tributaries over 5 miles in length. He found a total of 289 rivers protected by the act as of 2017. Still, the total number of actual river miles (12,734) is less than half of 1 percent of our nation's total river miles. The system has room for growth to say the least.

Alaska has 3,210 river miles protected, the most of any state. California comes in second with 1,999.6 miles, and Oregon at 1,916.7 miles, a close third. Oregon has the most number of rivers in the system, fifty-nine total, followed by California with forty-one rivers and Alaska with thirty rivers. However, while Alaska ranks high with these rankings, only 0.8 percent of the state's mileage is protected as Wild and Scenic. California does slightly better with a full 1 percent of miles protected and Oregon a whopping 2 percent. This will explain why we chose to feature so many rivers from both California and Oregon, and two longer trips from Alaska.

"AN UNSPOILED RIVER IS A VERY RARE THING IN THIS NATION TODAY. THEIR FLOW AND VITALITY HAVE BEEN HARNESSED BY DAMS AND TOO OFTEN THEY HAVE BEEN TURNED INTO OPEN SEWERS BY COMMUNITIES AND BY INDUSTRIES. IT MAKES US ALL VERY FEARFUL THAT ALL RIVERS WILL GO THIS WAY UNLESS SOMEBODY ACTS NOW TO TRY TO BALANCE OUR RIVER DEVELOPMENT."

—President Lyndon Johnson's remarks on signing the Wild & Scenic Rivers Act, October 2, 1968

THE ORIGINAL EIGHT RIVERS AND MAJOR TRIBUTARIES

Middle Fork Clearwater River, Idaho (including the Lochsa and Selway Rivers in Idaho)

Middle Fork Feather River, California

Eleven Point River, Missouri

Rio Grande, New Mexico (including the Red River in New Mexico)

Middle Fork Salmon River, Idaho

Saint Croix River, Minnesota and Wisconsin (including Namekagon River, Wisconsin)

Wolf River, Wisconsin

Rogue River, Oregon

CLASSIFICATIONS

Each segment of river carries one of three different classifications. We think of these as a spectrum that ranges from highly inaccessible and pristine to easily accessible with evidence of development:

1. *Recreational*: River sections easily accessed by a road, some development visible along shorelines and forms of impoundment (such as diversions or dams) may have existed in the past.

2. *Scenic*: Rivers with road access in a few places and mostly primitive shorelines.

3. *Wild*: Rivers only accessible by trail, flowing through largely intact landscapes that are remnants of America's past.

> The classifications also lead to naming convention confusion. Rivers can be classified as just *Scenic*, or just *Wild*, or just *Recreational*, or have a combination of classifications on different segments of river. All of these rivers are referred to as "Wild and Scenic rivers."

OUTSTANDINGLY REMARKABLE VALUES

Each designated river must have one or more Outstandingly Remarkable Values that make the place worth protecting. These could be cultural, recreational, scenic, historic, fisheries, wildlife, water quality, and more. Each river receives a comprehensive river management plan designed to protect and enhance these specific values, as well as to ensure no new dams or development projects be built that could diminish the free-flowing nature of the river or the integrity of the Outstandingly Remarkable Values. Because these values helped the river earn a designation, they are worth knowing before a visit to the river. They make these rivers extraordinary. Familiarity with this list may also lead to a greater sense of joint ownership for our public waterways, and the motivation to stand up and help protect more rivers.

HOW DOES A RIVER GET INTO THE WILD AND SCENIC SYSTEM?

"There is no such thing as an immaculate designation," comments Kevin Colburn, American Whitewater's national stewardship director. "The stork does not deliver Wild and Scenic Rivers. Designation takes action!"

Kevin and his team have helped local advocates protect many rivers. They know the process is far from easy. "Designations take an incredible amount of hard work by people with the vision and persistence to build support in local communities and take it all the way to the halls of Congress," he says. "And then, the political stars have to align in a complex and dynamic way so that Congress prioritizes and passes legislation."

Signage marks the Wild and Scenic Granite Creek in the Snake River Headwaters. ADAM ELLIOTT

To put it simply, in most cases citizens work with a senator or representative to propose one or more rivers for designation within a bill. Eventually it will be voted upon by all of Congress and signed into law by the President.

A second approach occurs when a state governor requests the Secretary of the Interior to designate a river. To take this path, the river must first carry a state-level designation or be administered by a federal agency.

Prior to designation, river management agencies study rivers to determine if they are potential additions to the system based on their free-flowing status and at least one Outstandingly Remarkable Value. The public can get involved in this stage and share what makes specific rivers worthy of protection. These agency-recognized streams are ideal candidates for future designation and are typically afforded some level of interim protection.

A FUTURE OF RIVER PROTECTION

While the Wild & Scenic Rivers Act protects many iconic river reaches, such as the Middle Fork Salmon, the Flathead, and the Delaware, these make up only a fraction of the free-flowing rivers necessary for healthy ecosystems and economies. "Without more designations, in 100 or even 500 years our nation will have lost many outstanding rivers," comments Colburn. And while rivers may be valuable when harnessed for development, they also provide great value as a wild resource. Free-flowing rivers perform vital ecosystem services for free that would be costly and cumbersome to recreate (see "The Science of Free-Flowing Rivers" on pages 204-205). As a reminder that we must continue to protect more or our rivers, we chose to include three "Future Wild and Scenic Rivers" in our top 50 (see #48 North Fork Blackfoot, #49 Nolichucky, and #50 Sol Duc Rivers). "Rivers belong to all of us," claims Colburn. "They are valuable for recreation-based economies, for the fish and clean water they bring us, and for the magnetic and inspiring solace of wild-flowing water."

How to Use this Book

We hope that this guidebook inspires you to explore the rivers that others have fought hard to protect. As you flip through the following descriptions keep in mind these few pointers:

- We chose to focus on sections of designated Wild and Scenic rivers with some of the best paddling opportunities. The mileage presented in the descriptions and maps reflects the specific paddling section and not the entire designated reach (total length).
- Always be prepared for changing weather, wear a personal flotation device (PFD), bring other important safety equipment, scout when you are unsure of a line, and employ more basic river-running skills. If you are new to paddling, great! Consider taking a swiftwater rescue course (Rescue3.com) if you want to be planning your own trips.
- Difficulty ratings are given for average flows. Rapids may increase in difficulty due to high or low flows. Additionally, one person's class III is also another person's class IV. Use the flow range provided and other Internet or guidebook resources to determine if the river is flowing low, medium, or high. When the difficulty rating is presented in parenthesis, such as the Jarbidge River's class III–IV (V) rating, the rapid in parenthesis can be portaged. This will help you understand how challenging the rapids may be.
- We generally only illustrate rapids at or above a class III rating and describe those that are most memorable. We avoid detailed descriptions of class V–V+ rapids. You'll need to do your own research there for safety reasons. Also, remember that free-flowing rivers change from year to year, and these descriptions may not include those continual changes.

Paddlers use the terminology "river right" and "river left" to orient themselves on a river. "River right" will always be the right side when facing downstream. Same with river left.

"We live in a van down by the river!" Adam and Susan pack up Gilly, the roadhome, while Wallace supervises. ADAM ELLIOTT

- We aim to entice you to plan a few Wild and Scenic trips through stunning images, richly descriptive prose, and basic logistics. In some cases, you'll want more information to prepare for your trip, especially for the multiday river trips. Use a river or state-specific guidebook to see campsite descriptions, read about hazards, understand regulations, and learn more about your Wild and Scenic sojourn. Most paddling trips can also be found in the national river database compiled at AmericanWhitewater.org.

Susan takes a break from her kayak to row the raft on the Illinois River. ADAM ELLIOTT

Map Legend

⟨84⟩	Interstate	⋏	Access	
⟨30⟩	U.S. Highway	⌣	Bridge	
⟨138⟩	State Road	⩕	Campground	
⟨33⟩	Local/County Road	▢	National Park	
-------	Trail	▣	National Forest/Recreation Area/Refuge	
— - — -	State Border	🅿	Parking	
⬭	Body of Water	▲	Peak	
∿	River/Creek	■	Point of Interest/Trailhead	
⋰⋅⋰	Intermittent Stream	⫽	Rapid	
〰	Wild River	⊡	Reservation	
〰	Scenic River	🗺	Scenic View	
〰	Recreational River	○	Town	
〰	Future Wild and Scenic River	❓	Visitor Center	
		≋	Waterfall	

Opposite: Susan and friends lower boats into one of the access points along the Elk River. ADAM ELLIOTT

Pacific
Northwest

The Rogue River is the quintessential western Wild and Scenic River, having nearly every single Outstandingly Remarkable Value. Adam Elliott

1

ROGUE RIVER

Section name	Grave Creek to Foster Bar
Distance	34 miles
Flow range	1,200–30,000 cfs
Season and source of water	Year-round season; dam release upstream and slow snowmelt
Gauge location	Agness, USGS #14372300
Time required	3–4 days
Classification	*Wild*
Difficulty	II–IV
Managing agency	Bureau of Land Management, Medford District; Rogue River–Siskiyou National Forest
Permit required?	Yes
Shuttle type	Vehicle
Outstandingly Remarkable Values	Fisheries, recreational, scenery
Why paddle this section?	Really fun rapids, superb mountain scenery, protected for over five decades, inevitable bear sightings

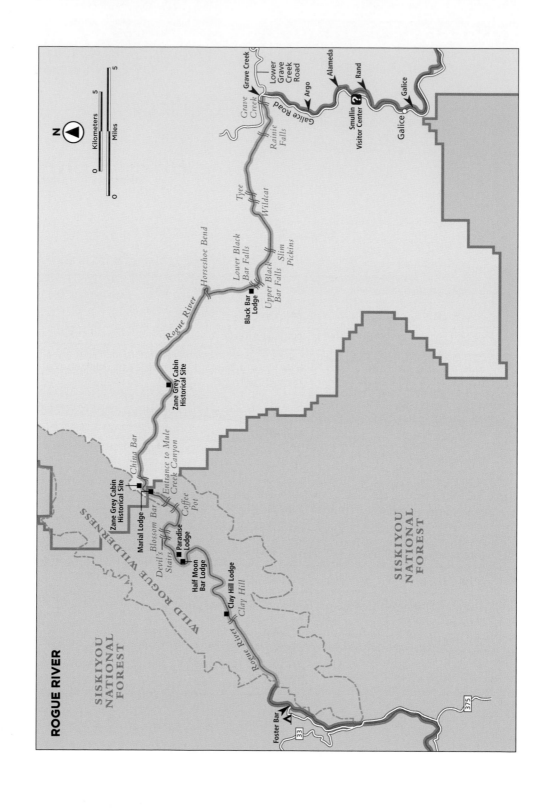

RIVER DESCRIPTION

Descending from Crater Lake National Park, in the high Cascade Mountains of south-western Oregon, to the Pacific Ocean, the Rogue River has long captivated American explorers. Native Americans flocked to the river's cold and powerful waters for the abundance of salmon and to the fertile lands alongside. Gold miners discovered riches along the river's banks. Today, every river runner yearns to add the legendary Rogue to his or her list of familiar watersheds.

Craggy but smooth rocks jut from the water that manipulate currents and create rapids that entice both intermediate river runners looking to paddle their own boats and novice adventurers joining a commercial trip. Along the banks of the river, the geologic foundation is covered by a rich and complex Siskiyou forest ecosystem with cascading mountain streams and rugged terrain. The Rogue's rich wildlife and remarkable beauty combine with a storied history of Native Americans and early settlers to make the Rogue many paddlers' favorite yearly river trip. It's no surprise that the Rogue joined the "original eight" rivers signed into the Wild & Scenic Rivers Act in 1968.

Takelma Native Americans lived in the upper Rogue River area until floods of settlers entered the valley in search of gold in the 1850s. Encounters between the groups were not pleasant, and soon the Natives were forced onto reservations far away. Evidence of all former residents can be found along the Rogue and within the valley.

Commercial outfitters have really upped their game on this classic river stretch: Specialty food and wine trips provide a gourmet camping experience; brewer-hosted trips provide guests with an opportunity to sample an impressive array of local craft beers; and classic lodge-to-lodge trips allow river runners to experience a river-accessible lodge each night. Check out Northwest Rafting Company (nwrafting.com) for some of these options.

We must apologize to the Rogue River for shortening this description to only the section between Grave Creek and Foster Bar. *Recreational* and *Scenic* designations extend both upstream and downstream of this *Wild* total length, which is simply the most iconic. Many groups begin their trips at or upstream of Galice, a small outpost and shuttle hub. This upper section also provides a day or two of class II warm-up before descending below Grave Creek. Other trips continue downstream past Foster Bar. You'll just have to plan multiple trips to this watershed to see it all.

PADDLER'S NOTES

Between May 15 and October 15 all river runners need a lottery-issued permit to float this section of the Rogue. All other times of year there is a self-issued permit system. Apply for a lottery system permit in December and January of each year at Recreation.gov. If you don't win the lottery, you can also call the BLM Smullin

Visitor Center at Rand (541-479-3735) to try to pick up cancellations for the near future or show up at Rand (just upstream from Grave Creek) first thing the morning of your desired launch and pick up same-day cancellation spots. Commercial outfitters will release their user days to the public a few days prior to launch if they have not sold them by then.

Numerous class II rapids fill the gaps in between the class III–IV rapids described here. The first of these comes within earshot of the put-in. Grave Creek Riffle and Falls, a typical Rogue whitewater specimen, will get you wet immediately.

A calmer float carries you to the pool above Rainie Falls. "Old Man Rainie," an early settler, lived in a small cabin at the base of the falls in the early 1900s. Take your time on the scout from river left. Often salmon can be seen jumping up the falls. The left channel will lead you over the actual falls, a class IV drop at most water levels and class V at high water. Most boaters opt to take the far-right line through the fish ladder. This involves a tricky dance of shipping your oars, lining through tight spots, and even using a bow paddler to prevent broaching. Some boats take the middle chute, just as narrow and technical as the fish ladder but with a steeper drop at the end. Above 3,000 cubic feet per second (cfs), guard rocks in the entrance to the middle chute could send you left over Rainie Falls.

The next class III, Tyee, at river mile 4.8, channels boaters to the right, where some zigzagging moves help avoid a pour-over or hole feature. Slim Pickins, at river mile 6.8, received its name from the early days of blasting the riverbed to open up the channel. A double-punch comes just 2 miles downstream at Upper and Lower Blackbar Falls rapids. A long class II straightaway leads to Horseshoe Bend rapid around— yes—a tight bend in the river at river mile 10.5.

Enjoy a peaceful stretch before whitewater returns at the China Bar rapid at river mile 21.5, just upstream of Rogue River Ranch. The ranch's historical museum is worth a peak and the big green lawn out front deserves an Ultimate Frisbee match.

Suddenly, just 1 mile downstream, rock walls pinch from both shorelines and force the entire river's powerful flow into the narrow slot between them. This is Mule Creek Canyon, a class IV reach. This one is hard to scout, but it's possible from the Rogue River trail. Geologic shifting has occurred in your favor here, with little gradient change within these walls. However, the boils and speed of the water absolutely keep smaller boats on their toes. The Coffee Pot churns about a quarter mile from the head of the canyon; it's a seething whirlpool boil that can flip a fully loaded raft at certain flows. Set safety just below here to throw a rope to any swimmers who may enter the Pot. Eddy out on the left toward the end of the canyon to enjoy Stair Creek Falls.

Blossom Bar, a class IV rapid, sits just around the bend. Pull over on the right to walk downstream to scout and watch other paddlers' lines. Rafts take the left channel with a quick ferry move back to the center to avoid a jumble of pinning rocks called

The Rogue River can be a quiet and peaceful place in the evenings.

the Picket Fence that extends from the left bank. There is a good chance you'll even see a deflated and pinned raft on the fence during busy summer months—not a fun way to end your trip.

Shortly after the pool at the base of Blossom Bar, the river enters the Devil's Stairs, where you follow the main tongue down the right, taking care to avoid the wall along river right.

The class III action dwindles after Devil's Stairs and you'll begin to see jet boat tours motoring upstream. Luckily, they aren't permitted above Blossom Bar during the peak whitewater season. Lots of great camping, hiking, swimming, and cliff jumping await you on the rest of the river trip, such as at Clay Hill camp or Flora Dell Falls.

The variety of river campsites along the Rogue River makes each night different. There are too many to include in this description or on the map, but you'll want to grab a copy of the Rogue River float guidebook anyway. The Bureau of Land Management (BLM) has a guide available for download from its website with detailed descriptions and locations of each campsite.

Bears have historically ravaged rafters' food stashes from coolers, dry boxes, and anything nylon. River managers worked hard to educate river runners about bear safety and have even constructed several electric bear enclosures at high-use camps. Thanks to this effort, far fewer incidents of curious and hungry bears are reported today, but bear sightings are still very common.

Warm summer afternoons and fine cliff jumping on the Rogue River.
NATE WILSON / NORTHWEST RAFTING COMPANY

DIRECTIONS TO TAKEOUT

Setting shuttle over Bear Camp Road takes nearly a full day, and for this reason most river runners hire a shuttle service. The Galice Resort, (541) 476-3818, offers shuttles, among others. From Merlin, continue on Galice Road until you arrive in Galice in 11.5 miles. To drop a car at the takeout, turn left (away from the river) on Galice Creek Road. Bring a map to navigate any unmarked junctions. Turn right at the T, when this road hits Agness Road. In 2 miles turn right to reach Foster Bar. Bear Camp Road closes for nearly all of November to May due to snow. Shuttles during these months involve a trip out to the Oregon coast and a dip into northern California.

DIRECTIONS TO PUT-IN

From Galice, Grave Creek access site is just 7 miles downstream. You'll pass other boat launch options along the way that work great as well.

NEARBY ATTRACTIONS

The Illinois Wild and Scenic River flows into the Rogue just downstream of the Foster Bar takeout. The mountains surrounding the Rogue also beckon more days of outdoor play, as well as the rugged southern Oregon coast. Oh, and you are practically a step away from Northern California, so head down toward the Smith River drainage for more excellent excursion options.

NORTH UMPQUA RIVER

Section name	Boulder Flat to Gravel Bin
Distance	14 miles
Flow range	500—5,000 cfs
Season and source of water	Occasionally all year; fall and winter rain, spring snowmelt into summer
Gauge location	Above Copeland Creek near Toketee Falls, USGS #14316500
Time required	1 day
Classification	*Recreational*
Difficulty	III (IV)
Managing agency	Umpqua National Forest
Permit required?	No
Shuttle type	Vehicle
Outstandingly Remarkable Values	Culture, fisheries, recreation, scenery, water quality
Why paddle this section?	Great balance of fun class III and spectacular scenery, incredible fisheries, and a vibrant forest ecosystem; a perfect weekend escape

RIVER DESCRIPTION

The North Umpqua's long season and plentiful class III rapids make the run a favorite of every Northwest paddler. The river flows off the steep volcanoes of Oregon's Cascade Range. Evidence of the molten history can be seen in the towering basalt columns along the upper stretch of river. Many giant old-growth trees throughout the watershed have

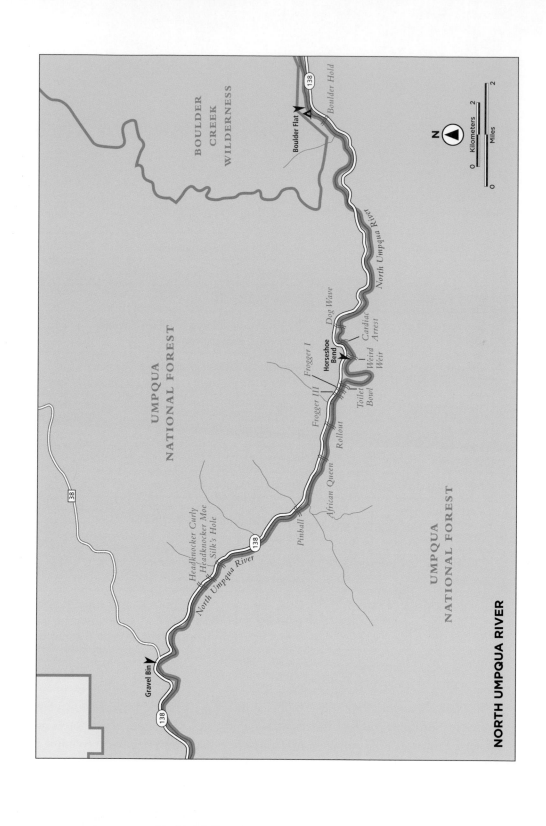

NORTH UMPQUA RIVER

Rafters bop down through one of the many class II boulder gardens. ADAM ELLIOTT

been preserved from the voracious logging days. Now surrounded by national forest land, where better long-term logging strategies are practiced, the Umpqua's riparian forest fills the corridor with the fresh, richly pure air of a healthy ecosystem.

Anglers began floating the run long ago. The North Umpqua's fish runs draw international notoriety. Beginning in the 1920s, prospectors, loggers, and explorers established fishing camps along the river to take home the legendary steelhead and salmon that use the river for spawning.

Today, fishing holes around the confluence of Steamboat Creek may offer the most popular angling in the country. For this reason, management plans dictate specific months when boating is restricted so that anglers can have the full right-of-way. These times of year mostly occur when flows are too low to float, or early or late enough in the day that river runners aren't inconvenienced. From July to October, paddlers can enjoy the river section described here from 10 a.m. until 6 p.m. Anglers get the dawn and dusk hours. Other months of the year, we're free to float anytime. Downstream of the Gravel Bin access site, boaters must stay off the water all day from July 15 to October 31.

For paddlers of any craft, the North Umpqua offers a quality day of whitewater and scenery without any major hazards or portages. Rafts, canoes, kayaks, and more can be seen throughout the season, as well as plenty of riverside relaxers in their camp chairs simply enjoying the river's famous blue pools and riffles.

PADDLER'S NOTES

The first class III rapid of the run, Boulder Hole, sits just below the launch site. A jumble of rocks and a ledge have boaters weaving through this rapid. Scouting can be done from eddies or shore. Float through some pools and mellow rapids before arriving at Dog Wave, where a sneaker hole pops up on the left at lower flows. Not far downstream you'll want to stay left of a large island and go over Cardiac Arrest rapid, a longer rapid that continues past the downstream end of the island. Weird Weir rapid will demand you stay right as well, avoiding some ledges on the left.

Horseshoe Bend river access immediately follows Weird Weir on the right. The campground is another quarter mile beyond the access site. To cut the float distance by about half, start or end your trip here.

After floating around the large bend that Horseshoe Bend is named for, you'll arrive at class III Toilet Bowl. Froggers I and III follow (no, Frogger II is not noteworthy). Pick your way through Rollout Rapid just downstream. In another mile you'll want to start right at the African Queen rapid, as the river bends to the left and lands you in some punchy waves or a hole at the bottom.

Float under a bridge in about a mile, signifying that Pinball rapid, class IV, is nearby. Scouting is advisable from river left because the rapid is not easily portaged. Above the scouting spot on the left is an alligator wave that has been known to flip unprepared rafters busy looking for the scout eddy. Be alert even before the rapid to avoid this embarrassing possibility.

The final class III rapids on the run are Silk's Hole, Headknocker Moe, and Headknocker Curly just downstream. Float your way the final few miles to the Gravel Bin takeout site on river right, just before Steamboat Creek enters the main river.

DIRECTIONS TO TAKEOUT

From OR 99 south outside of Roseburg, turn left on North Bank Road. In a bit less than 17 miles you'll hit OR 138. Turn left here and head up the river on OR 138. Gravel Bin takeout is well marked at mile 40 on OR 138, on the right just past where Steamboat Creek flows into the North Umpqua.

DIRECTIONS TO PUT-IN

Continue upriver on OR 138 from the Gravel Bin takeout. To reach the takeout (or put-in) at Horseshoe Bend, look for US Forest Service Road 4750 near mile 46. Turn

Susan guides a paddle raft through the first hole in Pinball Rapid, North Fork Umpqua.
ADAM ELLIOTT

right here and follow signs to the boat ramp. Parking is limited at the Horseshoe Bend river access site, so shuttle most vehicles to the takeout at Gravel Bin if possible. For the Boulder Flat put-in, look for Boulder Flat Campground around mile 54 on OR 138. The boat ramp and noncamper parking is located to the right.

NEARBY ATTRACTIONS

The Umpqua National Forest in this area contains more recreation options than you can imagine. Bring your hiking shoes, mountain bikes, fishing rods, and camping gear if you want to truly experience this watershed. An easy option is the North Umpqua Trail, which follows most of the river and can be accessed at twelve different trailheads.

Toketee Falls, upstream of the section described here, epitomizes the epic punchbowl-style waterfall known throughout the Pacific Northwest. The river flows over this two-tiered 113-foot (total) waterfall, with tall, columnar basalt cliffs sandwiching the falls in on either side. A pipeline diverts most of the river's flow around the drop for power generation downstream, but a portion of the river flows over the drop all year nonetheless. During heavy rains, this waterfall swells enough to attract the world's elite kayakers for the plunge.

LOWER DESCHUTES RIVER

Section name	Macks Canyon to Heritage Landing; confluence with Columbia River
Distance	24 miles
Flow range	3,000–8,000 cfs
Season and source of water	Year-round; winter rain, and spring snowmelt with dam released flow throughout the year
Gauge location	Moody, USGS #14103000
Time required	1–3 days
Classification	*Recreational*
Difficulty	II (III)
Managing agency	Bureau of Land Management, Prineville District; Oregon Parks and Recreation Department; Confederated Tribes of Warm Springs
Permit required?	Yes
Shuttle type	Vehicle
Outstandingly Remarkable Values	Culture, fisheries, geology, recreation, scenery, wildlife, botany
Why paddle this section?	Year-round flows; beginner-friendly multiday river trip; a central Oregon classic

The Lower Deschutes is a classic example of the Scenic designation. It feels remote and has very little infrastructure, yet has some roadside access. ADAM ELLIOTT

RIVER DESCRIPTION

Many boaters claim the Lower Deschutes as their first multiday river trip. The ease of access, quality of scenery, steady flows, and beginner-level rapids attract boating parties throughout the year. Located less than two hours from Portland, the Lower Deschutes's vibrant hillsides glow in greens and yellows. Basalt cliff faces strike up from the hills as the river sweeps around large meanders and valleys and over gentle whitewater rapids. Boaters from the temperate and rainy climates of the western Cascades especially appreciate the sunshine and drier climate commonly found in this part of central Oregon throughout the year.

Spending a few days on the Lower Deschutes means extra time to explore the landscape and relax at one of many great campsites, some of which come equipped with pit toilets. The broad valley makes for excellent stargazing at night, as your campfire apple pie sizzles in the coals.

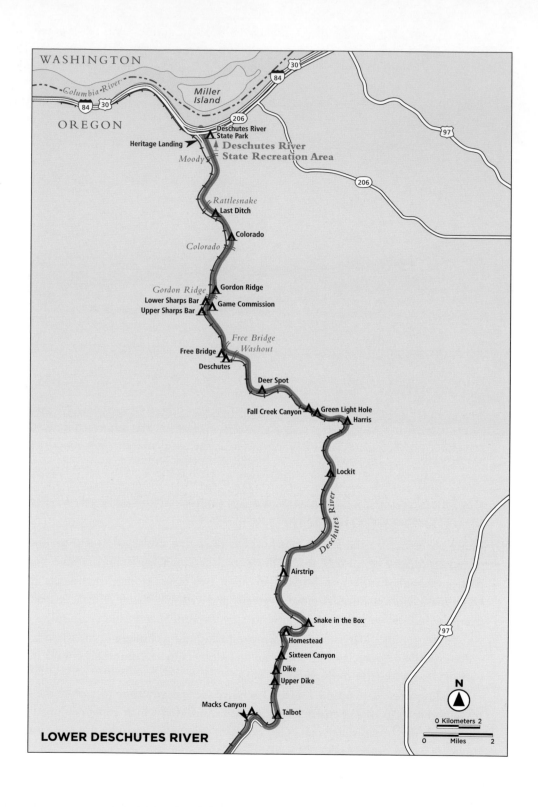

WASHINGTON

Columbia River

Miller Island

84
30

84 30

OREGON

206

97

Deschutes River
State Park

Heritage Landing

Deschutes River
State Recreation Area

Moody

206

Rattlesnake
Last Ditch

Colorado

Colorado

Gordon Ridge
Gordon Ridge

Lower Sharps Bar
Game Commission

Upper Sharps Bar

Free Bridge
Washout

Free Bridge

Deschutes

Deer Spot

Fall Creek Canyon
Green Light Hole

Harris

Lockit

Deschutes River

Airstrip

Snake in the Box

Homestead

Sixteen Canyon

Dike

Upper Dike

Macks Canyon

Talbot

N

97

0   Kilometers   2

0   Miles   2

LOWER DESCHUTES RIVER

From Mack's Landing to the confluence with the Columbia, no roads access the Lower Deschutes, making these final twenty-four miles particularly enjoyable. The lower river holds a *Recreational* designation for this entire reach, as well as for the seventy-six miles upstream. These hundred miles were included in the 1988 Omnibus Oregon National Wild & Scenic Rivers Act, along with thirty-nine other rivers. This act remains the largest river protection legislation effort in US history.

By the time the Deschutes approaches the Columbia River, it carries much of the water draining from the eastern Cascades. Upstream springs contribute a continuous flow, while Pelton Round Butte Hydroelectric Project also regulates the river to provide enough water for floating year-round. Motorboats are permitted on this stretch of river, but not all the time.

The Lower Deschutes's subsurface aquatic environment begs to be explored. Consider bringing your fishing pole or rod on your river trip. Expect to see several fishing parties out there taking advantage of the world-class steelhead and trout fisheries. Many boaters read the currents, eddies, and morphology of rivers from the surface, but those who understand fish behavior can read those currents underneath the surface as well. The two sets of knowledge complement each other and will inevitably increase your skills at reading and navigating water.

PADDLER'S NOTES

The BLM requires each boat to obtain a Boater Pass, found online at Recreation.gov. Check the Boater Pass schedule released by the BLM if you have trouble securing a permit, which is rare. The BLM releases more permits as launch dates get closer. Check the motor schedule to see if you'll be sharing the river with jet boats.

All rapids labeled on the map approach a class III difficulty level at average flows. Most of these are in the last ten miles of the run. Rafts often have few problems, while beginner kayakers may wish to follow someone more experienced to avoid swirly eddy lines and bigger waves.

Many more designated camps can be found as you float than the ones you'll see on the map. Look for the BLM maps of Lower Deschutes Section 4, downloaded from the website, for general locations of additional camps. Go for camps with a few trees to provide morning shade. The sun can be bright out there.

DIRECTIONS TO TAKEOUT

Heritage Landing river access site is located just off I-84. From Portland, take exit 97 for OR 206 toward Deschutes River State Park. In 2.5 miles turn right on Old Moody Road to reach Heritage Landing.

HOW TO COOK IN A DUTCH OVEN

The Dutch oven has long been hailed as the ultimate tool for backcountry gourmet mastery. Nothing bestows amazement at the campsite table like a warm and gooey cinnamon bun in the morning or a hearty chicken potpie after a long day's paddle. However, the Dutch oven also has a dubious reputation, as though you must possess a special sixth sense and decades of culinary expertise to use this antique kitchen appliance.

Well, we're here to help. Follow these simple tips to impress your river crew with a Dutch oven treat.

SET THE STAGE

Arranging your tools and prepping your coals greatly improves the finesse and success of your cooking performance. Gather the necessary tools and have them ready:

- *Oven*: Chose a model with feet and a lip around the lid.

- *Charcoal*: Don't skimp on the cheaper brands. They don't hold heat as well and can leave a dish only semi-cooked.

- *Fire pan*. We use two sturdy oil pans, but a proper fire pan can double as a grill.

- *Channel locks*: Indispensable. Keep a good 12-inch set of these pliers in your camp kitchen.

- *Hot mitts*: Because it will get hot.

- *Lighter*: Go with the long stick lighter variety.

- *Tongs*: A set of sturdy, long-handled tongs helps to move coals around. Mark them as the dedicated Dutch oven tongs so your salad doesn't end up with surprise bits of coal.

ASSEMBLE YOUR DISH

Begin food prep early. Chop veggies, braise your meat, or mix your brownie batter first, and then assemble your dish.

FIRE UP THE OVEN

Assemble 30 percent more coals than your dish needs into a briquette pyramid. The extra coals will keep as a small reserve on standby. Soak the pyramid with lighter fluid and light. Ash will cover the coals when they are ready, usually in about fifteen minutes.

ARRANGE THE COALS

Generally, brownies and cakes require about six coals on the bottom of your Dutch oven. The top will get a full outer ring of coals plus two coals placed in the center of the lid on the top. A casserole will get the same number of coals on top with a few extra on the bottom. A loaf of bread will get fewer both on top and bottom: six briquettes on the bottom with a sparser full ring on top (about three less than the other dishes).

TURN ON YOUR NOSE

The most impressive moment of the Dutch oven meal occurs as the chef simply "knows" the dish has finished cooking. To the non-Dutch chef this timing seems magical, when really it is all about the smell. Position your oven upwind of the camp circle and check in on the scents of your dish wafting through the air every few minutes. When the smell of cake, lasagna, baked bread, or whatever you chose to bake begins to tickle your nostrils, open the oven and check it. From here, keep a close eye on the oven until your food is fully cooked.

Crushed aluminum cans make for proper spacing and support for multiple Dutch ovens. ADAM ELLIOTT

Susan and Wallace drift the Lower Deschutes on a sunny winter day. ADAM ELLIOTT

DIRECTIONS TO PUT-IN
In Tygh Valley, turn left onto OR 216 east from US 197. In 8.4 miles, turn left after crossing the Deschutes onto the BLM access road that follows the river for 17.4 miles on river right. The road ends at Macks Landing.

NEARBY ATTRACTIONS
More great river running opportunities await upstream on the Deschutes, as well as the Wild and Scenic tributaries of the Metolius and Crooked Rivers.

CHETCO RIVER

Section name	Carter Creek to Steel Bridge
Distance	Upper Gorge: 18 miles; Lower Gorge: 10 miles
Flow range	500–2,000 cfs
Season and source of water	Spring; rainfall
Gauge location	Brookings, USGS #14400000
Time required	1 day hiking; 2–3 days on the river
Classification	*Wild* and *Scenic*
Difficulty	II–IV+
Managing agency	Rogue River–Siskiyou National Forest
Permit required?	No
Shuttle type	Hire a shuttle with Bearfoot Brad
Outstandingly Remarkable Values	Water quality, fisheries, recreation
Why paddle this section?	Pristine and remote; deep blue pools; challenging, committing, and stunningly beautiful

Supplemental description provided by Matt Curry.

RIVER DESCRIPTION

Translucent blue water and large, smooth boulders fill the Chetco River's tight and narrow canyon. Astonishingly clear water displays the river's bottom like a live aquarium

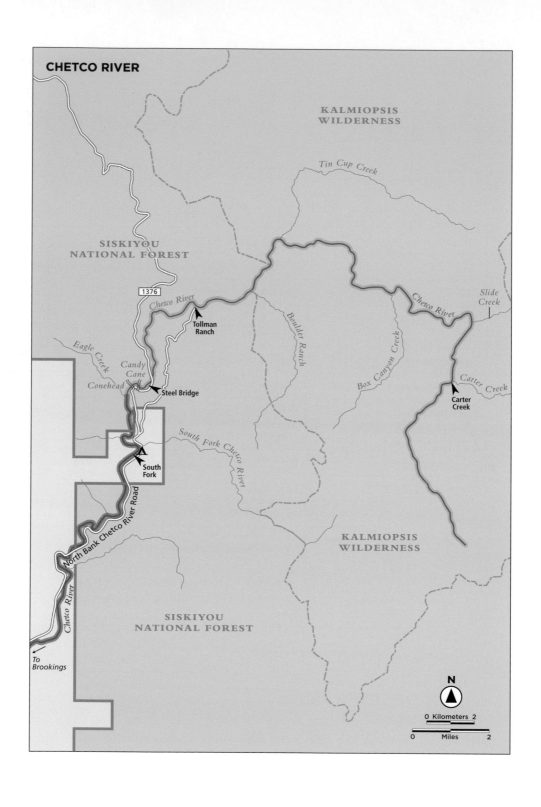

CHETCO RIVER

KALMIOPSIS
WILDERNESS

Tin Cup Creek

SISKIYOU
NATIONAL FOREST

1376

Chetco River

Chetco River

Slide
Creek

Tollman
Ranch

Boulder Ranch

Box Canyon Creek

Eagle Creek

Candy
Cane

Carter
Creek

Conehead

Steel Bridge

Carter
Creek

South Fork Chetco River

South
Fork

North Bank Chetco River Road

Chetco River

KALMIOPSIS
WILDERNESS

SISKIYOU
NATIONAL FOREST

To
Brookings

N

0 Kilometers 2

0   Miles   2

Andy Maser charges one of many tight rapids on the upper Chetco River.
Thomas O'Keefe / American Whitewater

exhibit. Salmon and trout dart about as your boat's shadow drifts over them, and colorful rocks glisten in a chromatic flurry at the bottom of the river.

The Chetco flows freely from source to sea. Nearly all of its length, forty-six miles, is classified as either *Wild*, *Scenic*, or *Recreational*. Only the final eleven miles, as the river flows into the ocean, were left out of the designation. The headwaters and upper stretches flow through the incredible and little-known Kalmiopsis Wilderness, the largest wilderness area in Oregon, which also encompasses the nearby Wild and Scenic Illinois and North Fork of the Smith Rivers. Prior to protection, early mining claims released toxic chemicals into these waterways. Today, nickel strip mines still threaten many of the headwater streams in this area, which produce some of the cleanest and clearest water in the nation.

In the slow meanders of the lower river, the fishing contingent floats in full force. Just like the other rivers along the Wild Rivers Coast, the Chetco harbors important runs of winter steelhead, fall Chinook salmon, and sea-run cutthroat trout. Winter months see more recreation on the lower reaches with the fishing industry, while spring attracts whitewater boaters into the upper gorges. And, of course, summer swimming and camping opportunities entice many more.

Northwest Rafting Company operates guided trips to the Upper Chetco.
NORTHWEST RAFTING COMPANY

PADDLER'S NOTES

Most explorers of Chetco's upper gorge opt to take a creek boat, a packraft, or an inflatable kayak due to the 10-mile hike to the put-in. You know a run is truly wild when the access includes trail instructions. Some groups even camp along the hike as it can be strenuous and long, especially carrying your boats and camping gear, and even more especially when snow blankets the ground. However, the perspective of starting high on a ridge and descending into a river should be experienced at least once by every paddler.

Boaters with hard-shell kayaks will find a flow around 1,500 cubic feet per second (cfs) to be on the low side. If taking packrafts or inflatable kayaks, the river can be run with much lower water. At flows above 3,000 cfs, rapids will connect more and the whole run will be much tighter and pushier.

Some describe this run as a miniature of the nearby Wild and Scenic Illinois River. At times, the river feels narrow and "creeky," with large boulders that choke the channel to create class IV+ rapids. The turquoise-blue and emerald-green water will distract you, but keep an eye out for regular class III–IV ledges and boulder gardens strewn throughout the run. Boulders can be as large as houses, making a boater feel tiny even in this small drainage. Expect solid class IV between Slide Creek and Granite Creek, and don't be too scared to scout and portage anything that looks risky. Additional class IV+ awaits downstream but is separated by more class III. You're deep in the wilderness here; take risks carefully.

Campsites along the Chetco River are typically small and on cobble bars, which can change slightly after every high-flow season. Some years Tin Cup, Box Canyon, and Boulder Creeks have nearby camping options that fit several boaters.

If you opt to take out at the South Fork Camp on river left rather than the Steel Bridge access, you'll hit two of the more difficult class IV–V rapids: Candy Cane and Conehead. You'll encounter these just after you pass under the bridge. Both can be scouted and portaged on river right.

DIRECTIONS TO TAKEOUT

From Brookings, drive east on North Bank Chetco Road as it follows the Chetco River out of town. From US 101, you'll drive almost 16 miles until you reach the South Fork Chetco River. Turn into the campground before crossing the South Fork. Or, continue traveling up the Main Chetco River by crossing the South Fork and turning left onto High Prairie Road/FR 1376. In 4.2 miles you'll reach a bridge where you can access the river.

DIRECTIONS TO PUT-IN

Babyfoot Lake trailhead is the beginning of the strenuous 10-mile hike in. Bring at least one good topo map. Depending on snow conditions you can go high on Trail 1126 to Hungry Hill, or lower on Trail 1124a toward Babyfoot Lake. Take trail 1124 to Trail 1129, then take Trail 1131 to Bailey's Cabin, which has a small spring. Trail 1109 drops you at Carter Creek, which you can follow to put in at the confluence. Trails can be difficult to follow and may change due to recent forest fires. Thanks to the Siskiyou Mountain Club for doing their best to maintain these remote paths!

Bearfoot Brad Camden, the local southwest Oregon and northern California shuttle driver, can take you to the trailhead. Give him a call at (707) 457-3365. If you want to drive yourself, head to Crescent City, California, and take US 101 north to exit 794 for US 199. Follow the Smith River on US 199 for 53.3 miles. Just past Cave Junction, Oregon, turn left on 8 Dollar Road/FR 4201. Follow this road for 14.6 miles to a "Y," where you'll go left toward the Babyfoot Lake trailhead, less than a mile down the road.

NEARBY ATTRACTIONS

Brookings, Oregon, is a great town to peruse and enjoy a coastal culture. Chetco Brewery makes a great post-river stop. Hiking options abound, and the beach itself is one of the more spectacular coastlines in the country. Head south to paddle in the Smith River drainage, or north to the Rogue, Illinois, and Elk Rivers.

ILLINOIS RIVER

Section name	Miami Bar to Lower Oak Flat
Distance	31 miles
Flow range	500–3,500 cfs
Season and source of water	Spring; snowmelt and winter rains
Gauge location	Kerby, USGS #14377100
Time required	3–4 days
Classification	*Wild* and *Scenic*
Difficulty	IV (V)
Managing agency	Rogue River–Siskiyou National Forest
Permit required?	Yes
Shuttle type	Vehicle
Outstandingly Remarkable Values	Fisheries, recreation, scenery, botany, water quality
Why paddle this section?	Technical whitewater in a remote wilderness canyon; stunning scenery and wildlife

RIVER DESCRIPTION

The Illinois River is the wilder, younger sibling of the famous Rogue River in southwestern Oregon. The Illinois's narrow flow window, steeper gradient, tendency to flash, and remote location make the river harder to catch but more satisfying when you do. Rafters and kayakers should prepare for difficult whitewater, study the weather patterns and gauge info, and bring all the appropriate safety equipment.

Kayakers enjoying a mellow rapid on the Illinois River. ADAM ELLIOTT

The Illinois flows toward the northwest along the northern edge of the Kalmiopsis Wilderness to its confluence with the Rogue at Agness. Fairly consistent gradient whisks paddlers through decade-old wildfire regrowth, past countless waterfalls, over too many boulder gardens to count, and beneath deep grey bedrock cliff walls. Most of the rapids are read-and-run, with the exception of Green Wall Rapid, a class V that can be portaged on the left. There are around ten or eleven class IV rapids, including York Creek, Pine Creek, Fawn Falls, Little Green Wall, and Submarine Hole, and numerous class III rapids. Campsites are adequate for small and medium-size groups. Because permit size is limited to twelve, this works great.

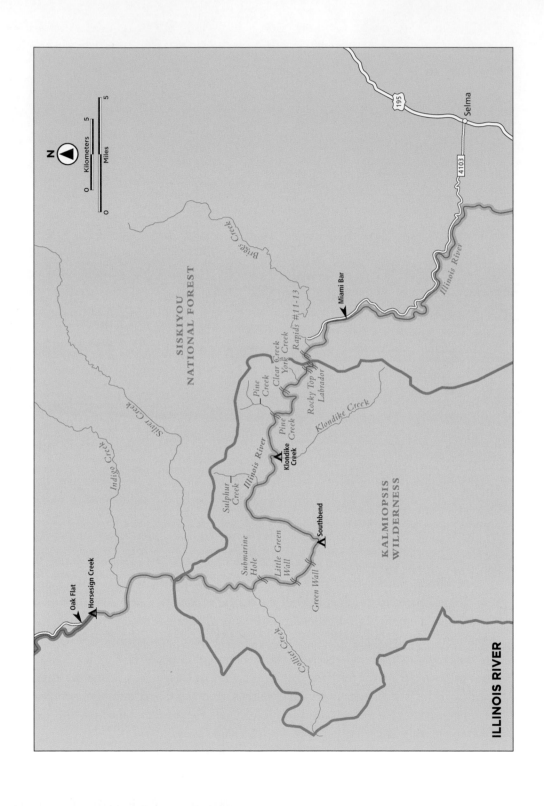

ILLINOIS RIVER

The Illinois was included in the original set of Wild and Scenic rivers proposed in 1968 but was dropped. Finally, it joined the system in 1984. A dam had been proposed above Oak Flat, but Wild and Scenic status protected the river from it.

PADDLER'S NOTES

Take your time out here; it is a true wilderness splendor. A private trip can be a great way to see the river but going with a guided tour will give you more opportunity to experience the full beauty of the place. Learn more at NWRafting.com or ARTA.org. Know your weather before entering this watershed. River levels spike during and after storms, quickly making the run dangerous. Don't get caught in the canyon when heavy rains are headed that way.

Arrange your shuttle logistics before going to the put-in. You can find shuttle services through Galice Resort, (541) 476-3818, on the Rogue River or through Bearfoot Brad Camden, (707) 457-3365. If you want to run the shuttle yourself, spending nearly a day on either end of your trip, there are two main routes: one over Bear Creek Road, and the other out to the coast and into California. Each cover considerable distances wrapping around the wilderness area.

While the whitewater is not to be underestimated, the pool-drop nature (at average flows) offers opportunity to pick up the pieces and prepare for the next one. The class III begins about three miles into the run, with the first class IV, Rocky Top, at four miles. Over the next four miles York Creek, Clear Creek, and Pine Creek rapids arrive, before or after their namesake tributaries, and all reach class IV difficulty.

The exception to the pool-drop rule here is Green Wall Rapid, a class V 18 miles into the run. Prelude is the class III lead-in to Green Wall, and if botched this could make the whitewater below significantly worse. Scout on the left, and when you do push off from shore, make sure you make all the moves, not just the hard ones. Rafts would have a hard time portaging here.

Little Green Wall rapid, class IV, is just downstream, followed by several miles of continuous class III. Three miles downstream from Green Wall is Submarine Hole—a raft flipper. Below Collier Creek you won't find any more class IV. Take time to explore the side streams if you can; their mossy granite boulders and perfectly blue water are enchanting.

Kayakers love self-support kayak trips on the Illinois because of easier logistics, plus easier navigation of the whitewater. However, we prefer to bring rafts. We just love having a full kitchen, a tarp shelter for in the inevitably rainy weather, and extra friends who may not have the skills to kayak.

A group scouts Green Wall Rapid, a technical class IV drop for both kayakers and rafters.
ADAM ELLIOTT

DIRECTIONS TO TAKEOUT

From Gold Beach, along US 101 at the mouth of the Rogue River, drive east on Jerry Flat Road (Agness Road; FR 33) for 27 miles. At Agness, turn southeast on Oak Flat Road and drive 3 miles to the river access point at Lower Oak Flat.

DIRECTIONS TO PUT-IN

In Selma, the Selma Market is adjacent to US 199 and Illinois River Road. After obtaining your permit at the kiosk here, drive west on Illinois River Road (which becomes FR 4103 at mile 13.6) for just over 16 miles to reach Miami Bar access.

NEARBY ATTRACTIONS

The Rogue River should not be missed. If you are driving from out-of-state to get on the hard-to-hit Illinois, it is likely outside of the lottery permit period for the Rogue River. Get yourself a drop-in permit and have a great time seeing the river at a higher flow. The camping and hiking in this corner of Oregon, especially out on the coast or within the Kalmiopsis Wilderness, is some of the best as well.

6

CROOKED RIVER

Section name	Lone Pine Bridge to Crooked River Ranch
Distance	16.5 miles
Flow range	1,000–4,000 cfs
Season and source of water	Usually March and April; unpredictable dam releases
Gauge location	Smith Rock State Park, American Whitewater gauge #43093
Time required	1 day
Classification	*Recreational*
Difficulty	IV (V)
Managing agency	Bureau of Land Management, Prineville District
Permit required?	No
Shuttle type	Vehicle
Outstandingly Remarkable Values	Geology, recreation, scenery, wildlife, hydrology, botany, ecology
Why paddle this section?	Best big-water paddling in Oregon; awesome scenery through central Oregon's high desert canyons

River description supplemented by Nate Merrill.

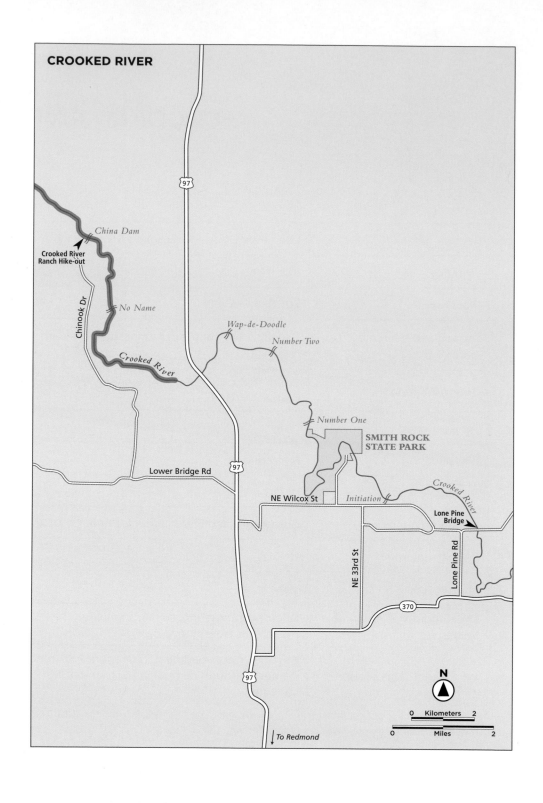

Looking down from the cliffs of Smith Rock, you can barely see kayakers on the Crooked River just upstream of the Wild and Scenic section. Susan Elliott

RIVER DESCRIPTION

The whitewater found on the Crooked River as it meanders around Smith Rock State Park would be considered the best big-water, class IV river running in the Northwest if dam managers upstream released regular flows. Between the scenery of floating through Oregon's iconic Smith Rock State Park, the massive hydraulic features, and the pool-drop nature of the run, the Crooked River quickly turns into an advanced boater mecca when water fills the channel. Unfortunately, this only occurs when generous snowpack fills Ochoco and Prineville Reservoirs, resulting in surprise dam releases that bring the river to life every few years.

When word spreads that water is churning through the Crooked River canyon, boaters flock to the region. Multiple large groups float the run daily during this time, often for multiple laps as long as the water holds out.

The geologic Outstandingly Remarkable Value here cites the colorful layers of volcanic basalts, ash, and sedimentary rock seen in the tall canyon walls. While Smith Rocks State Park sits upstream of the designated *Recreational* section of the Crooked, floating the flat meanders around the park's impressive rock formations makes the long flat-water paddle a delight. From the water, scan the rock walls for climbers and high-liners (individuals walking on a piece of webbing between two cliffs) as you drift toward your own extreme adventure-sport session downstream.

The Wild and Scenic designation begins midway through the run, and continues for the final four miles. This *Recreational* classification extends for another 5 miles downstream of the takeout until the Crooked flows into the Opal Springs Hydropower Project. Boaters rarely paddle from Crooked River Ranch all the way to the Billy Chinook Reservoir, but it is possible. This run can be floated at lower flows with spring water increasing the volume, but requires a long paddle out on the lake or a long, steep hike out at Opal Springs.

PADDLER'S NOTES

You happen to be near Central Oregon and have heard the Crooked has water. First, consider yourself lucky. Next, find a solid crew to paddle with you. Due to the last-minute nature of this run, groups of less experienced paddlers often jump on the run to take advantage of the narrow flow window, despite not having sufficient class IV–V skills. You'll want a team that can respond to any rescue situation out there, whether from your crew or from someone else's. More class III–IV action should be expected interspersed between the named rapids described here. Scouting is always a good idea on the Crooked.

From Lone Pine Road downstream, expect a few miles of flat-water warm-up before Initiation Rapid. This first taste of Crooked whitewater actually extends for a long stretch downstream. Expect around a mile of this initial class III–IV. At higher flows, above 2,800 cubic feet per second (cfs), this section is quite continuous and a swim or flip here would probably result in a long time in the water. Paddlers have been known to hike out of the Crooked at Smith Rocks after feeling overwhelmed in this first gorge.

Below here, enjoy the gentle float around Smith Rocks before arriving at Number One, the next class IV rapid. This pool-drop rapid hides a large hole halfway down that is surrounded by pushy and surging waves and hydraulics. Most boaters stick to the right to cut through the weaker, right side of the hole.

Number Two rapid sits around a sharp left-hand bend in the river, a little less than two miles downstream from Number One. Stopping above Number Two can be difficult when water levels are higher, especially for rafts. The left-hand bend is a blind corner and sneaks up on beginners. Look for a private road bridge to signal this rapid sits around the next turn. A large volcanic rock island in the center of the river pinches the right and left channels, and hints at the underlying rock type that creates the whitewater. The standard line is through the left channel.

Another mile downstream is Wap-de-Doodle rapid, at the next sharp left-hand bend. While this one intimidates most boaters when looking at it for the first time, it actually consists mostly of large waves that can be run a number of ways. Downstream,

Early spring rafting on the Crooked River is challenging and chilly, but delivers some of the best whitewater in all of Oregon. BRENDAN WELLS

paddle more class III rapids for a few miles as you pass under three bridges in one of the more dramatic stretches of the Crooked River gorge.

No Name rapid may have the worst reputation despite its name. It contains the biggest, nastiest hole on the Crooked toward the bottom of the drop. Whitewater continues after the hole, making any swim less than desirable. Scout or portage on the right-side trail.

Where the dirt road reaches the river, the final rapid awaits. China Dam rapid can be run moving right to middle, or avoid it by taking out above the drop. This is probably the nastiest looking drop on the river, but don't be fooled. A clean line can be seen from scouting on river right.

Hollywood Road, a dirt road, leads from Crooked River Ranch to the river just below China Dam rapid. This access point was privately owned and threatened by development until it was acquired by the Trust for Public Land, which has been working to establish a trail network to formalize public access to the river.

DIRECTIONS TO TAKEOUT

In Terrebonne, turn left onto Lower Bridge Way, drive for 2.2 miles, and then turn right onto NW 43rd Street. In 1.8 miles turn left onto NW Chinook Drive. You'll

Central Oregon in all of its glory: Basalt, pine trees, blue skies, and excellent whitewater on the Crooked. BRENDAN WELLS

begin seeing signs for Crooked River Ranch before turning right on Club House Road. Drive straight back around the main buildings, and veer to the right toward the yurts. Park at the end of this road.

DIRECTIONS TO PUT-IN
From Terrebonne, head east on Smith Rock Way toward the state park. Continue straight until Smith Rock Way ends at Lone Pine Road in 4.8 miles. Turn left onto Lone Pine Road. Put in where the road crosses the Crooked River, in about a quarter mile. Be mindful of parking off the road as there isn't a great parking lot for boaters here.

NEARBY ATTRACTIONS
Take time to explore Smith Rock State Park by foot or with rope and harness. While the climbing here attracts visitors from all over the West, the hiking is just as sweet. Consider a paddle on the Wild and Scenic Metolius or Deschutes Rivers, too. Both have sections that flow into the Billy Chinook Reservoir as well.

MCKENZIE RIVER

Section name	Ollalie to Paradise
Distance	8.3 miles
Flow range	600–9,000 cfs
Season and source of water	Year-round; spring-fed, snowmelt, and rainfall
Gauge location	Near Vida, USGS #14162500
Time required	Half day to full day
Classification	*Recreational*
Difficulty	II–III
Managing agency	Willamette National Forest
Permit required?	No
Shuttle type	Vehicle, mountain bike
Outstandingly Remarkable Values	Fisheries, scenery, recreation, hydrology, geology, water quality
Why paddle this section?	Continuous class II–III waves and boulder gardens; thick forested watershed

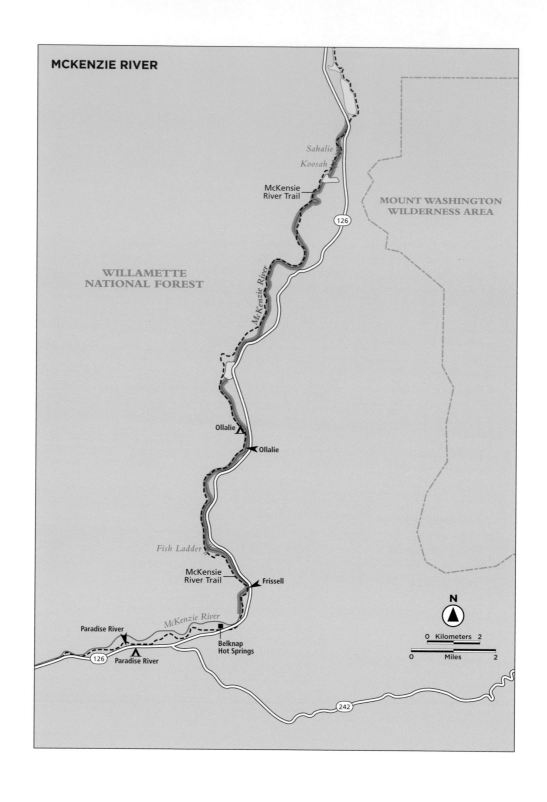

MCKENZIE RIVER

Sahalie
Koosah

McKensie
River Trail

MOUNT WASHINGTON
WILDERNESS AREA

126

WILLAMETTE
NATIONAL FOREST

McKenzie River

Ollalie

Ollalie

Fish Ladder

McKensie
River Trail

Frissell

McKenzie River

Paradise River

126

Paradise River

Belknap
Hot Springs

242

N

0   Kilometers   2

0   Miles   2

Adam throws a "blunt" at Neil's Wave on the Mackenzie River, downstream of the Wild and Scenic section. Susan Elliott

RIVER DESCRIPTION

For a taste of a spring-fed watershed with deep aquifers and rich national forest terrain, head straight to Oregon's McKenzie River watershed on the western slope of the central Cascade mountains. This Wild and Scenic river flows year-round due to the slow release of snowmelt from deep aquifers within the porous, volcanic bedrock. Expect a delightfully swift and splashy day while paddling on the McKenzie, with smaller features to navigate around or launch yourself over.

The bright blue hue of the river, seen in the deep pools and bubbling riffles, makes the water quality Outstandingly Remarkable Value an obvious one. Ancient underground reserves preserve the water's temperature and quality for decades or more after melting from the high Cascade Range and before it is released into streams. This combination of a geologic storehouse and a slow-melt hydrologic system is also cited as an Outstandingly Remarkable Value for the McKenzie River. One result of this combination is healthy populations of native wild trout (rainbow, bull, cutthroat), as well as a thriving spring wild Chinook salmon run. For this reason, the McKenzie River attracts many boaters who bring their rods and reels as well.

The steady flows and healthy fish stocks fostered the design and creation of the McKenzie River drift boat, also called a dory. These flat-bottomed narrow boats, with

Rowing down the Mackenzie can be a great family activity. Adam rows friends and family down for their first river trip. SUSAN ELLIOTT

a pointed stern and flat "transom" bow, have continuous rocker (the hull's curve) that allows boaters to swiftly turn and navigate smoothly through whitewater rapids while also fishing. The revolutionary design opened up Oregon's wild rivers to fishing in the mid-twentieth century. Today, craftsmanship of the McKenzie River drift boat, and similar designs in Grand Canyon and Rogue River dories, seduce river runners who seek a smooth and organic ride on whitewater.

The recreational Outstandingly Remarkable Value on the McKenzie River extends into the surrounding forested watershed with exceptional hiking and biking opportunities. The McKenzie River Trail runs from the river's headwaters at Clear Lake for 26 miles downstream. While most mountain bikers and hikers explore segments of the trail starting uphill, you could use your feet or bike for a shuttle back upstream for one spectacular adventure day.

While the section between Ollalie and Paradise campground appeals to most boaters, a few elite-level kayakers have descended both Sahalie and Koosah Falls at higher water flows. At about 70 feet and 60 feet, respectively, with highly consequential class V rapids above and below both drops, these waterfalls should not be attempted without significant experience and risk evaluation. However, anyone can hike the 2.5-mile loop to view these spectacular exhibits of plummeting water over volcanic ledges.

PADDLER'S NOTES

Both the put-in and takeout for this stretch of the McKenzie River are located within beautiful forested riverside campgrounds. More parking can be found at Paradise, the takeout, but both would be great places to spend the night.

The most significant rapid on the run is Fish Ladder, about 3 miles downstream from Ollalie. You'll see power lines on river right, close to the river at the top of the rapid. Because wood can collect in this boulder garden, scout from the road beneath the power lines on the right. This is the only class III rapid at normal flows. Higher flows cover more of the rocks and make tighter navigation skills less necessary, but demand a high level of attention due to the lack of eddies and potential for wood hazards.

Less than 3 miles downstream from Fish Ladder you'll see hot steam rise from the left bank, which marks Belknap Hot Springs. The lodge maintains the two developed pools here at 104 degrees Fahrenheit, a stark contrast from the cold spring water you've been paddling. Pulling over here and paying for hourly access to the pool is pretty sublime. You may not want to get back into the cold river, however.

The remainder of the run moves along at a steady pace, with lots of class II waves and features. At some water levels, a fun wave can be found downstream of Frissell boat launch at a location known as Blue Pool. The pool below the small rapid invites sweaty mountain bikers on the river-left trail in for a cool dip.

DIRECTIONS TO TAKEOUT

From the Ollalie Campground, head back out on OR 126 westbound by turning right, and drive 7.8 miles to Paradise Campground and river access site. Look for signs pointing you to the boat launch area within the campground.

DIRECTIONS TO PUT-IN

Ollalie Campground is located at mile 13 on OR 126 east of Springfield. Turn into the campground and turn left immediately to drive about 0.5 mile to the boat ramp.

NEARBY ATTRACTIONS

The waterfalls of the McKenzie River attract elite kayakers and throngs of sightseers every year. Sahalie Falls, a 70-foot cascade flowing over a natural lava dam, can be seen from a trail close to a parking area. Hike the trail on either side of the river (it forms a loop) and you'll find Koosah Falls, a 60-foot fall into a deep pool. The loop hike, including both falls, is 2.6 miles.

The volcanic activity of the region creates several nearby hot springs. Belknap Hot Springs appeals to those seeking more of a developed experience, while Terwilliger Hot Springs requires a short hike and offers a much more natural experience—*au naturel* for many. A hike or mountain bike ride on the McKenzie River Trail complements a paddle to please the multisporters seeking to embrace more of this river's natural wonders.

METOLIUS RIVER

Section name	Upper and Lower
Distance	Upper: 11.5 miles; Lower: 17.1 miles
Flow range	1,300–3,000 cfs
Season and source of water	Year-round but preferably in spring, summer, or fall; spring-fed and snowmelt
Gauge location	Near Grandview, USGS #14091500
Time required	1–2 days
Classification	*Recreational* and *Scenic*
Difficulty	II–III
Managing agency	Deschutes National Forest; Warm Springs Indian Reservation
Permit required?	No
Shuttle type	Vehicle
Outstandingly Remarkable Values	Cultural, fisheries, geology, history, recreation, scenery, wildlife, botany, ecology, hydrology, traditional cultural use
Why paddle this section?	Up-close eagle and osprey viewing; epic clear blue water; wilderness-quality immersion experience in a day trip

The Upper Metolius provides excellent views of Jefferson Peak (pictured), the Three Sisters, and Black Butte. MICHAEL HUGHES / NORTHWEST RAFTING COMPANY

RIVER DESCRIPTION

Gushing from the basalt rocks of Oregon's Central Cascade Mountains, the spring waters of the Metolius River flow powerfully right from the source. So much water pours from the ground that a boat can float upon it almost immediately. Frigid and bright blue, the river begins by meandering through mountain marshes and thick old-growth ponderosa pine forests. The Wild and Scenic designation begins at the river's source, an act that has promoted and strengthened one of the most intact river ecosystems within the national system.

Dipping your paddle blades into this icy stream, you'll immediately begin to appreciate the litany of Outstandingly Remarkable Values protected. First, the combination of geology and hydrology deliver the clean water from the depths of the mountains, allowing for extraordinarily high water quality and diverse botanic and ecological systems. The Green Ridge Fault releases cold, snowmelt water from the aquifer to the

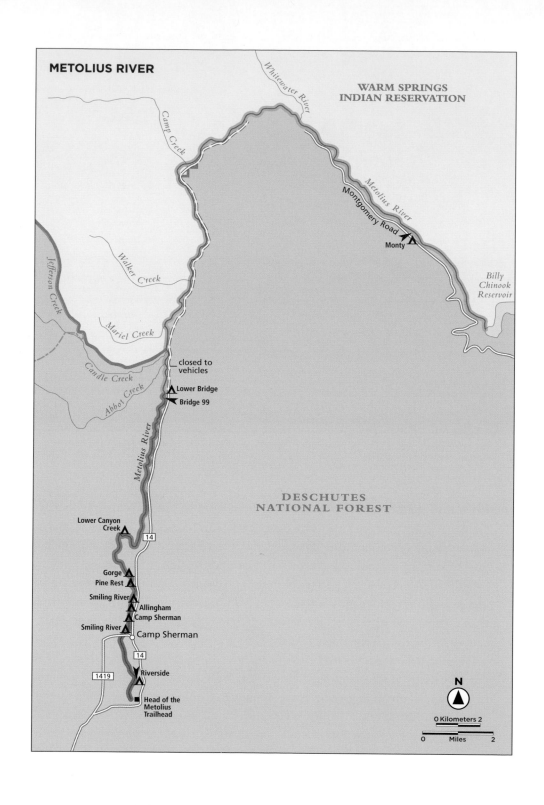

METOLIUS RIVER

WARM SPRINGS
INDIAN RESERVATION

Whitewater River

Camp Creek

Metolius River

Montgomery Road

Monty

Billy
Chinook
Reservoir

Jefferson Creek

Walker Creek

Mariel Creek

Candle Creek

Abbot Creek

closed to
vehicles

Lower Bridge

Bridge 99

Metolius River

DESCHUTES
NATIONAL FOREST

Lower Canyon
Creek

14

Gorge
Pine Rest
Smiling River
Allingham
Camp Sherman
Smiling River

Camp Sherman

14

1419

Riverside

Head of the
Metolius
Trailhead

N

0 Kilometers 2

0   Miles   2

earth's surface at the Head of the Metolius. Geologists believe the water actually originates in the high Cascades, rather than at nearby Black Butte.

The spring's stable flow regime creates a steady and reliable habitat for wildlife. Minimal flow variation makes for predictable boating levels as well. That's six of the Outstandingly Remarkable Values right there: geology, hydrology, wildlife, ecology, botany, and recreation.

You'll float past anglers enjoying this blue-ribbon fly-fishing spot, even on the more remote lower river stretch. They compete with a healthy eagle and osprey population for the fish. As we floated downstream, we observed eagles sitting on logs practically an arm's length away, and unperturbed by our presence. The fishing must be good, hence Outstandingly Remarkable Value number seven.

Campgrounds and the small cabin outposts of Camp Sherman dot the entire 11.5 miles of upper river, classified as *Recreational*. Access for floating can be found just a few miles downstream from the river's source. Camp Sherman's beloved rural scenic landscape attracts thousands of tourists in the summer and contributes to two more Outstandingly Remarkable Values: cultural and historic. Management plans for the area restrict development outside the historical rustic character of the buildings, which maintains the simplistic mountain culture that attracts river users to the Metolius.

The lower river, classified as *Scenic*, stretches for 17 miles until it reaches the backwaters of Billy Chinook Reservoir. The riverside campgrounds and cozy lodges fade away in this primitive reach, leaving you alone with the mountains and continuous class II whitewater. Instream wood may contribute to a varied habitat for fish, but it also poses a challenge to paddlers. For this reason, intermediate boaters should be ready to jump on shore to avoid surprise strainers on the Metolius.

The Warm Springs Tribe administers the landscape on river left, and continues to use it for traditional gathering and hunting, the final Outstandingly Remarkable Value recognized in Wild and Scenic designation. In the development of the management plan for the Metolius, the tribe held the position that it retained jurisdiction over the entire riverbed and both banks. However, the state of Oregon's navigability laws hold all riverbeds and banks in trust for the state's residents. Recreation has been found to be a value, which allows us to paddle here, but we must respect tribal values and stay off the river-left shoreline as much as possible to avoid conflicts.

PADDLER'S NOTES

While the Metolius may technically be full of class II whitewater, we would recommend this run for at least class III boaters due to the continuous nature of the run (it's a nonstop freight train) and the inevitability of portages around nasty logjams. You'll need to stay alert for hazards at all times, even as you are lulled into a routine by continuous class II wave trains and incredible Central Oregon scenery.

Starting the Metolius on the Upper stretch, classified *Recreational*, allows you to easily paddle some of the run in a day with minimal shuttle. Start at Riverside Campground on river right and take out at any of the campgrounds, or at Bridge 99/SW Resorts Road (the final access point before the *Scenic* stretch).

Low bridges cross the river in several places along the *Recreational* reach. Scout carefully to determine if there is sufficient clearance. For this reason and because of logjams, we don't recommend rafts for the Metolius. An inflatable kayak allows you to hop out onto shore the easiest, making it the watercraft of choice here. Rapids are mostly class II, with the potential for logs everywhere. Have we mentioned there is wood in the river yet?

The *Scenic* stretch extends about 17 miles from Bridge 99 to Monty Campground. You'll enjoy continuous class II wave trains with the added spice of several portages around river-wide logs. The eagles and ospreys have been known to sit at river level as you float by; you'll be stunned by their proximity. Bring your rod to get in on some of the best fishing in central Oregon. Be sure to check regulations before launching.

Monty Campground may be difficult to recognize as you float down. As you approach the campground, you'll see a gauge station on the right. Look for eddies on the right to take out in the next half mile of river. The campground is officially open from about June to September. It may be possible to camp outside of the season, but you may also find a closed gate. If that's the case, you will have to park along Montgomery Road/FR 64 and walk your boat through the campground.

The shuttle for the *Scenic* stretch is purely Forest Service dirt roads with plenty of washboards. It takes at least one-and-a-half hours to make the shuttle one-way on a day with decent weather. While two-wheel-drive vehicles can make it, a four-wheel drive with some clearance will make it a whole lot smoother.

DIRECTIONS TO TAKEOUT

Just north of Terrebone, after you pass signs for Crooked River Ranch, take a slight left onto SW Culver Highway. In 2.3 miles take the slight left (not the hard left) onto SW Iris Lane, also called H Street. In 1 mile turn right onto SW Feather Drive. In 1.2 miles turn left onto SW Fisch Lane, which you'll follow in a right turn as the road becomes SW Frazier Drive. Take the first left onto SW Peck Drive, which turns into SW Jordan Drive. Stay hard left on Jordan Drive as you get close to the lake and begin to meander around its coves. In 8.6 miles turn right to stay on Jordan Drive for another mile before turning left onto SW Graham. This becomes Montgomery Road/FR 64. Veer left to stay on Montgomery where it is also called SW Fly Road. At this point, you'll be driving west and getting close to the lake again. Note that you'll see FR 1170 on the left soon after you veer left. From that juncture, Monty Campground is about 7.5 miles. You'll take FR 1170 to the put-in.

Wild and Scenic designation of the Metolius River has made this a world-class fishery for steelhead, salmon, bull trout, and more. ADAM ELLIOTT

DIRECTIONS TO PUT-IN

From Monty Campground, go back east 7.5 miles and turn right on FR 1170/SW Prairie Farm Road. There are lots of forest roads along this route, so look for the brown and white signs at all intersections to confirm you are on the correct road. For the next 9 miles, stay on FR 1170/SW Prairie Farm Road/SW Alder Springs Road (it will switch back and forth between these names). Mostly, stay due west or straight through any intersections. The first major turn will be a slight left onto FR 1140. In 0.5 miles this will change into FR 1149; turn right to stay on FR 1149. You'll descend into the Metolius canyon for the next 6 miles. At the T intersection with FR 14, you'll either turn right to reach Bridge 99 (put-in for the Lower 17 miles) or left to get to Riverside Campground if you include the Upper Metolius in your run.

NEARBY ATTRACTIONS

Check out the Head of the Metolius overlook area to see the actual source of the river, which is just upstream from Riverside Campground. The amount of water gushing out of the ground is astounding. A trail can be found along most of the lower Metolius on river right as well. Bring your bike for a big human-powered shuttle day.

9

ELK RIVER

Section name	Butler Bar to the Fish Hatchery
Distance	11 miles
Flow range	3–4 feet on the stick gauge
Season and source of water	Year-round; rainfall
Gauge location	Visual or by phone (541-332-0405 during fishing season), located downstream from the fish hatchery
Time required	Half day to full day
Classification	*Recreational*
Difficulty	II–III (IV)
Managing agency	Rogue River–Siskiyou National Forest
Permit required?	No
Shuttle type	Bike or vehicle
Outstandingly Remarkable Values	Fisheries, scenery, botany, water quality
Why paddle this section?	Clear water; tiered spring waterfalls over mossy granite ledges; easily scoutable pool-drop rapids; roadside access

RIVER DESCRIPTION

The Elk River flows quietly into the Pacific Ocean along Oregon's southern coast, off the radar of many boaters. When one of the frequent rainstorms hit, this run becomes a gem of southwestern Oregon. As rain subsides, the river reverts to a placid

Winter fog and ice blanket the Elk River in southwest Oregon. ADAM ELLIOTT

turquoise-blue hue and reveals the thriving ecosystem and fantastic geology hidden below the water's surface. Even deep pools are remarkably clear. Above the surface of the river, springs form waterfalls that flow over tiers of mossy rock ledges. As the sun breaks through the tall riparian old-growth trees and bounces off the steep bedrock walls of the gorges, you'll find there is just too much beauty to absorb all at once. Your best shot for taking it all in is from the seat of a boat.

The primary form of recreating along the river is done with a fishing rod in hand, mostly because of the high quantity of other classic rivers to paddle in the area. A study found the Elk River to be the most productive salmon stream of its size left on the West Coast south of Alaska. With no history of dams and a temperate old-growth forest filling the headwaters and most of the river banks, the river boasts an incredibly high quantity of Chinook salmon, sea-run cutthroat trout, winter steelhead, and some coho salmon. This healthy ecosystem would not be here, however, without significant efforts from local activists after the heyday of logging.

While the perfect water level may be tricky to catch, the Elk River provides a great paddling opportunity when other local rivers are too high or low. There is no online gauge for river levels. Instead, paddlers can call the Elk River Fish Hatchery, (541) 332-7025, during fishing season to inquire the river level. A reading of 3 to 4 feet on

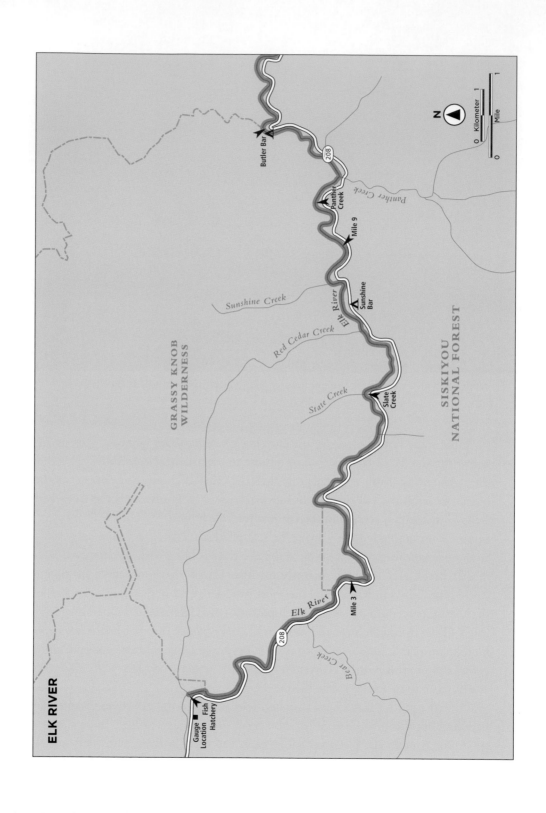

the stick gauge is preferable, although some say above 5 feet is more fun. You'll have to take your chances on this one and look at the river when you arrive to determine if the level is right for you. Outside of fishing season, boaters will need to guess water levels based on recent storms. Typically, the Elk runs within a good paddling range when a storm has ended a day or two prior.

PADDLER'S NOTES

Kayakers and canoeists can pick apart the run with multiple river access points along Elk River Road. Most rapids can be scouted once on the river due to the pool-drop nature of the run, and a few can be seen from the road. Thick riparian vegetation and cliffs obscure the view of most rapids from the road. To get in the full 11 miles of paddling, start at Butler Bar and take out at the fish hatchery. A few class IV rapids should be scouted within tighter gorges near the top and bottom of this section. You'll want to both pick a line through the rapid and also see if wood blocks the channel. The rapids change year to year, even in the bedrock gorge sections. This is mostly due to wood, but also some movement of boulders.

If class II is your style, try starting at the Mile 9 river access site (simply a pullout around mile 9 on OR 208/Elk River Road). Take out at the Slate Creek access site about 4 miles downstream. Cars can drive down to the large cobble bar on river left here. Below Slate Creek the river picks back up again into the class III–IV range depending on flow levels.

DIRECTIONS TO TAKEOUT

From Port Orford, head north on US 101 for 3 miles. Turn right on Elk River Road, which heads east. The fish hatchery takeout is about 8 miles up the road on the left (best to set the trip odometer when you turn up the main road). Park near Elk River

"PERHAPS MOST IMPORTANT, RIVERS REMIND US THAT WE ARE INSEPARABLY PART OF THE NATURAL WORLD. THE SWIRLING CURRENTS APPEAL TO CANOEISTS, RAFTERS, AND KAYAKERS, NOT ONLY FOR THE THRILL AND CHALLENGE OF WHITEWATER, BUT FOR THE RIVERS' GIFT OF PEACE AND SERENITY. PADDLING ON JOURNEYS OF A DAY OR A WEEK OR A MONTH IS A CAPTIVATING WAY TO TRAVEL AND TO EXPERIENCE THE FINEST OF NATURE IN EXTRAORDINARY PLACES SEEN NO OTHER WAY."

—*Tim Palmer in* Wild and Scenic Rivers: An American Legacy

Susan takes the right line as Tim Palmer lines his canoe down the left bank. ADAM ELLIOTT

Road on the right side of the parking area. This allows parking spaces to remain open for the hatchery staff on the left.

DIRECTIONS TO PUT-IN
Continue driving up Elk River Road from the fish hatchery, and keep an eye on the mileage to reach the various river access sites. Choose which works for you depending on how much time you have or how adventurous you feel.

NEARBY ATTRACTIONS
Spending the weekend camping, swimming, and fishing along the Elk extends this wilderness experience. Try Butler Bar or Sunshine Bar Campground for easy river access, or head farther up the canyon to Laird Lake Campground for a more remote experience. Stop at one of the Samuel H. Boardman scenic viewpoints on US 101. The Oregon Coast Trail connects these pullouts for views of this famously rugged shoreline and access to secret beaches, waterfalls tumbling into the ocean, and even a natural bridge.

CLACKAMAS RIVER

Section name	Sandstone Bridge to Moore Creek
Distance paddled	4–12 miles
Flow range	700–10,000 cfs
Season and source of water	Fall, winter, spring, and most of summer; rainfall and springs
Gauge location	Above Three Lynx Creek, USGS #14209500
Time required	Half day to full day
Classification	*Recreational*
Difficulty	II–III+
Managing agency	Mount Hood National Forest
Permit required?	No
Shuttle type	Vehicle, bike, hitchhike
Outstandingly Remarkable Values	Recreation, fisheries, wildlife, history, vegetation
Why paddle this section?	Great intermediate whitewater; roadside access but surrounded by national forest; close to Portland

RIVER DESCRIPTION

Surrounded by national forest land, the Clackamas River's remote and mountainous feel, pool-drop class III+ whitewater rapids, and great wilderness camping may help you forget that Portland's metropolis sits just an hour to the northwest. Paddlers in the city retreat to the cool, blue waters of the Clackamas after work, on weekends, and any

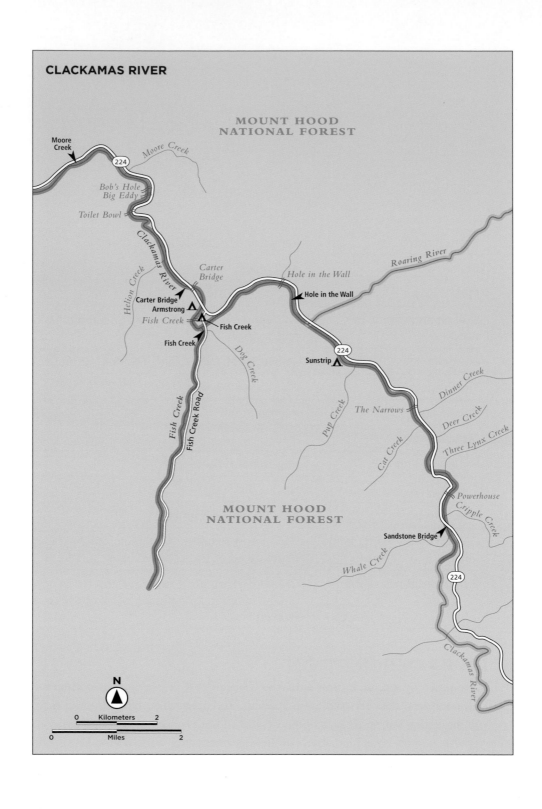

CLACKAMAS RIVER

MOUNT HOOD
NATIONAL FOREST

Moore
Creek

224

Moore Creek

Bob's Hole
Big Eddy

Toilet Bowl

Clackamas River

Helion Creek

Carter
Bridge

Carter Bridge
Armstrong

Fish Creek

Fish Creek

Fish Creek

Dog Creek

Fish Creek

Fish Creek Road

Hole in the Wall

Roaring River

Hole in the Wall

224

Sunstrip

Pup Creek

The Narrows

Cat Creek

Dinner Creek

Deer Creek

Three Lynx Creek

Powerhouse

Cripple Creek

Sandstone Bridge

MOUNT HOOD
NATIONAL FOREST

Whale Creek

224

Clackamas River

N

0   Kilometers   2
0   Miles   2

The USA Rafting Team competes in a slalom race during the Clackamas River Festival.
ADAM ELLIOTT

chance they can get. While intermediate paddlers will love the upper section described here, easier class I-II sections can be found farther downstream, below the North Fork Reservoir. These beginner-friendly sections have helped many paddlers prepare for the whitewater in the upper section.

Old-growth Douglas fir trees, rich riparian communities, and a healthy forest make the vegetation along the Clackamas an official Outstandingly Remarkable Value. While the road follows the river, this deep forest canopy prevents even a hint of noise from penetrating into your floating ambience. Naturally, these large swaths of public land invite wildlife and support the rich ecosystem required to support healthy fish stocks—both also Outstandingly Remarkable Values. The wild salmon populations reign over the river because the fish ladder mechanisms at the reservoir downstream prevent hatchery fish from moving into the designated upper watershed. This effort has helped boost wild populations while neighboring river systems have found hatchery fish outcompeting wild fish.

Susan catches some air as she passes through a gate during the Clackamas River Festival.
ADAM ELLIOTT

Deep forests mixed with multiple well-maintained river access sites, a healthy wild anadromous fish population, and riverside trails attract outdoor recreation enthusiasts of all kinds to the Clackamas watershed. However, the river draws Portland's thriving boating community more than other forms of outdoor play. In the rainy winter months, paddlers head farther upstream into tributary drainages to find more paddling options on the Collawash, Fish Creek, or the headwater reaches of the Clackamas, all designated Wild and Scenic as well.

PADDLER'S NOTES
Most rapids on the Upper Clackamas are classified as class II or III, but winter storms can take the hydraulics up a notch and create class IV action. Even at flows as high as 10,000 cubic feet per second (cfs), the river can be a big, fun mess, with boils and waves everywhere and no major portages, albeit less recovery time between rapids.

Putting in at the Sandstone Bridge provides the most time on the river. You'll hit two class III rapids, Powerhouse and the Narrows, within just a few miles. Many boaters use the new Hole in the Wall access point, just downstream at mile 41 on OR 224, for a slightly shorter paddle but easier entry into the river. The rapid with the same name just downstream pushes boaters into a nasty recirculating eddy on the left. Keep to the right here to avoid getting pushed to the wall in an uncomfortable way.

You'll arrive at Carter Bridge rapid after passing the Fish Creek access boat ramp and bopping over some fun class II. The rapid sits upstream of the actual Carter Bridge. Keep far left for the standard line but be ready to paddle through big waves and even holes at higher flows.

Big Eddy class III rapid comes next, and can be scouted from the road or river. The final class III rapid is Toilet Bowl, which can be scouted on either side of the river but not so well from the road. The wave and play features at Bob's Hole, around the bend, have entertained boaters year-round, but parking on the road to avoid a shuttle is discouraged. In another half mile you'll see the trail leading to Moore Creek access site. Biking your shuttle if you plan to just play at Bob's Hole will avoid any conflicts and save you gas money.

Rafters will find luxurious ramps to slide equipment to the river at the Fish Creek and Hole in the Wall access sites, as well as a wide trail at Moore Creek. You may guess by now, but the plethora of access locations makes the Clackamas easy to break apart into sections.

DIRECTIONS TO TAKEOUT
From Estacada, drive east on OR 224 and climb the hill into the upper watershed, above the North Fork Reservoir. The Moore Creek takeout access is located at road mile 35.3 on OR 224. At mile 37.4, Big Eddy access can also be used as a takeout.

DIRECTIONS TO PUT-IN
Continuing south from the Moore Creek takeout on OR 224, turn right on Sandstone Road toward Indian Henry Campground at mile 45.7. The put-in is on the left a quarter mile up the road. You can also put in at the Hole in the Wall access site, which is at mile 41 on OR 224. This is a better option especially when flows are low.

NEARBY ATTRACTIONS
Bagby Hot Springs offers individual cedar log tubs—a very Northwest, rustic feel. To reach the hot springs, drive farther into the headwaters on OR 224 and follow the signs. Snow in the winter will close these roads. Hiking trails can be found at several of the access locations and great camping options exist around Carter Bridge.

OWYHEE RIVER

Section name	Lower: Rome to Birch Creek Ranch
Distance	65 miles
Flow range	750–10,000 cfs
Season and source of water	March to early June; snowmelt and spring rain
Gauge location	Rome; USGS Station #13181000
Time required	4–6 days
Classification	*Wild*
Difficulty	II–III+
Managing agency	Bureau of Land Management, Vale district
Permit required?	Yes
Shuttle type	Four-wheel-drive vehicle
Outstandingly Remarkable Values	Scenery, recreation, wildlife, geology, prehistoric culture
Why paddle this section?	Riverside hot springs; castle-like rock formations; deep red and green canyon; great beach camps

RIVER DESCRIPTION

The Owyhee River's colorful canyon landscape grows in magnitude every day on this awe-inspiring multiday river trip. The southeastern Oregon desert hides the Owyhee Canyonlands, an area that spans over 2.5 million acres, with spires and calderas,

Susan and Wallace looking at bighorn sheep on the Owyhee. ADAM ELLIOTT

bighorn sheep, and golden eagles, and the 346-mile-long Owyhee River at its core. The Lower Owyhee, from Rome to Birch Creek Ranch, provides a no portage run with a few whitewater challenges, a wealth of wildlife, and a week's worth of wilderness bliss.

The landscape begins humbly in Rome, with rolling desert hills and ranches. Slowly moving downstream, the hills morph into colorful chalk sandcastle formations. By the last few days of the float, red and green canyon walls shoot up directly from river's edge, with the occasional eroded spire attached to the steep slopes. Pelicans, hawks, mergansers, golden eagles, songbirds, and more all share the skies and the water. Mammals such as pronghorn antelope, coyotes, marmots, and jackrabbits find homes on the land. The canyon's remote nature and rugged terrain have helped the Owyhee River remain a secret treasure, but following several high snowpack years, the river has steadily become more well known. Especially when word got out of the riverside hot springs.

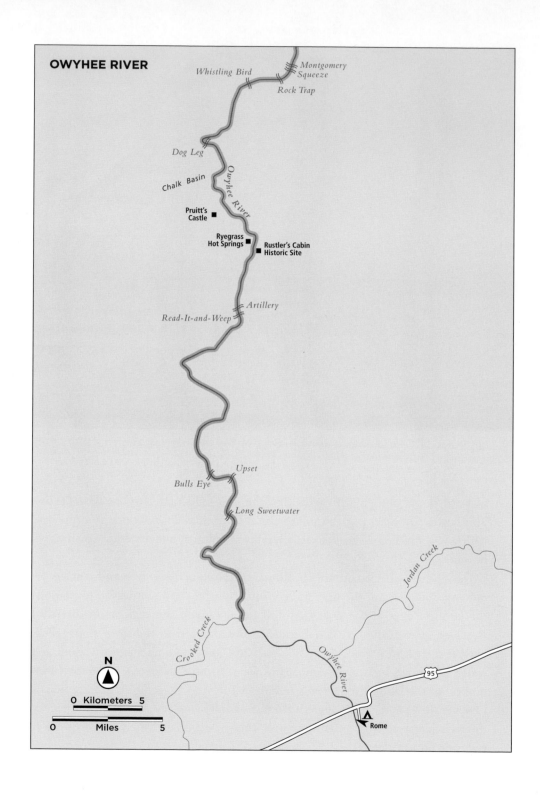

OWYHEE RIVER

Whistling Bird

Montgomery Squeeze

Rock Trap

Dog Leg

Chalk Basin

Owyhee River

Pruitt's Castle

Ryegrass Hot Springs

Rustler's Cabin Historic Site

Artillery

Read-It-and-Weep

Upset

Bulls Eye

Long Sweetwater

Jordan Creek

Crooked Creek

Owyhee River

95

N

0 Kilometers 5

0 Miles 5

Rome

A huge portion of the Owyhee watershed was brought into protection in 1984 under the Wild & Scenic Rivers Act. This includes the three forks of the Owyhee and three tributaries. A total of 120 miles, all designated as *Wild*. This is truly a wild place. The BLM publishes the *Owyhee, Bruneau and Jarbidge: Wild and Scenic Rivers Boating Guide*, and as of 2017 this is being reprinted. Download one for free online or contact the BLM to find where to purchase a copy of the new edition.

The geologic story of the Owyhee River is as twisted as the sinuous meanders of the river. Rhyolite lava flows originating from the Yellowstone hotspot's eruptions some 15–17 million years ago created the brownish-red canyon walls that deeply contrast with the green sage and moss perched on small ledges in Iron Point Canyon. Lava flows continued in the region after the rhyolite deposits, creating layers of basalt over most of the rhyolite as well as deep valleys where lakes would intermittently form. As hot lava periodically flooded the lake sediments, they baked the sand and mud into the hard, red-brick layer we see today. The layers of chalk sandstone, siltstone, and gravel appear as weathered layer-cake formations from these ancient lakebed deposits around mile 24. We couldn't help imagining massive layers of chocolate, vanilla, and strawberry cream pie. As the Owyhee River formed and eroded the land around the layers to create intricate patterns, it also exposed them to elements that molded them into tightly packed spires and cliffs, particularly in the Lambert Rock area.

Archaeologists have identified over one hundred prehistoric habitations throughout the lower Owyhee River valley. These sites often include petroglyphs and are largely kept secret from the general public to avoid destruction. A curious hiker may be able to discover a treasure, but should always respect the site and leave no trace. Evidence of difficult river crossings and abandoned cabins and ranches show the hardships early American homesteaders faced in crossing the harsh landscape. Floating toward the Birch Creek Historic Ranch takeout, a dilapidated waterwheel still sits on the edge of the river, along with other equipment from the early settlers.

PADDLER'S NOTES

Generally, the difficulty of rapids on the lower Owyhee River increases as the water level drops below about 1,000 cubic feet per second (cfs) to reveal tighter lines around small boulders. At medium flows, most rapids can be run down the middle in the wave train. At high water (above 8,000 cfs), expect lots of washed-out rapids, but new features such as holes and waves that will keep you on your toes and could quickly surprise you with a flipped raft.

The trip begins with a placid float through a wide valley sprinkled with historic buildings from the days of westward wagon trips. Class III rapids begin around mile 11, with Long Sweetwater, Upset, and Bulls Eye (class IV at low water). Fill up your

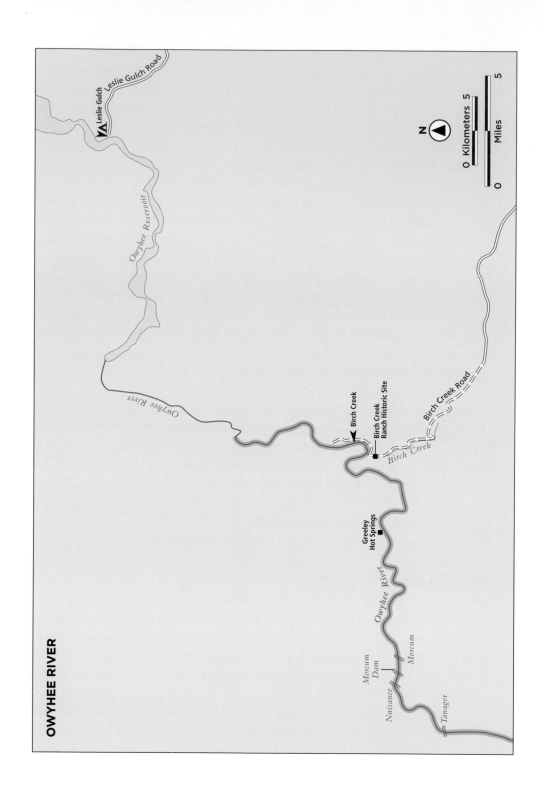

OWYHEE RIVER

Leslie Gulch
Leslie Gulch Road

Owyhee Reservoir

Owyhee River

Owyhee River

Birch Creek

Birch Creek
Ranch Historic Site

Birch Creek Road

Birch Creek

Greeley
Hot Springs

Morcum
Dam

Nuisance

Morcum

Owyhee River

Tanager

N

0 Kilometers 5

0 Miles 5

water jugs at Weeping Wall springs on river left around mile 17.5. While this is a natural spring, you'll still want to treat the water.

The class III returns with Read-It-and-Weep at mile 21, followed by Artillery. The next rapids of note lie just before and within Iron Point Canyon, starting at mile 31. First is the class IV Whistling Bird rapid, where the river pushes into the right cliff wall. A slice of the canyon wall fell into the river on the right, along with many boulders, to create a hazard. Expert kayakers may find it thrilling to navigate through these boulders and underneath the spliced cliff wall resting in the river. Rafts will want to pull away from the right.

Rock Trap and Squeeze rapids (class III) lead into Montgomery, the other class IV. The river pushes left here, and over a large pour-over hole. Most rafts stick to the inside of the bed as much as possible. Low water reveals other tricky rapids below here around mile 38, but mostly the river mellows for your final days of floating.

We found a trip length of six days to be optimal. This included a layover day about a mile downstream of the hot springs at mile 24, with hiking options into the Chalk Basin canyons and a toasty fire all day long (burning wood we packed in and out). Aim to spend time hiking in the Chalk Basin area between miles 24-28, just before Iron Point Canyon around mile 31, or in Jackson Canyon at mile 37. Remember, camping directly below or above a hot spring is restricted to one night only. Many camps have great beaches, including Hackberry at mile 15 and Honeymoon at mile 19.5, while others are gateways to geologic explorations, such as Exit Camp at mile 35.

As of 2017, permits could be acquired at the Rome launch site. Private groups of boaters are limited to twenty people. Contact the BLM for updates and other private party regulations on fires, toilet systems, and more.

DIRECTIONS TO TAKEOUT

There are two takeout options. The first is at the historic Birch Creek Ranch, and includes a rugged, mandatory four-wheel-drive vehicle to climb the steep roads back up toward US 95. When heavy rain strikes, the road has been known to close and leave boaters stranded due to impassable mud and creeks. Luckily, camping and potable water can be found at Birch Creek. Birch Creek Road is located off US 95.

Trips can also float another 17 miles to the Leslie Gulch access, where a much friendlier road exits the canyon. However, this option requires a reservoir slack-water paddle of about 12 miles, often with heavy wind. Bring a motor or plan for a workout. Succor Creek or McBride Creek Roads lead from US 95 to Leslie Gulch. All takeout roads branch off US 95 north of Jordan Valley.

Montgomery rapid in Iron Point Canyon. ADAM ELLIOTT

DIRECTIONS TO PUT-IN

Rome is located on US 95 in Oregon's southeastern corner. The launch site is about 77 miles from the Snake River if you are coming from Boise, Idaho. Campsites and potable water can be found at Rome put-in site.

NEARBY ATTRACTIONS

While few towns or services can be found in the Owyhee Canyonlands, the mountains and tributaries themselves are full of recreation opportunities, from biking and hiking to boating and canyoneering. Try driving back toward Boise on the Owyhee Uplands Backcountry Byway. A great road map and guide can be found on the BLM website.

12

WHITE SALMON RIVER

Section name	Middle and Lower
Distance	7 miles
Flow range	1–5 feet on the stick gauge in Husum, or about 500–2,000 cfs
Season and source of water	Year-round; flows from rain, glacier melt, and aquifer storage
Gauge location	Underwood, USGS #14123500, or a visual stick gauge in Husum
Time required	Half day to full day
Classification	*Scenic*
Difficulty	II–III (IV)
Managing agency	US Forest Service; Columbia Gorge National Scenic Area
Permit required?	No
Shuttle type	Vehicle, bike, hitchhike
Outstandingly Remarkable Values	Whitewater boating, White Salmon River Gorge, hydrology, culture, fisheries
Why paddle this section?	A quintessential Northwest whitewater run; narrow gorges; cold spring water; exciting class III with an optional waterfall

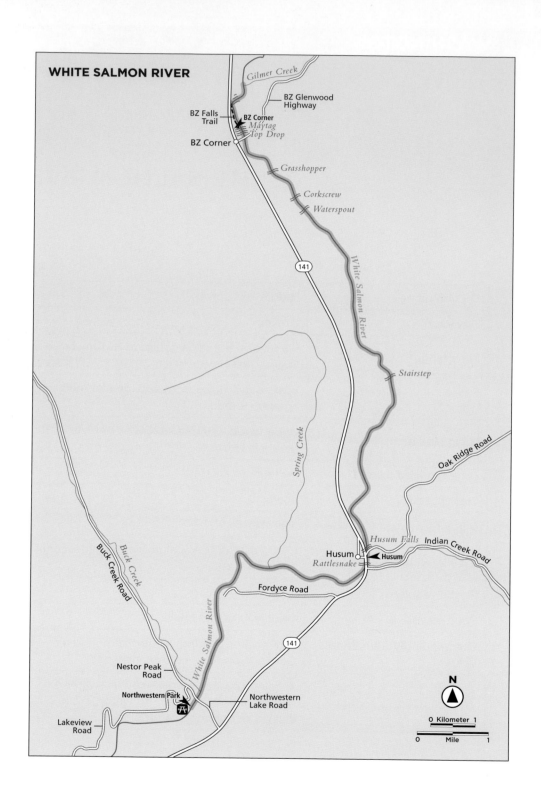

WHITE SALMON RIVER

Gilmer Creek

BZ Glenwood
Highway

BZ Falls
Trail

BZ Corner

BZ Corner

Maytag
Top Drop

Grasshopper

Corkscrew

Waterspout

141

White Salmon River

Stairstep

Spring Creek

Oak Ridge Road

Buck Creek Road

Buck Creek

Husum Falls

Husum

Indian Creek Road

Rattlesnake

Husum

Fordyce Road

141

White Salmon River

Nestor Peak
Road

Northwestern Park

Northwestern
Lake Road

Lakeview
Road

N

0   Kilometer   1

0   Mile   1

Fall kayaking and rafting on below Husum Falls, White Salmon River.
WET PLANET WHITEWATER CENTER

RIVER DESCRIPTION

Of the countless rivers that flow from southern Washington's Mount Adams, the White Salmon River is the one that provides year-round sustenance and everyday paddling opportunities for local and visiting paddlers. In the Columbia River Gorge along the border of Washington and Oregon, the rivers have attracted a thriving paddling community of beginner, intermediate, and elite kayakers and rafters. The White Salmon River is the heart of this community.

The White Salmon is a gem of Pacific Northwest whitewater and the go-to after work run for fun class II eddy-catching all the way up to thrilling class V waterfall-dropping (in upper sections). On the river, columnar basalt walls and deep lava caves line the banks of the region's longest vertical wall gorge. Springs pour and seep from every crevice. Crowds quickly spread out along the narrow river even on busy summer days. With glacial water kept cold in underground aquifers and a narrow canyon that prevents direct sun exposure, you'll find paddlers in dry tops or dry suits all year here.

Snow melts from Mount Adams and fills the porous lava-rock aquifers, preserving the cold temperature and slowly releasing water throughout the entire summer. For this reason, hydrology has been identified as an Outstandingly Remarkable Value. When other rivers in the Columbia River Gorge, in both Washington and Oregon, have dropped too low to paddle during the hot summer months of the Pacific Northwest, the White Salmon always provides flow.

The river's class II–V whitewater provides sections for nearly every level of paddler. The most popular stretch, the Middle White Salmon, offers intermediate class III action for a healthy commercial rafting and private boating scene, with the option of a class IV waterfall experience over Husum Falls. After the river passes through the town of Husum, it becomes known as the Lower White Salmon to the takeout at Northwestern Park. A *Scenic* designation begins at the BZ launch site, where the Middle White Salmon begins, and continues 8 miles downstream through the Lower White Salmon to the takeout at Northwestern Park. This designation, along with the Wild and Scenic headwaters designations and the tenacity of locals, has kept threats of hydropower at bay on the entire length of the river. The class IV-V whitewater can be found on the upstream Farmlands and Green Truss sections of the river.

PADDLER'S NOTES

Both rafters and kayakers put in at BZ Corner, either above the Maytag hole (directly opposite the end of the metal stairs), or just below to run the first class III rapid, Top Drop. The next few miles provide the highest concentration of whitewater on the Middle. First, the river pushes into a cave on river right. Next, a small but tricky and often log-choked boulder garden leads into Grasshopper rapid, which has a narrow right line, a wide center-left line around a large boulder and a pour-over hydraulic, or a line to thread between the two. Next comes Corkscrew rapid, where boaters stick to the right bank just as a waterfall pours in from the top of the right cliff wall. After a surf spot, you'll find Waterspout. This narrow pinch in the river can be run on the middle left at nearly every flow.

For the next few miles, class II read-and-run rapids keep the trip moving smoothly. A big eddy on river left can be a great lunch spot and signals the next class III rapid is nearby. Stairstep rapid is longer and contains several smaller ledges with many different lines. Some boaters choose to run right at the top or look for the nublike boof off the center-right of the ledge. Run down the middle of the second drop with slight left angle. At higher flows (above 3.5 feet on the Husum stick gauge), a fun boof line opens just a few feet off the right bank. While seemingly the smallest, the third ledge (or pinch, rather) provided the most raft flips when the author, Susan, guided commercial here for many seasons, perhaps because it is the most unassuming. Finally, head left of center for the final drop.

FREEING THE WHITE SALMON RIVER: REMOVING CONDIT DAM

We rarely get to witness the rebirth of a river. For nearly a century the White Salmon River flowed freely to where it met Northwestern Lake created by Condit Dam. In 2011, the stagnant lake water disappeared when PacifiCorp blasted a hole in the base of 125-foot-tall dam. The hole rapidly drained the reservoir and much of the trapped sediment that had deposited over a hundred years of river flow. As giant mudslides cascaded into the moving water, the river found its historic course, initiating the return of a free-flowing river ecosystem and the rebirth of the river. Salmon swam to historic headwater spawning grounds again. Vegetation recolonized the old river banks. Whitewater rapids formed in a deep, sinuous, and magical canyon that had been buried for over one hundred years.

Over the course of the next year, PacifiCorp slowly dismantled all evidence of Condit Dam. As the owner of the dam, the power company opted to remove the structure because the upgrades required to meet current environmental standards would cost more for ratepayers. The decision was economic. However, the benefits go beyond savings for ratepayers. The free-flowing river now provides increased commercial and private recreation opportunities for rafters and anglers. The entire river valley ecosystem also benefits from a connected upper and lower watershed, which allows the river to move nutrients, wood, and sediment freely. The only thing left to do is protect this new river reach, the Lower Gorge of the White Salmon River, as a part of the Wild and Scenic system.

Looking upstream from Condit Dam at the newly free-flowing White Salmon River, you could watch a river carve the landscape to find its path after spending one hundred years under the reservoir. ADAM ELLIOTT

Cave Wave on the lower White Salmon River is a locals' favorite soul-surfing spot.
ADAM ELLIOTT

Husum Falls grows closer now. It isn't hard to imagine the thrill of rafting over this for the first time. Thousands of commercial rafters claim Husum Falls as their first waterfall experience. The entire river drops over a 10- to 12-foot ledge just upstream of the WA 141 bridge, making this rapid excellent for spectators and scouters. Generally, the line is to the right of center where the water falls more vertically. Commercial raft trips begin running the drop when the stick gauge downstream reads about 2.5 feet, although the falls have been known to change after every winter. Best to get out and watch others run this one before taking the plunge yourself.

The Lower White Salmon is generally class II, although the continuous nature of the rapids and the water temperature make swimming more consequential than on most class II rivers. Therefore, it isn't a great place for someone without a combat roll. Late summer flows extend the recovery time between rapids, while winter flows bump this run up to a big-wave class III playground with catch-on-the-fly surf spots everywhere. And never miss the opportunity for a soul surf session on the cave wave about two-thirds of the way down the Lower. The cave eddy on the left and cobble bar on the right have some boaters spending hours here on warm summer evenings.

Directly upstream of the Middle White Salmon is the class IV–V Green Truss section, and the Class IV Farmlands stretch of the river is farther upstream. These two sections of river hold a very special place in both the authors' hearts. The steep, narrow gorge, dripping springs over mossy ledges, and absolute incredible quality of whitewater are simply incomparable to anywhere else. If your skills allow, be sure to check them out. Or inquire about hopping on a commercial trip on the Farmlands with Wet Planet Whitewater Center in Husum, WetPlanetWhitewater.com.

> "IF OUR SALMON ARE NOT HEALTHY, THEN OUR WATERSHEDS ARE NOT HEALTHY—AND IF OUR WATERSHEDS ARE NOT HEALTHY, THEN WE HAVE TRULY SQUANDERED OUR HERITAGE AND MORTGAGED OUR FUTURE."
>
> —*John Kitzhaber, Governor of Oregon, August 16, 2000*

DIRECTIONS TO TAKEOUT

From Hood River, Oregon, cross the Columbia River into Washington and turn left on WA 14 for less than a mile. Turn right onto Alt WA 141, which connects to WA 141 proper. Tack on the Lower White Salmon and takeout at Northwestern Park, or leave a car in Husum to run only the Middle.

DIRECTIONS TO PUT-IN

Continue north on WA 141 from the takeout to the small town of BZ Corner where you'll find the US Forest Service's BZ Corner launch site on the right.

NEARBY ATTRACTIONS

Countless guidebooks describe recreation in the Columbia River Gorge. Summer finds kiteboarders and windsurfers flocking to the Columbia River's swells, while kayakers enjoy rivers all year long on both the Oregon and Washington sides. Hiking to waterfalls, mountain biking over desert hillsides, and more make a trip here (multisport) to say the least. After grabbing a lunch and a beer at Wet Planet Whitewater Cafe in Husum (open spring to early fall), go explore the bountiful outdoor splendor. We particularly love the Sleeping Beauty hike near Trout Lake, biking at Syncline near the Klickitat River, and the Falls Creek Falls hike north of the Wind River.

SKAGIT RIVER

Section name	Marblemount to Rockport
Distance	10 miles
Flow range	1,500–12,000 cfs
Season and source of water	Year-round; rain and snowmelt
Gauge location	Marblemount, USGS #12181000
Time required	Half day to full day
Classification	*Recreational*
Difficulty	I–II
Managing agency	Mount Baker–Snoqualmie National Forest
Permit required?	No
Shuttle type	Vehicle
Outstandingly Remarkable Values	Fisheries, scenery, wildlife
Why paddle this section?	Highest concentration of eagles in the Lower 48; views of North Cascade peaks; gentle beginner paddle

Massive trees line the Skagit River, making prime habitat for eagles, osprey, and heron.
ADAM ELLIOTT

RIVER DESCRIPTION

With a backdrop of the rugged, sharp peaks in North Cascades National Park and surrounded by wide and fertile floodplains, the Skagit River will knock you over with its beauty. On your float through the Skagit River Bald Eagle Natural Preserve, you'll see 60-pound salmon dart upstream through the clear, turquoise water. Along the gentle meanders, you'll watch eagles hunt and nest—sometimes up to a few hundred on a single day floating. Mostly, you'll experience a dynamic and important waterway that, along with its major tributaries, has been protected for nearly forty years.

In 1978, the Skagit River joined the ranks of Wild and Scenic rivers, along with several of its major tributaries: Cascade, Sauk, and Suiattle Rivers. In total, 158.8 miles of river received protection that year. In 2014, 14.3 miles of Illabot Creek was added. Designating more than just the main stem allows a greater continuity and connectivity within the watershed. Both paddlers and wildlife benefit from this, with more miles for recreation and more miles for high-quality habitat.

SKAGIT RIVER

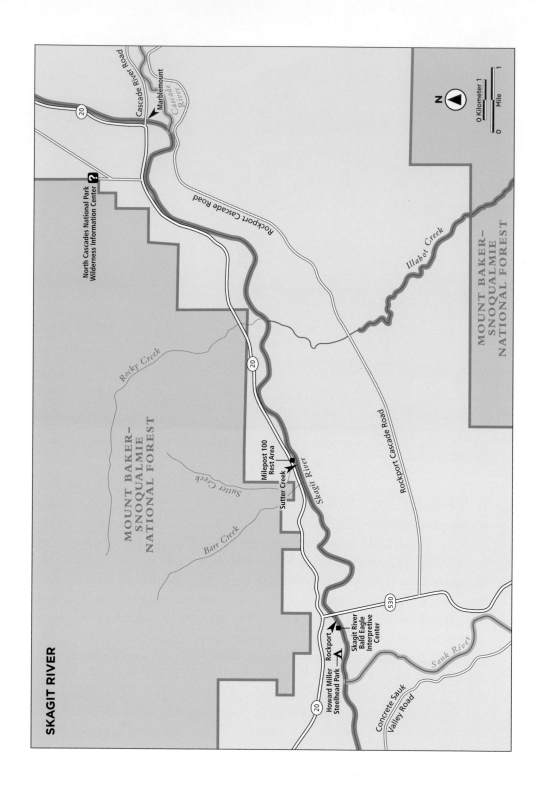

MOUNT BAKER–
SNOQUALMIE
NATIONAL FOREST

MOUNT BAKER–
SNOQUALMIE
NATIONAL FOREST

North Cascades National Park
Wilderness Information Center

Marblemount

Cascade River Road

Cascade River

Rockport Cascade Road

Illabot Creek

Rocky Creek

Sutter Creek

Barr Creek

Milepost 100
Rest Area

Sutter Creek

Skagit River

Rockport Cascade Road

Howard Miller
Steelhead Park

Rockport

Skagit River
Bald Eagle
Interpretive
Center

Concrete Sauk
Valley Road

Sauk River

N

0 Kilometer 1
0   Mile   1

On a clear day, you can see the glaciers of the northern Cascades to the north of the Skagit Valley. ADAM ELLIOTT

The Skagit has been labeled the most important and largest river draining into Washington's Puget Sound. Originating among North Cascades National Park's sharp peaks, the Skagit watershed ranges in elevation from sea level to over 8,000 feet. The lower river's floodplain provides a rich agricultural resource for residents in the Seattle metro area and beyond, while the floodplain narrows to just a few miles wide within the designated Wild and Scenic reach. Farther upstream, streams pour off the steep mountain slopes and no floodplain exists at all.

If you have never witnessed a convocation of eagles, a trip to the Skagit in the winter should be near the top of your list. The section of river described here flows within the Skagit River Bald Eagle Natural Preserve between Marblemount and Rockport. The largest concentration of eagles in the Lower 48 migrate to the Skagit River in the winter from Alaska and northern Canada. The National Park Service and US Forest Service recorded the official high number of individual birds within the Skagit River at over 850 in one week in 2007. Boaters report that numbers in the hundreds can commonly be seen each day during the peak season.

The higher quality of water allows for five species of salmon and three species of sea-going trout to thrive within the watershed, including the designated tributaries of the main stem Skagit River. Despite great habitat, numbers of wild steelhead in the basin plummeted to levels that forced the population onto the Endangered Species List by 2007. In 2010, the Washington Department of Fish and Wildlife closed the river to fishing starting February 1 each year. While the run has revived in numbers, as of 2017 the open fishing season continues to be limited to December and January only. A plan to reopen in the later winter months to catch-and-release is in the works and may be implemented by the time you make it to the river.

PADDLER'S NOTES

Most paddlers seek out this stretch of river in the winter months to view eagles. Snow may line the banks, and the West Coast marine climate will certainly chill your bones if you forget adequate warm gear. When properly prepared, the eagle viewing and gentle paddling is a phenomenal combination. During the eagle season, public recreational boaters must launch after 11 a.m. and guided tours must launch after 12 noon. Eagles have sole use of the river during those morning hours, but you can see them feeding on cobble bars in those early hours from a designated viewing location on shore.

The class I–II riffles on the Skagit can be navigated fairly easily. Stay alert as the channel divides over shallow bars when flows begin to drop, but, otherwise, just enjoy dipping your paddle blades into the calm flow as you take in all the scenery. Pull over at any of the large cobble bars to enjoy a lunch break with ample opportunity for rock skipping.

Be sure to turn around and look upstream, especially in the second half of your paddle. On clear days, the glaciers on the jagged North Cascades peaks create quite the magnificent backdrop to your scenic float.

Upstream sections of the river offer more whitewater, particularly between Goodell Creek and Copper Creek. Intermediate paddlers from British Columbia to Seattle love the S-bends and great class III waves in this reach. Seattle City Light originally slated this section for hydropower development, hence it was not included in the 1978 designation. However, the utility has since dropped the proposal and now supports the extension of the Wild and Scenic designation farther upstream.

Advanced paddlers should keep an eye on flows for the Cascade, a designated tributary flowing into the Skagit just below the Marblemount access site. This class V run dishes out continuous whitewater with classic features characteristic of Washington's North Cascades mountain terrain. Another tributary gem is the Sauk River, which suits the beginner and intermediate paddlers more.

Thomas O'Keefe and Susan share a canoe on a fall day. ADAM ELLIOTT

DIRECTIONS TO TAKEOUT

The Rockport river access site is located on the downstream side of the bridge in Rockport. From the south, turn left onto Rockport Park Road just after you cross the Skagit and park in the lot on the left just downstream of the bridge.

DIRECTIONS TO PUT-IN

From the takeout, continue on Rockport Park Road toward the WA 530 bridge and turn left to get back on WA 530, but on the river-right side of the Skagit. You'll quickly reach WA 20 eastbound, and need to turn right to continue upstream. Stay on WA 20 for 8.4 miles. In Marblemount, you'll technically be turning right to cross the Skagit on Cascade River Road, but it is more like staying straight. Turn right into the boat launch area just after you cross the river.

NEARBY ATTRACTIONS

The North Cascades National Park entrance is just upstream from this section of the Skagit. Taking a few days to experience the headwaters within this park is a great way to extend your Skagit River trip. Also look into floating the other designated tributaries, like the Sauk or Cascade. They typically have optimum flows throughout the rainy winter and spring seasons.

MIDDLE FORK SNOQUALMIE RIVER

Section name	Taylor River to Concrete Bridge (Upper Middle)
Distance	7.5 miles
Flow range	1,000–4000 cfs
Season and source of water	Fall, rainstorms; spring, snowmelt
Gauge location	Tanner, USGS #12141300
Time required	1 day
Classification	*Scenic*
Difficulty	II (III)
Managing agency	Mount Baker–Snoqualmie National Forest
Permit required?	No
Shuttle type	Vehicle, bike
Outstandingly Remarkable Values	Recreation, fisheries, wildlife
Why paddle this section?	Towering peaks and deep forests around every bend; scenery always changing; swift current and class II rapids.

The Middle Fork Feather River changes character several times as it cuts through the northern Sierras. THOMAS O'KEEFE / AMERICAN WHITEWATER

RIVER DESCRIPTION

Just outside of the Seattle metropolis, the Middle Fork Snoqualmie River provides a popular entry point to one of Washington's most extraordinary and popular outdoor recreation destinations. The upper stretch of river, described here, sweeps boaters beneath wide views of Mount Garfield, with deep riparian forests along the banks. Class II rapids produce just the right amount of thrill and action for a chill day floating through this majestic landscape.

Draining Chains Lake and the Alpine Lakes Wilderness, the Middle Fork Snoqualmie's water quality remains high despite its proximity to such a large city. Old-growth trees can still be found in the headwaters forests, which provide habitat for countless wildlife species including large mammals like elk, cougars, and bear.

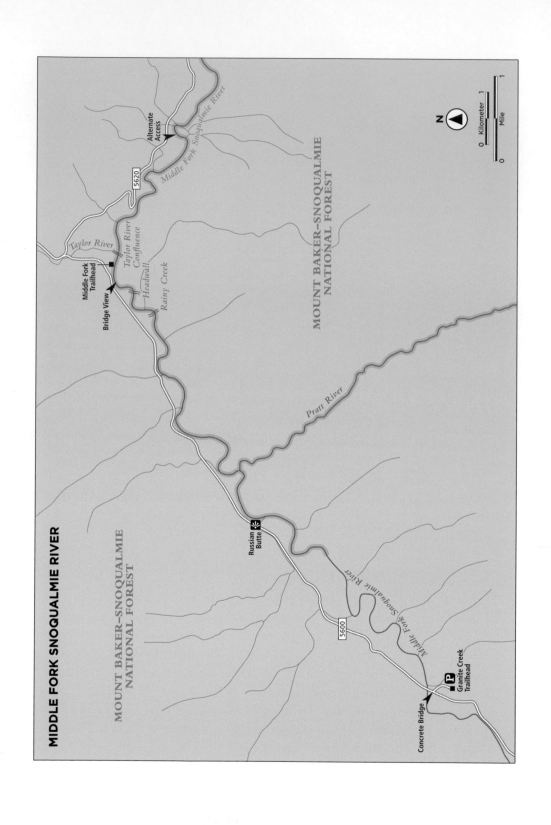

Superb native trout habitat exists in both the main stem river and tributaries like the Pratt River.

Access into the upper watershed became much easier as of 2016 with the paving of nine additional miles of Middle Fork Road. Boaters now find better parking, trails, and ramps leading to the river as well. These improvements, including facilities for boaters, would not have been provided had it not been for the work of American Whitewater. This nonprofit helped local planners understand the value of recreation in this corridor.

The Middle Fork Snoqualmie is one of the more recent Wild and Scenic designations. In 2014, twenty-seven river miles received protection from the headwaters to just downstream of the Pratt River confluence. Classified as *Wild*, the Pratt River also entered the Wild and Scenic system in 2014.

PADDLER'S NOTES

The gauge reads the river level at the downstream end of this section. Generally, if you see 1,000–3,000 cubic feet per second (cfs) on the gauge, the section should have enough water to paddle. We recommend the Bridge View put-in near the Middle Fork Snoqualmie trailhead. Boaters (both rafters and kayakers) should park at the pullout at mile 11.3 along the road, rather than parking at the trailhead and scrambling under the footbridge. If you want to add a few miles to the trip and more iconic vistas of Mount Garfield, continue up Middle Fork Road less than a mile to cross the Taylor River. Within a short distance, Middle Fork Road will spur to the right up a small hill. This spur is easy to miss. At mile 14.8 along this spur road you'll see a trail to the river marked by several large boulders

The current will keep you moving as you meander around each bend of the upper Middle Fork Snoqualmie. Fresh vistas of surrounding peaks pop up behind the old-growth riparian forest as you make your way downstream.

One of the most popular sections of river for Seattle's whitewater paddlers is the middle Middle Snoqualmie, just downstream from the section described here. Class III–IV rapids here challenge the intermediate boater and can be reached in less than an hour from the city. You'll find most of the crowds frequent this section, rather than the more tranquil float on the upper.

DIRECTIONS TO TAKEOUT
Take exit 34 from I-90 east to 468th Ave SE. Turn left (north) on 468th Ave. In 0.6 miles turn right on Middle Fork Road. Stay on this road for 5.6 miles to the reach Granite Creek trailhead, where you can park your vehicle. Take out on river left after floating under the bridge, and walk back to your car. You can also take out 3 miles up the road at Russian Butte View (a good option when flows are lower, as the whitewater is tamer and the views are less dramatic).

Taka O'Keefe takes the plunge from a midstream boulder on the Middle Fork Snoqualmie at one of many great midsummer swimming holes. Thomas O'Keefe / American Whitewater

DIRECTIONS TO PUT-IN

Keep driving upstream for a little over 6 miles on Middle Fork Road to reach Bridge View access site, a small parking area on the right side of the road just before the Middle Fork trailhead parking. An alternate upstream put-in can be reached by continuing to mile 14.8 to a small parking area.

NEARBY ATTRACTIONS

If your skills allow, continue floating into the class III–IV middle Middle Snoqualmie downstream. It is a classic stretch of whitewater in the region. Or consider exploring the watershed by foot via one of the many trailheads along Middle Fork Road. If your route takes you by Snoqualmie Falls, downstream of this paddling section, take a few minutes to walk to one of the overlooks. While much of the river's volume is diverted into powerhouses, the river can still span across the entire 286-foot-tall ledge at high flows, sending blinding spray hundreds of feet up into the air.

Opposite: It would be great to spend more than three days on the Middle Feather, but for the lack of plentiful campsites. Adam Elliott

California

15

MIDDLE FORK FEATHER RIVER

Section name	Devil's Canyon
Distance	32.7 miles
Flow range	700–3,000 cfs
Season and source of water	Spring; snowmelt
Gauge location	Merrimac, AW gauge ID #42691
Time required	3 days
Classification	*Wild* and *Scenic*
Difficulty	V
Managing agency	Plumas National Forest
Permit required?	No
Shuttle type	Vehicle
Outstandingly Remarkable Values	Fisheries, geology, history, recreation, scenery
Why paddle this section?	Remote wilderness kayak self-support, from class fun to full-on class V.

The Middle Fork Feather feels quite different in different sections. ADAM ELLIOTT

RIVER DESCRIPTION

The Devil's Canyon run on the Middle Fork Feather is often described as three distinct sections, with three distinct difficulty levels. Kayakers start the first day paddling numerous class III rapids, a few excellent class IV rapids, and one class V rapid. On day two more distinct, mostly class IV and V rapids are encountered while paddling through Franklin Canyon, including Franklin Falls, a sloping 10-foot drop into a frothy hole. Paddlers enter Devil's Canyon proper on day three, and the paddling is mostly class V rapids consisting of large granite boulders and cliffs. The whitewater and scenery will easily take your break away.

Downstream of Devil's Canyon, below Milsap Bar, the river drops through the steeper class V+ Bald Rock Canyon. The entire 108 miles of the Middle Fork Feather downstream from Beckwourth to Oroville Reservoir carries a *Wild*, *Scenic*, or *Recreational* classification. In 1968, when the Middle Fork Feather joined the first batch of rivers in the Wild and Scenic system, the designation extended farther than today. In 1978

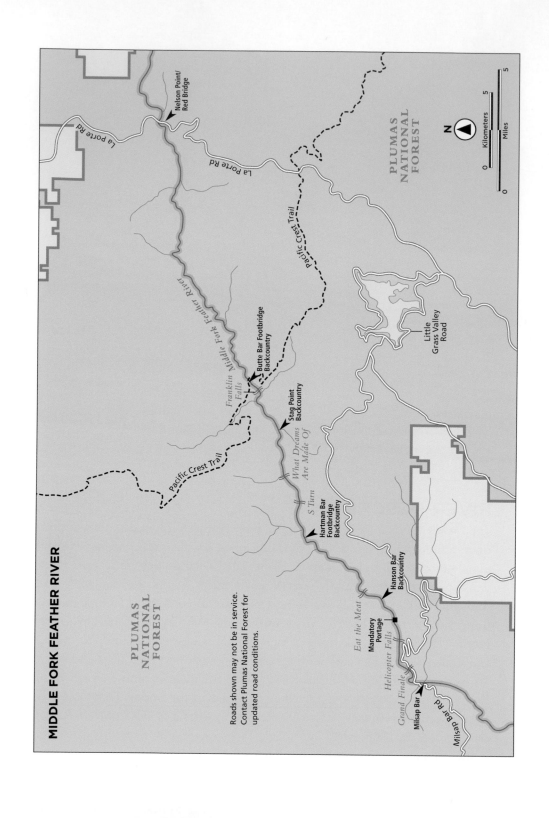

MIDDLE FORK FEATHER RIVER

Roads shown may not be in service.
Contact Plumas National Forest for
updated road conditions.

PLUMAS
NATIONAL
FOREST

PLUMAS
NATIONAL
FOREST

La Porte Rd

La Porte Rd

Nelson Point/
Red Bridge

Pacific Crest Trail

Pacific Crest Trail

Franklin
Falls

Middle Fork Feather River

Butte Bar Footbridge
Backcountry

Stag Point
Backcountry

What Dreams
Are Made Of

S Turn

Hartman Bar
Footbridge
Backcountry

Hanson Bar
Backcountry

Eat the Meat

Mandatory
Portage

Helicopter Falls

Grand Finale

Milsap Bar

Milsap Bar Rd

Little
Grass Valley
Road

N

Kilometers   5

Miles   5

0

0

several miles near a private ranch were delisted. This stripping of designation status is the only instance where protections have been lifted from a Wild and Scenic river.

Even with a designation, mining threatens this river. In 1970, a dredging permit was issued to an Arizona mining company without the need for an environmental impact statement. Sportsmen and environmental groups fought and stopped the dredging. Resource extraction in the many watersheds of Wild and Scenic rivers continues to threaten their Outstandingly Remarkable Values.

PADDLER'S NOTES

Any wilderness run, regardless of difficulty, should be approached with caution. Early season (April or May) often has higher water from snowmelt, and can be cold with unstable weather patterns. Late season—June or July—often has great weather but lower flows. Although the run can be done in two days, we highly encourage groups to take three or four days.

You'll lose count of how many class IV and V rapids you encounter. Many can be portaged and some are must-run. Make sure to plan contingency time for inclement weather, spikes in flow, or group mishaps. The whitewater labeled on the map are what we consider some of the more notable class V rapids. They are not the only difficult rapids on the run. Be ready for lots of class IV–V for the duration of this run.

Day one has only one class V rapid, a manky boulder garden best run in a tight slot left of a big boulder. Franklin Falls, run on day two, often has a very retentive hydraulic, but is easily portaged on the left with a big seal launch. Day three has the most whitewater, with more class V than we can mention here. At about mile 29, a large pool with many small waterfalls on river left will help you identify the mandatory portage on river right. Don't miss it.

About a mile downstream, class V Helicopter Falls is best scouted on river right, but there is no good portage around this drop. Find the best line from shore, then lace up and drop in. Finale rapid is the last major drop before the takeout at Milsap Bar, with many challenging rapids to keep things interesting in between.

DIRECTIONS TO TAKEOUT

From Oroville, drive east on CA 162, Oroville-Quincy Highway, for about 22 miles to the tiny town of Brush Creek. Turn right on Bald Rock Road, and then almost immediately left onto Milsap Bar Road. Unfortunately, the road is not open all the way to the river; you should see a sign telling you that the road is closed (this is a "temporary closure," but it could be years before it reopens). As of this writing, there was a good place to park and pick up river runners about 2 miles up from the river. We don't advise leaving a vehicle parked here for the entirety of your run, as there have been break-ins and vandalism in the past. Check with the Feather River Ranger

Adam prepares to boof the center line in one of the few class V rapids in Franklin Canyon, Middle Fork Feather River. DAVE HOFFMAN

District at (530) 534-6500 for current information about road access, as well as any other emerging hazards or safety issues. Another good resource is the Plumas National Forest website.

DIRECTIONS TO PUT-IN

The put-in for Devil's Canyon, Nelson Point, or Red Bridge is on La Porte Road just south of Quincy, California. There are multiple ways to get there from the Lake Oroville area, but don't trust Google for your decision. If you are driving your own shuttle and are going directly to the put-in from the takeout, continue east on CA 162 for about 40 miles to the town of Quincy. Continue straight on to CA 70 east for 3.5 miles. Turn right on La Porte Road. Drive 8 miles to Red Bridge Campground.

NEARBY ATTRACTIONS

Bald Rock Canyon on the Middle Fork Feather is a classic Sierra Cali granite class V run directly downstream from the Devil's Canyon section. For all of you hard-core paddlers out there, try to hit this run later in the season. After the Devil's Canyon flows drop out, Bald Rock will come into appropriate flows. Feather River Falls on the Fall River, tributary of the Middle Fork Feather, is a horsetail falls totaling 410 feet, and a beautiful sight.

NORTH FORK SMITH RIVER

Section name	Major Moore's to Gasquet
Distance	14.8 miles
Flow range	8–12 feet
Season and source of water	October to April, during the rainy season
Gauge location	Crescent City, USGS #11532500
Time required	1 day
Classification	*Recreational, Wild,* and *Scenic*
Difficulty	IV
Managing agency	Six Rivers National Forest
Permit required?	No
Shuttle type	Vehicle (hiring a driver recommended)
Outstandingly Remarkable Values	Fisheries, geology, recreation, scenery
Why paddle this section?	Miles of dreamy class III–IV rapids; chromatic spectrum in both water and mountains; a day-long wilderness paddle

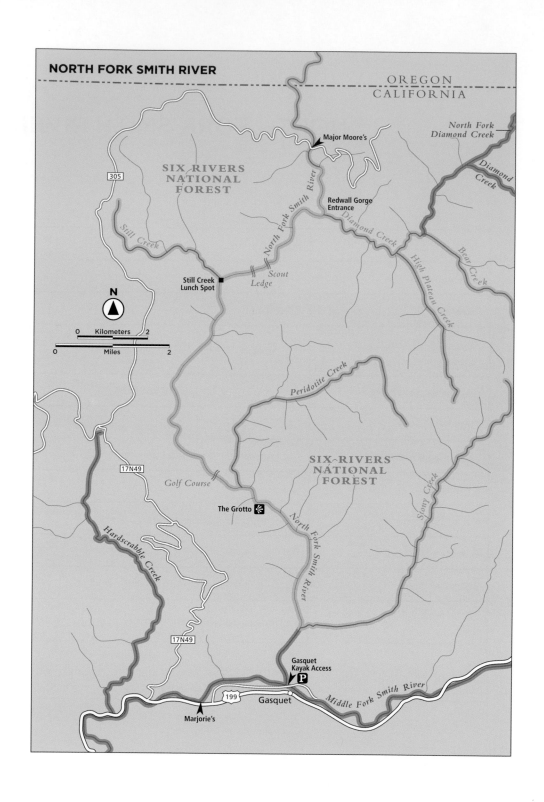

NORTH FORK SMITH RIVER

OREGON
CALIFORNIA

SIX RIVERS
NATIONAL
FOREST

305

North Fork
Diamond Creek

Major Moore's

Diamond Creek

Redwall Gorge
Entrance

Still Creek

North Fork Smith River

Diamond Creek

Bear Creek

High Plateau Creek

N

Still Creek
Lunch Spot

Scout
Ledge

0 Kilometers 2

0 Miles 2

Peridotite Creek

SIX RIVERS
NATIONAL
FOREST

17N49

Golf Course

Stony Creek

The Grotto

North Fork Smith River

Hardscrabble Creek

17N49

Gasquet
Kayak Access

P

199 Gasquet

Middle Fork Smith River

Marjorie's

View of the Smith watershed from the drive in to the put-in. LORI TURBES

RIVER DESCRIPTION

The North Fork Smith River is one of the more remarkable yet generally unknown rivers to paddle in California. Many whitewater kayakers seek class "fun" rapids, the type that challenge skills and technique but don't instill too much nervous energy or fear. For most paddlers, class fun rapids fall into a class III–IV range. If this speaks to you, then the North Fork Smith may just be your dream kayak or raft trip.

Imagine miles of playful rapids in a dramatic, wild, and remote canyon that can be accessed in just a day. Steep, forested hillsides reminiscent of an Idaho landscape climb from the rocky, canyon walls at river level. Jagged red rocks juxtapose with the absolutely clear turquoise water flowing around granite boulders polished so smooth as to appear silver. As the river draws flows into the Middle Fork Smith River, the landscape shifts to the moss-laden, redwood-thick Northern California rainforest ecological zone.

Minerals in the serpentine rock found in this watershed make it difficult for plants to grow, unlike in the lush forests just to the south, in the other forks of the Smith River. This is why hillsides appear more like a desert than a rainforest. One of the plants that thrives here, however, is the carnivorous California pitcher plant, which eats insects to obtain more nutrients.

Paddlers bounce down one of many class II and III wave trains on the North Fork Smith River. LORI TURBES

With its source in Oregon's Kalmiopsis Wilderness, the North Fork Smith is designated from its headwater streams across the California state line all the way to its confluence with the Middle Fork Smith in Gasquet. From there, the designation continues all the way to the ocean. Four tributaries of the North Fork are also protected as Wild and Scenic, making the watershed incredibly pristine. Despite this, proposals to mine threaten the headwaters.

With no hydropower upstream to falsely manipulate the river's water, boatable flows come and go throughout the long rainy winter season with minimal notice. For this reason, only a small handful of outfitters offer commercial trips on any of the Smith River tributaries. When nature gifts you perfect flows while you happen to be in this remote corner of Northern California, you will treasure your day paddling and this deeply special place that much more.

PADDLER'S NOTES

Paddlers launch on the North Fork Smith at a range of flow levels. Generally, a good medium flow is 9 to 10.5 feet. Rapids get really big with minimal time to regroup at levels above 11 feet. Always keep in mind the wilderness character of this run. Hiking out could turn into a multiday epic.

Don't expect a long flat-water stretch on this river until the last few miles. Nope, this paddler's gem provides back-to-back, pure fun, class III read-and-run rapids, with several class IV rapids to keep things spicy. We're talking nearly fourteen miles of this.

First, hire a driver to take you up to the put-in and leave your car at the takeout. The shuttle would take you several hours on top of a long day paddling. Plus, you'll want to meet "Bearfoot" Brad Camden, a Gasquet local who knows everything about the North Fork Smith River. As of this writing, you could reach him at (707) 457-3365; bradcamden@earthlink.net. He lives near the takeout, next to She-She's Restaurant on CA 199. With at least a day's notice, he can find multiple cars to help run shuttles for larger groups.

From the put-in at Major Moore's, you'll find class III immediately. After Diamond Creek enters on river left, about 1.5 miles downstream, look for Scout rapid. You may have guessed, but most boaters scout this one on the right. It may be the most difficult rapid you encounter. Ledge rapid is about a quarter-mile downstream from Scout rapid. This one is hard to scout.

As Still Creek flows in on the right, you'll see a great rocky outcrop where most boaters rest and enjoy a lunch break. Four more miles of class III, and you'll encounter the class IV Golf Course, with lots of holes to pick your way around. Just after Peridotite Creek flows in on the left you'll see the Grotto on river right. Paddle under these dripping falls for a surreal view. Waterfall Alley extends for another mile downstream.

DIRECTIONS TO TAKEOUT

See our recommendation in the Paddler's Notes section about hiring a shuttle driver. If you want to do it yourself, a wooden sign on CA 199 in Gasquet will direct you to the turn for Marjorie's access takeout.

DIRECTIONS TO PUT-IN

To reach Major Moore's from Marjorie's, continue west on CA 199. After you cross the river, turn right onto Low Divide Road/FR 17N49. Keep left at the first fork, within half a mile, and settle in for 19.5 miles of slow dirt-road driving. Junctions are not well labeled so bring a map, or hire Brad to drive you.

NEARBY ATTRACTIONS

Spend as much time as you can in the Smith watershed. Paddle any section that fits your ability level, and you won't be disappointed. Camp at Jedediah Smith Redwoods State Park or Redwood National and State Parks to feel the awe that redwood trees naturally instill in anyone. Go for a hike anywhere within those parks to really have the magic of redwoods soak into your soul. Between the crystal-clear water and blissful bewilderment of the size of the redwood groves, you will be forever altered. We promise.

TRINITY RIVER

Section name	Hayden Flat to Cedar Flat
Distance	6.7 miles
Flow range	500–5,000+ cfs
Season and source of water	Year-round; dam release, rainfall, and snowmelt
Gauge location	Near Burnt Ranch, USGS #11527000
Time required	Half day to full day
Classification	*Recreational*
Difficulty	II+
Managing agency	Shasta–Trinity National Forest
Permit required?	No
Shuttle type	Vehicle
Outstandingly Remarkable Values	Fisheries
Why paddle this section?	Great weekend riverside camping; surfing galore; forested watershed with clear and refreshing water

CA 299 follows the Trinity River and allows great views of both the Del Loma and Burnt Ranch Gorge sections. ADAM ELLIOTT

RIVER DESCRIPTION

The Trinity River's vibrant waters, on-the-fly surf, and sinuously sculpted boulders provide paddlers with ample enjoyment any time of year. A major tributary of the Wild and Scenic Klamath River, this river welcomes families for weekends of camping and floating in a majestic mountain setting.

The Trinity Alps mountain range in the coastal mountains of Northern California formed as the oceanic plate collided with the continental plate, causing uplifting and mountain building. Glaciation and repeated cycles of erosion all contributed to the diverse concoction of rock types we see today, including gabbro, chert, granite, diorite, limestone, sandstone, serpentine, schist, and marble. Large outcrops of these rocks, many perfectly smoothed from the river's power, can be seen around every bend as you float. The Mediterranean climate brings ample precipitation to the watershed,

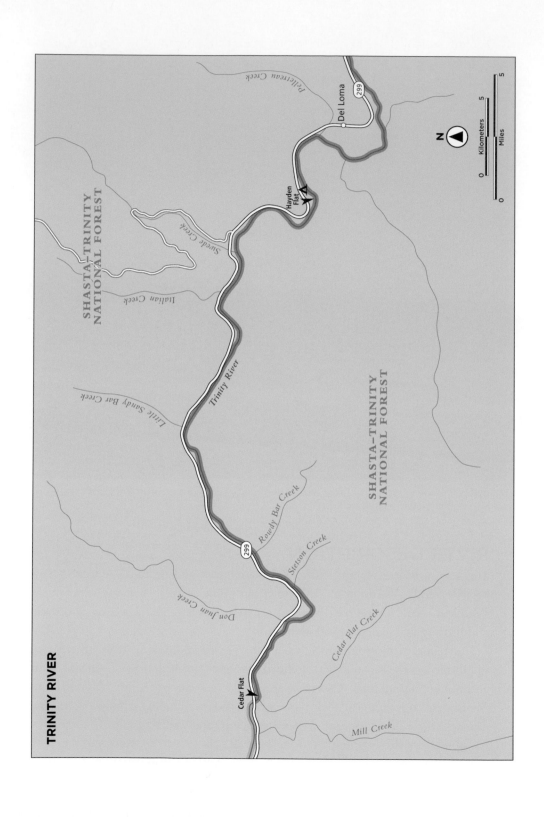

TRINITY RIVER

helping sustain flows for boating throughout most years. The watershed is almost entirely forested, with a mixed coniferous and hardwood ensemble of trees. Along with this come the animals who prefer to live in a healthy, intact forest, such as large and small mammals, bald eagles, bats, and more.

At one time the river was known for its salmon, steelhead, and sturgeon runs. While the ecosystem continues to recover from the resource extraction of the past, these runs have not yet returned to historical numbers. Despite this, fishing for salmon and steelhead remains popular, along with the nonnative trophy brown trout, hence, the Outstandingly Remarkable Value for fish on this river.

The rush for gold hit the Trinity River hard. Placer mining chewed up gravel bars, and hydraulic mining blasted hillsides. However, hostile Native Americans in the Burnt Ranch area (downstream of the section of river described here) and the treacherous nature of the river gorges prohibited much mining upstream, leaving these areas a little less impacted.

After the gold rush, the Trinity River continued to provide for hungry and eager settlers through dredging. These claims soon ended, and the remaining settlers turned to ranching and logging, an economic staple even today. As you wind your way up the Trinity River, you'll see a strong recreational economy as well, with campgrounds and rafting outfitters sprinkled in the valley.

PADDLER'S NOTES

River levels vary widely for this section of the Trinity. Some argue that flows up to 40,000 cubic feet per second (cfs) make for a fun day, while the majority of paddlers stick to flows below 5,000 cfs. Generally, there is enough water to run this section all year long.

The Trinity does not see the same crowds as the popular South Fork American River but offers a similar range of difficulty. Upstream of Hayden Flat, you'll find fantastic class III whitewater, and downstream lies the famous class V Burnt Ranch Gorge. The section featured here, Hayden Flat to Cedar Flat, is the best paddling for the widest variety of skill levels. Beginning boaters will find challenges in the small hydraulics and wave trains, while advanced boaters can surf their hearts out.

Class II waves and maneuvers dominate this stretch. We enjoyed catching lots of eddies and as much surf-on-the-fly as possible. While the road follows this *Recreational* stretch, it is far enough above the river level that you barely notice it, making the run feel more remote than it actually is.

DIRECTIONS TO TAKEOUT

From Redding to the east or Arcata to the west, the road to the Trinity is CA 299. The road follows the river, and can be blocked in places by landslides or snow during the winter. The Cedar Flat access site is at milepost 56.2 from Arcata. You'll pass the

December snows adorn the Trinity Alps above the Del Loma section of the Trinity River.
SUSAN ELLIOTT

access points for the class V Burnt Ranch Gorge section of the river from Arcata, and the Pigeon Point section from Redding.

DIRECTIONS TO PUT-IN
The Hayden Flat Campground access point is at milepost 62.9 along CA 299, just before Del Loma when driving from the west (Arcata).

NEARBY ATTRACTIONS
The Trinity provides class I–V paddling options throughout most years. Plan to camp and explore this canyon for a few days. The Klamath and Smith Rivers, just north of here, and the Eel River to the south, make for more Wild and Scenic paddling options. Of course, the national forests in this region offer plenty of multisport adventures too.

18

LOWER AMERICAN RIVER

Section	Sailor Bar Park to River Bend Park
Distance paddled	8.25 miles
Flow range	600–12,000 cfs
Season and source of water	Year-round; dam releases with added water from spring snowmelt
Gauge location	Nimbus Fish Hatchery
Time required	Half day to full day
Classification	*Recreational*
Difficulty	Class I–II
Managing agency	Sacramento County Regional Parks
Permit required?	Yes: parking and boating permit at county launch sites
Shuttle type	Bike, vehicle
Outstandingly Remarkable Values	Fisheries, recreation
Why paddle this section?	Best urban recreation section in the system; beginner friendly

RIVER DESCRIPTION

The Lower American River below Folsom Dam provides excellent beginner paddling, beautiful scenery, and very little evidence that the river flows through one of California's biggest metropolises. Almost entirely surrounded by Sacramento County's American River Parkway system of river access and recreation areas, the river feels like

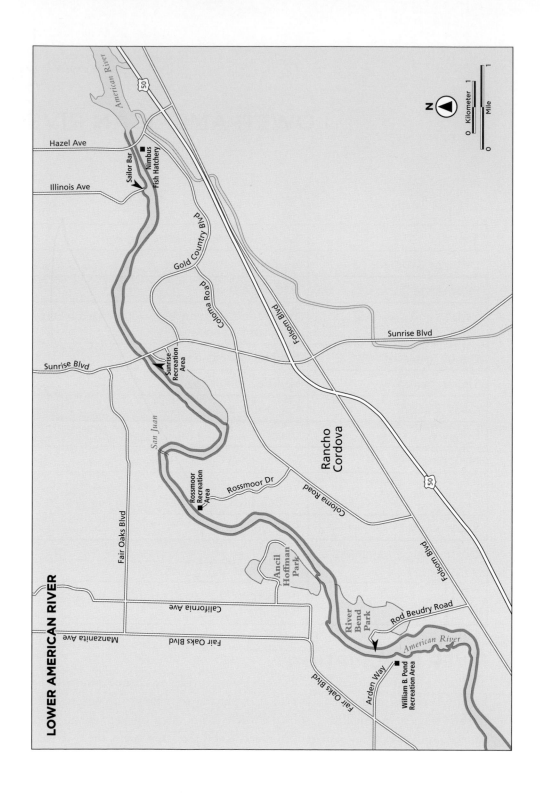

a fully natural corridor lined with thick vegetation, riverside cliff walls, and interesting clay and rock formations.

In 1981, the Lower American River joined the Wild and Scenic system with twenty-three miles of *Recreational* river starting at the outflow of Nimbus Dam and continuing to the confluence with the Sacramento River. While most *Recreational* rivers have a road visible from river level, the American River does not. However, plenty of fellow paddlers, bikers, walkers, swimmers, sunbathers, and more will be seen. A bike path follows the entire course of the river, allowing both bikers and walkers to easily access the water. On hot days, people can be found under every shady tree, especially those with a rope swing attached, enjoying intermittent swims, welcoming shade, and the occasional blast of hot California sunshine.

PADDLER'S NOTES

The high water level on our spring paddle on this stretch must have discouraged other boaters, as we had the whole river to ourselves. We hear this is rare. On hot summer days, rafters, tubers, recreational kayakers, and more flock to this urban watering hole, many for their first experience floating along a river. Rangers patrol access points to check permits and remind river users to wear their personal flotation devices (PFDs). They also help discourage unprepared paddlers on high water days. While mostly flat water, the river's power can easily flip and pin any watercraft, especially at bridge piers. Beginning paddlers should stick to flows under 6,000 cfs.

The class II San Juan rapid may add a dash of excitement to your day on the water. The rapid changes at different flow levels, but generally has larger waves and a swirly eddy in the center-right of the river. Stick to the left, or the inside of the bend, if you want to avoid it, or take your chances with a swim and head for the meat of the rapid itself.

Rafts, PFDs, and paddles can be rented from a number of outfitters in the area. Or take a class from the local California Canoe & Kayak (calkayak.com) (510) 893-7833, outpost to improve your technique and start venturing to other rivers in the area. The Lower American is a great place to start a life of river-running explorations.

DIRECTIONS TO TAKEOUT

River Bend Park, one takeout option, can be accessed from exit 15, Mather Field Road, from US 50 east of Sacramento. Turn right on Mather Field Road and then make a sharp left onto Folsom Boulevard. Turn right on Rod Beaudry Drive to head into River Bend Park. Purchase your parking and boating permits at the kiosk near the entrance to the park if no one is at the booth. Head left at all turns to park at the farthest downstream parking lot. From the river, you'll recognize this takeout as a

Bluffs line the American River on the north side, creating a nice buffer from residential neighborhoods. ADAM ELLIOTT

long cobble bar on the left at the end of a large left bend in the river. A path with two concrete strips leads up over a berm and to the parking lot.

DIRECTIONS TO PUT-IN

To reach Sailor Bar from River Bend, get back on US 50 eastbound and exit onto Hazel Avenue. Turn left on Winding Way in 1.5 miles. Turn left again onto Illinois Avenue, and head into Sailor Bar Park. Don't forget to purchase a parking and boating permit.

NEARBY ATTRACTIONS

The Jedediah Smith Memorial Trail provides a great complement to a day on the river, especially if using bikes for your river shuttle. The trail runs for 32 miles from Discovery Park to Beals Point. The Nimbus Fish Hatchery provides great educational opportunities in the efforts required to raise and release fish into the river.

MERCED RIVER

Section names	Yosemite National Park; Indian Flat to Briceburg
Distance	In Yosemite: 5 miles; Indian Flat to Briceburg: 12 miles
Flow range	800–8,000 cfs (<7 feet on Pohono Bridge)
Season and source of water	Spring and summer; snowmelt
Gauge location	Pohono Bridge, USGS #11266500
Time required	Half day to full day
Classification	*Recreational, Scenic,* and *Wild*
Difficulty	Yosemite: I–II; Indian Flat to Briceburg: III
Managing agency	Yosemite National Park; Sierra National Forest
Permit required?	Permit required within Yosemite; not required outside park
Shuttle type	Shuttle bus within Yosemite; vehicle or hitchhiking outside the park
Outstandingly Remarkable Values	Culture, geology, recreation, scenery, biology, hydrology
Why paddle this section?	Most unique way to experience Yosemite; roadside whitewater through California alpine meadows and forests; beginner and intermediate options

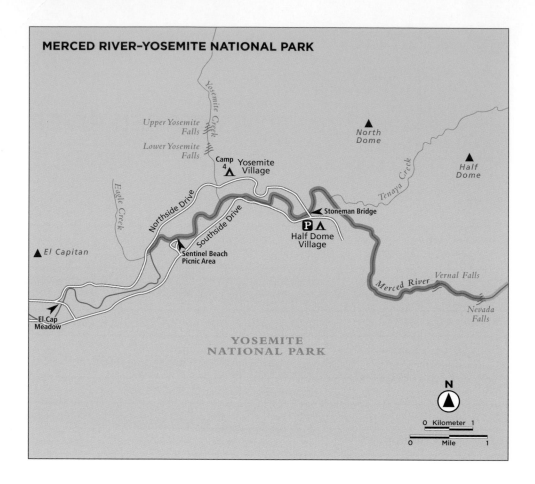

RIVER DESCRIPTION

Turned off by the crowds visiting Yosemite these days? As a paddler, you're in luck. Floating along the valley's central waterway, the Wild and Scenic Merced River, may be the best way to experience the solitude and magnificence of this iconic American landscape. Imagine slowly taking in the view of Half Dome just upstream from your launch as you lazily drift around a forested river bend, away from campgrounds and trails. Yosemite Falls comes into view next, and you imagine the line of hikers waiting to reach the top. You take another relaxed stroke in the placid river meander, far away from the chaos. As you get closer to the takeout at the base of El Capitan, enjoy the serene moments and scan the wall for climbers. Paddling the Merced is the way to go.

The dreamy paddling does not stop at the park boundary. Whitewater rapids have long been adored from El Portal to beyond Briceburg. Advanced paddlers begin in the steeper sections upstream, while intermediate paddlers launch near Indian Flats for a long and scenic day in the foothills of California's Sierra.

Much of the Merced through the heart of Yosemite National Park is placid and reflective.
MICHELLE FRANCESCO / AMERICAN WHITEWATER

Love for this river began thousands of years before paddlers took their plastic boats to these waters. While John Muir claimed that the glaciated valleys, roaring waterfalls, and surrounding mountains of Yosemite Valley deserved to be protected from human impacts, Native Americans had already been living in the Merced Valley for at least 8,000 years. The Indian village of Ahwahnee, located behind the current visitor center, provides a glimpse into the life of the Southern Sierra Miwoks' way of life. The gold rush days in 1849 initiated a swift and violent end to this lifestyle by greedy settlers. By the 1930s, the Indians still holding onto their homes were relocated and eventually evacuated. It is a sobering reminder of the efforts we've made to preserve wild landscapes.

Today, most visitors know the Merced only from driving over its bridges or picnicking alongside its banks. Paddling the Merced within the Yosemite National Park just became legal in 2015. For decades, the National Park Service did not recognize paddling as a legitimate form of recreation. American Whitewater worked with park

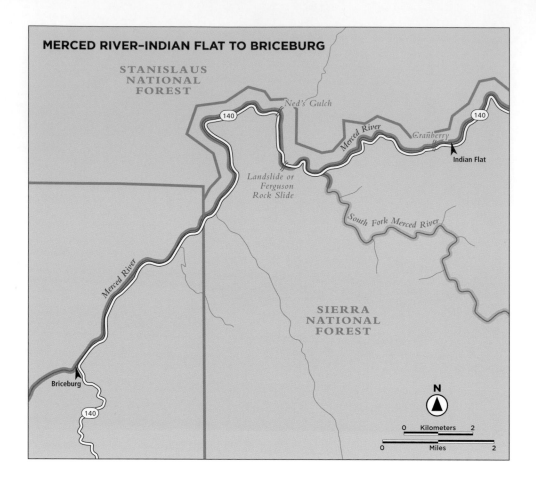

managers to show that the river can be seen as a "water trail," similar to other back-country routes. Through a collaborative and research-based process, the park opened the Merced to river recreation, and paddlers across the state rejoiced. The Merced River Management Plan not only addressed river activities but also provided a balance between resource use and multiple user groups. At least in Yosemite, boating has gained equal footing to other forms of low-impact recreation.

PADDLER'S NOTES
Before launching your boat within the national park, check in with a ranger for updates on regulations, conditions, and river access locations. To protect the Merced's wild nature, large wood will be left in place and certain sensitive riparian zones will be off-limits for riverside picnics. We can paddle here now, but with the understanding that we will help protect these resources. Do your part to get educated.

The section within Yosemite technically begins at the Stoneman Bridge. However, the classified *Recreational* reach begins farther upstream at Nevada Falls. The designation thus includes the iconic hike to Nevada and Vernal Falls. Don't let the crowds deter you from seeing these two falls, and the beginning of the quintessential John Muir Trail. Hit the trail as early as possible (before 8 a.m.) to catch some solitude on the way up. To fully take in the Merced's Wild and Scenic designation, plan a backpacking trip farther into the headwaters. For experienced whitewater boaters looking for a class V challenge, throw that packraft (and special use permit) into your pack and float the *Wild* reach above Nevada Falls (see Priscilla Macy's account of an adventure into the Upper Merced on page 109).

To stick to Yosemite's mellow class I–II rapids and gentle flat water, plan to take out at Sentinel Beach Picnic Area or El Capitan Meadows. Remember that the park limits the number of boaters each day, similar to backcountry trail regulations. This likely won't be an issue for you because it is estimated that less than 5 percent of Yosemite visitors look to float the Merced. Additionally, the specific number of daily float permits may change as Yosemite managers study the use and impact to the resources. This form of continuing analysis will help maintain this exquisite paddling resource for many years to come.

For a bit more whitewater action, look to the roadside stretches of the Merced just outside the park boundary. While we focus on the stretch beginning at Indian Flat, the whitewater upstream can be a blast if your skills are up for it. Starting at the river access site at Indian Flat seems most obvious, but feel free to put in anywhere along the road where you can park your car safely. This will actually help on busy weekends when the parking at Indian Flat gets tight.

Just below Indian Flat, you'll hit your first big wave train in class III Cranberry Rapid. Sometimes just big waves and sometimes something a little "munchier," the rapid always starts off the run with a bang. The next rapid of note is Landslide, just beyond the first bridge. You'll recognize the bare mountainside on river left that pushed debris into the river to create this rapid, also known as Ferguson Rock Slide rapid. A long straightaway ends in Ned's Gulch, a heartier rapid that gets into the class IV range at higher flows, but mostly just contains big waves.

Briceburg river access makes for an easy takeout, but can also get crowded. Again, anywhere you can safely exit the river and park a car works along this stretch of the Merced. A dirt road continues downriver right after Briceburg, and more rapids can be found farther downstream for another 2 miles.

DIRECTIONS TO TAKEOUT

Heading toward Yosemite and the Merced from the west on CA 140, you'll reach Briceburg at 11.7 miles from the junction with CA 49. This is the first point that you

Downstream from El Portal, the Merced River has many class III rapids, with a few class IV rapids in the upper section. Susan Elliott

see the river. If you are paddling within the park, head to the put-in first and retrieve your vehicle via the park's shuttle system. Thus, from the put-in at Stoneman Bridge, you'll travel around the Yosemite Valley's loop road to either El Capitan Meadow (heading west on the loop; river right) or Sentinel Beach (heading east; river left).

DIRECTIONS TO PUT-IN
Indian Flat access is 12 miles from Briceburg. To paddle through the park, continue driving toward Half Dome Village and park anywhere you can in that general area. It may be worth dropping your boats and gear off near the river at Stoneman Bridge first, or just snagging a parking spot as soon as you can.

NEARBY ATTRACTIONS
If you can't find enough to do in Yosemite, you may need to see a doctor. Plan your visit well in advance because campgrounds fill immediately. We recommend the campgrounds near Half Dome Village. Wild and Scenic paddling options surround you in this part of California. Head north into the Tuolumne River valley for several sections of this California favorite. Other national parks nearby include Kings Canyon and Sequoia National Parks to the south, both of which include other designated rivers to check off your list (the Kings and Kern Rivers).

PADDLING THE UPPER MERCED RIVER

By Priscilla Macy with support from Jacob Cruiser

We finally made it to Glacier Point after traveling all night and enduring thunderstorms and gumdrop-size hail as we began our hike in to paddle the Upper Merced River. It was our second attempt at paddling the newly opened reach through Yosemite National Park. With a permit in hand, we were already closer to exploring the river than we had been on our first trip.

We slept well by using our inflatable kayaks (IKs) as sleeping pads near Moraine Dome, our first camp just 8 miles from our vehicle. We dreamt of smooth granite and open spaces. Leaving our tent at Moraine Dome and hiking 6 more miles the next day, we arrived at Merced Lake, our put-in. Our excitement to finally be paddling far outweighed our fatigue from hiking.

We found the first half mile below Merced Lake through Echo Gorge to be a class-fun boater's dream come true, with back-to-back slides the whole way, including two about 100 feet long and about 40 feet tall. Partway down this gorge I plunged into a small hole that filled my boat with water and caused me to miss an important eddy—a downside of paddling an IK. A downstream hole flipped me over and sent me uncomfortably deep. A bit shaken but not about to give up, we continued downstream. Sunny skies and some of the largest-scale class III–IV whitewater we had seen to date helped lift the spirits.

A footbridge signaled the entrance to the most committing gorge of the trip. We ran a few fun and challenging rapids before reaching the point of commitment. With waning mental and physical stamina, we decided to walk around the gorge and finish our run the next day. At camp we ate ravenously as the joy that comes with a wilderness adventure started setting in.

The next day started with a few steep, bouldery rapids and a quick portage or two, with another long, fun, and forgiving slide at the end. We made the easy walk around Bunnell Gorge along the trail, but opted to run Bunnell Cascade, one of the most fun drops we had ever run.

Below the cascade was an island and a meadow. We made an easy log portage or two before running a couple of class IV rapids leading up to the final large cascade just above our camp. The lead-in rapids were fun and the campsite cascade was divine: tall, fast, and straightforward.

We napped and swam before deciding to paddle out that afternoon through the pleasant Little Yosemite Valley meadow. Paddling is illegal below here as the river enters a gorge ending in Nevada Falls.

We began the beautiful, but knee- and back-busting descent down the Mist Trail toward Yosemite Valley. If you are carrying a boat, use the longer but less steep John Muir Trail.

For us, the trip was a unique and intimate way to experience the Yosemite landscape, and in the way we most enjoy. We hold out hope that the collaborative work of Yosemite National Park and American Whitewater, which opened the Merced River to human-powered boat traffic, can serve as a model for other national parks, including Yellowstone.

The last move of the crux gorge, called Hard Twist. The eddy visible on river right at the base of the drop must be caught to portage up and around an as-of-yet unrun pile of boulders. PRISCILLA MACY

TUOLUMNE RIVER

Section name	Merals Pool to Wards Ferry Bridge
Distance	18 miles
Flow range	600–10,000 cfs
Season and source of water	Summer to early fall; dam release
Gauge location	Cherry Creek Confluence, American Whitewater Gauge #43519
Time required	1–2 days
Classification	*Scenic* and *Wild*
Difficulty	IV–V
Managing agency	Stanislaus National Forest
Permit required?	Yes: May 1 to Oct 15
Shuttle type	Vehicle
Outstandingly Remarkable Values	Cultural, fisheries, geology, history, recreation, scenery, wildlife, ecology
Why paddle this section?	A California classic; fantastic camping and side hike options for a quick trip

A gear boat for OARS' commercial raft trip pulls to the right at Stern Rapid, Tuolumne River. Sam Swanson

RIVER DESCRIPTION

With its headwaters in the glacial grassy meadows of Yosemite, the Tuolumne River plummets between high Sierra ridges to churn through steep, granite boulder-strewn canyons in a magnificent spectacle. Imagine waterfalls raging off sheer cliffs, long chutes and slides ending in a tumultuous upheaval of spray, all surrounded by wildflower aromas, tall ponderosas, oak savannahs, and mountain scenery. Below Lumsden Falls, the river calms to an advanced-paddler, class-IV pace and becomes one of California's most iconic Sierra paddling destinations for kayakers and rafters alike.

The protection of the Tuolumne River as Wild and Scenic came in 1984, and encompasses the river from its pristine source to the backwaters of the Don Pedro Reservoir—minus the stretch of river buried under Hetch Hetchy Reservoir. From Merals Pool to Wards Ferry Bridge you'll float a few miles of the *Scenic* classified section and the entire reach of the lower *Wild* stretch. Upstream of the unnaturally placid water of the reservoir, sections of the river range between all three designation types, with *Recreational* stretches referring more to the exceptional trout fishing rather than paddling.

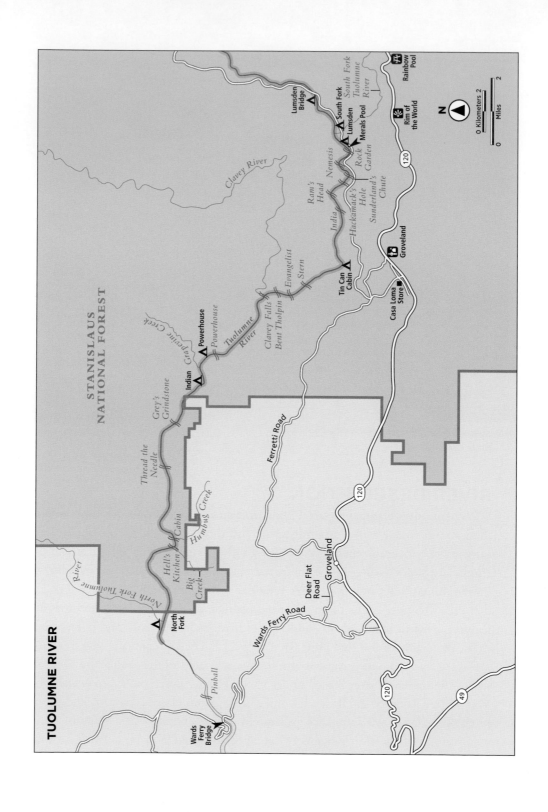

TUOLUMNE RIVER

STANISLAUS NATIONAL FOREST

Clavey River

Clavey River

North Fork Tuolumne River

Tuolumne River

South Fork Tuolumne River

Rainbow Pool

Rim of the World

Lumsden Bridge

Lumsden

South Fork

Merals Pool

Rock Garden

Nemesis

India

Hackamack's Hole

Sunderland's Chute

Ram's Head

Evangelist

Stern

Clavey Falls

Bent Tholpin

Powerhouse

Powerhouse

Indian

Grapevine Creek

Grey's Grindstone

Thread the Needle

Hell's Kitchen

Cabin

Humbug Creek

Big Creek

North Fork

Pinball

Wards Ferry Bridge

Wards Ferry Road

Deer Flat Road

Groveland

Ferretti Road

Groveland

Casa Loma Store

Tin Can Cabin

120

120

120

49

N

0 Kilometers 2

0 Miles 2

A raft finishes up a long day on the "T," approaching Don Pedro reservoir. ANNA WAGNER

The gap in designation around the O'Shaughnessy Dam makes the drowning of the Hetch Hetchy Valley even more obvious and painful. The Tuolumne River's twin, the Merced River, flows through the storied Yosemite Valley, yet the Tuolumne's own granite cathedral valley is entombed by the needs of downstream urbanites. In his essay titled "Dam Hetch Hetchy," John Muir proclaimed, "Hetch Hetchy Valley, far from being a plain, common, rock-bound meadow, as many who have not seen it seem to suppose, is a grand landscape garden, one of Nature's rarest and most precious mountain temples."

The fight over Hetch Hetchy Valley is said to be the first modern conservation battle, fought between 1908-1913. San Francisco needed water and the National Park system did not necessarily protect rivers from damming and diversion. The utilitarian argument won over the aesthetic and moral arguments made by the Sierra Club and other wilderness advocates, and Hetch Hetchy Valley was flooded. Today, Hetch Hetchy Water and Power Company releases reliable flows all through busy summer paddling months for our enjoyment on lower reaches. It is, however, still interesting thinking about the rapids that rest underneath that reservoir.

PADDLER'S NOTES

Paddlers must grab a permit at the Groveland Ranger Station between May 1 and October 15. Permits are free but can be reserved ahead of time for a small fee. Be sure to arrive during office hours. Take a look at the Stanislaus Forest Service website for more river regulations.

The shuttle is a bit of a beast. Stop by the Casa Loma Store, just past Groveland, to look into hiring a shuttle driver or at least finding others who are also making the descent into Tuolumne canyon. Hiring a shuttle is the best way to go for two reasons: Lumsden Road is sometimes closed to regular traffic in early season but open to commercial and shuttle drivers, and cars have been broken into overnight at the Wards Ferry takeout lot. Look for a sign at the put-in that will inform you which camps are designated commercial and which are open to the public. The list changes every year.

At average flows (600–4,000 cfs), most rapids on the Tuolumne fall into the class IV category. This means you may want to hop out and scout any horizon lines you encounter, or at least follow a trusted friend. We'll highlight a few of the more iconic class IV–V rapids here, but know that more information will make your run smoother.

You'll start a whitewater extravaganza with Rock Garden, located just downstream from Merals Pool. Rafts may find tight channels here at low flows, but kayaks can generally take multiple routes at all flows. Nemesis rapid appears in the next bend, named after a rock jumble at the end of the rapid where most of the flow feeds. Another bend and another class IV rapid, with Sunderland's Chute as the river turns right.

You'll pass through Hackamack's Hole, named after a long time Sierra Club activist involved in the campaign to restore Hetch Hetchy Valley, on your way to Ram's Head rapid, less than a mile downstream. The "ram's head" feature is the center hole at the bottom of the rapid. Pass through India rapid next, named after the first female paddler to descend this advanced run. The rapid is a longer set of drops and maneuvers. Farther downstream, the river takes a sharper bend to the right at a popular campsite, Tin Can Cabin, on the left.

A mile downstream is Stern rapid. Large boulders make for tight lines in rafts here. Scouting is advisable to pick your route. Evangelist rapid follows, with a series of drops. Rafters know Bent Tholpin rapid well, at least those who have broken oars on the left wall at the bottom.

Stay alert for Clavey Creek, a large tributary, which enters on the right and signals that you're about to drop into Clavey Falls, a true class V rapid. Scout on the right for this one. A large drop (sometimes up to 8 or 9 feet) and crashing holes offer several lines.

> ## "RIVERS BELONG TO ALL OF US. THEY ARE VALUABLE FOR RECREATION-BASED ECONOMIES, FOR THE FISH AND CLEAN WATER THEY BRING US, AND FOR THE MAGNETIC AND INSPIRING SOLACE OF WILD-FLOWING WATER."
> —*Kevin Colburn, National Stewardship Director, American Whitewater*

After a long straightaway, Powerhouse rapid and camp appear. An old powerhouse remains on the right shore, where you can pull over to reach camp. At flows between 6,000–8,000 cfs, a stellar wave appears in this rapid. Just downstream, a beach on river right known as Indian Camp makes for a great overnight spot, too.

Grey's Grindstone, a long rapid that deserves a scout to avoid a long swim, comes next. Thread the Needle, Cabin, and Hell's Kitchen rapids, more class IV fun, arrive around a few river bends before the North Fork Tuolumne River confluence, a popular campsite. Hike a bit up the small tributary to find great jump rocks and deep swimming holes. Finally, Pinball rapid may or may not appear, depending on the level of the Don Pedro Reservoir.

DIRECTIONS TO TAKEOUT
From Groveland, head southwest on Main Street/CA 120, and turn right on Deer Flat Road just out of town. Deer Flat Road runs into Wards Ferry Road in 1.5 miles. Turn right on Wards Ferry and continue for 5.8 miles until you cross the river. Most people park on the river-right side of the bridge.

DIRECTIONS TO PUT-IN
To reach Merals Pool from Groveland, head northeast on CA 120 for 7.6 miles. Turn left on Ferretti Road. The Casa Loma Store is on the left. Stop in for beta, a shuttle, or an amazing burrito. A mile down Ferretti Road take a sharp right onto FR 1N10/Lumsden Road. The next 5 miles of the one-lane, dirt road to Merals Pool will be slow and steady.

NEARBY ATTRACTIONS
You are at the foot of Yosemite and next door to the Merced River. Don't leave this region without experiencing both of these majestic places. Hike the Grand Canyon of the Tuolumne in the park if you have a few days, or just visit any place along the Tuolumne headwaters for incredible scenery and five-star camping, fishing, and swimming.

Southwest

21

VERDE RIVER

Section name	Beasley Flats to Gap Creek
Distance	8 miles
Flow range	600–30,000 cfs
Season and source of water	Winter and spring, rainfall; summer, sporadic monsoons
Gauge location	Camp Verde, USGS #09506000
Time required	1 day
Classification	*Scenic*
Difficulty	II-III (IV)
Managing agency	Coconino, Prescott, and Tonto National Forests
Permit required?	No
Outstandingly Remarkable Values	Cultural, scenery, fisheries, history, wildlife
Shuttle type	Vehicle
Why paddle this section?	Desert cliffs and narrow vegetation chutes; fantastic wildlife corridor; fun yet optional waterfall rapid

RIVER DESCRIPTION

The pulse of Arizona's biodiversity resides in and around the cool waters of the Verde River. Flowing south through the central valley, the Verde River supports more than

Opposite: Susan finds a smooth ramp in the left line at Verde Falls. ADAM ELLIOTT

117

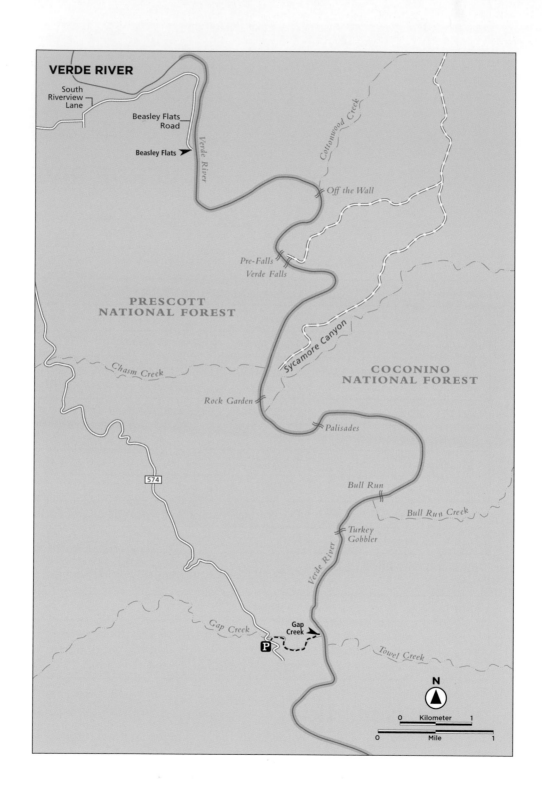

VERDE RIVER

South Riverview Lane

Beasley Flats Road

Beasley Flats

Verde River

Cottonwood Creek

Off the Wall

Pre-Falls
Verde Falls

PRESCOTT NATIONAL FOREST

Sycamore Canyon

Chasm Creek

COCONINO NATIONAL FOREST

Rock Garden

Palisades

574

Bull Run

Bull Run Creek

Turkey Gobbler

Verde River

Gap Creek

Gap Creek

P

Towel Creek

N

0   Kilometer   1

0   Mile   1

A paddler in an inflatable kayak navigates a chunky bedrock rapid on the Verde River.
ADAM ELLIOTT

75 percent of the state's total biodiversity, and sustains a paddling community in a region where rivers may not flow at all some years. The day run starting at Beasley Flats immediately transports paddlers into the wilderness without requiring multiple days on the water. The river channelizes around islands, and rapids carry boaters around bends and over boulders. Serene pools also promote wildlife viewing and soaking in the colorful desert canyon and free-flowing river.

Lush green reeds, cottonwoods, mesquite, and willows fill the riparian zone. Often tunnels through this thick vegetation make boaters feel like they are on a jungle cruise rather than a southwestern river. Narrow chutes create waves and fun rapids before exiting into large pools where the sun once again kisses your skin. Vegetation can become unruly in this unkempt and wild section of river, and with the help of beavers, logjams often plug up side channels or insert river-wide logs across the river. Habitat for river otters and native fish form because of this natural channel modification.

In a state with a growing population and a lack of freshwater resources, many communities in Arizona depend on the water quality of the Verde River. However, development within the watershed threatens the aquifer that holds most of the river's water. This would starve the important ecosystem that depends on the river. The river's Wild and Scenic status, as well as collaborative efforts to conserve water throughout the watershed, will help preserve this resource for generations.

PADDLER'S NOTES

The Beasley Flats access begins in a large pool where vegetation slightly obscures the direction of downstream flow. The river bubbles around bends and over cobbles for a mile and half until the class II–III Off the Wall rapid at about 1.7 miles. Here, the river pushes into the right wall. Starting at mile 2.3 boaters are asked to not stop on the river banks for the next 2 miles to camp or linger due to critical eagle nesting habitat (Dec 1–June 30).

Just downstream is Pre-Falls rapid. The 3- to 5-foot drop (depending on flows) is found on the left channel and can be scouted from the left. High flows create holes here rather than ledges. Pre-Falls rapid signals that class IV Verde Falls sits just downstream. The drop is larger at 8 vertical feet, and the rapid has boulders spaced throughout, making a scout for first-time boaters essential. Both rapids can be portaged on the left.

Palisades, Bull Run, and Turkey Gobbler rapids, all class III, are spaced about 2 miles apart for the rest of the run. Each of these has unique characteristics, like sharp channels that bend against a wall, long boulder-garden lines, and possible wood in play. The takeout at Gap Creek, on the right at about mile 8, can typically be recognized by a large cobble fan from the higher flows in Gap Creek itself. However, this can change year to year. Due to the presence of wood, always scout blind corners and channels on the Verde River to determine if hazards are present downstream.

Many paddlers opt to turn the Wild and Scenic stretch of the Verde into a multiday trip. Continuing beyond Gap Creek allows for another few days of floating and camping along the banks. Childs is a popular takeout for the multiday stretch, considering there are riverside hot springs there. Look for the online boater's map and guidebook on the Forest Service website that lists campsites and rapid descriptions.

DIRECTIONS TO TAKEOUT

Some of this drive is better suited for a four-wheel-drive vehicle, especially in wet weather. From I-17 south outside of Camp Verde, take exit 287 for AZ 260 east. Turn left onto AZ 260. In 2 miles turn right on Oasis Road. In 0.5 mile turn right onto Salt Mine Road. In another 6.2 miles, turn left to stay on Salt Mine Road. In 4 miles, the road will turn into FR 574, just after you pass Fence Line/Beasley Flats Road (to the

Evenings in central Arizona are magical. Multiday trips on the Verde are the only way to truly experience it. Adam Elliott

put-in) on the left. From Fence Line/Beasley Flats Road, travel 5 miles to the turn for the parking lot. Turn left into the dirt lot and scope out the trail that follows the creek 0.25 mile to the river so you know where to pull over.

DIRECTIONS TO PUT-IN
From the takeout, head back on FR 574 for 5 miles. Turn right on Fence Line/Beasley Flats Road. Turn right onto Desert Dawn/Beasley Flats Road. You will see the Verde on your left and hit the parking area and river access in less than a mile.

NEARBY ATTRACTIONS
Fossil Creek, another designated river, flows into the Verde below this stretch. While you're in the area, plan a stop here. The blue waters juxtaposed with the hot desert landscape are a swimmer's paradise. Parking permits are necessary, especially on busy summer weekends. To paddle the run, take a look at the following river description.

FOSSIL CREEK

Section name	Waterfall to Bridge
Distance	7 miles
Flow range	35–500 cfs
Season and source of water	Year-round; artesian springs with supplemental flow from rain
Gauge location	Near Strawberry, USGS #09507480
Time required	1 day
Classification	*Recreational*
Difficulty	III–IV
Managing agency	Coconino and Tonto National Forests
Permit required?	Yes, parking permit prior to arrival
Shuttle type	Vehicle
Outstandingly Remarkable Values	Cultural, fisheries, geology, history, wildlife, recreation, botany
Why paddle this section?	One of a few travertine paddling destinations in the country; bright emerald water; pure paradise in this arid landscape

RIVER DESCRIPTION

A mesmerizing desert oasis, Fossil Creek is a vivid blue-green stream gushing straight from the rocks as artesian springs. A steady 43–48 cubic feet per second (cfs) pours from rocks, full of calcium carbonate that deposits to create the travertine geologic character and brilliant water colors. All of this exists in a region of Arizona where summer brings sizzling temperatures in arid landscapes devoid of flowing water.

Skilled paddlers can run Fossil Falls. DANIELLE KEIL

Fossil Creek offers respite and immediate relief from the Southwest heat with deep, emerald swimming holes, as well as diverse wildlife and shady groves to set up a picnic and spend the day. For whitewater paddlers, the small stream transforms into a very special destination with travertine waterfalls, slides, and narrow chutes. As the Forest Service develops future management plans, paddling here may become even easier—or harder.

This remote river valley has experienced a surge in popularity in the past decade, following decommissioning of a hydropower project that returned the flow to this desert oasis. Word spread rapidly that a tropical Eden sat in central Arizona and soon over-visitation began to destroy this paradise. In 2016, a parking permit system helped

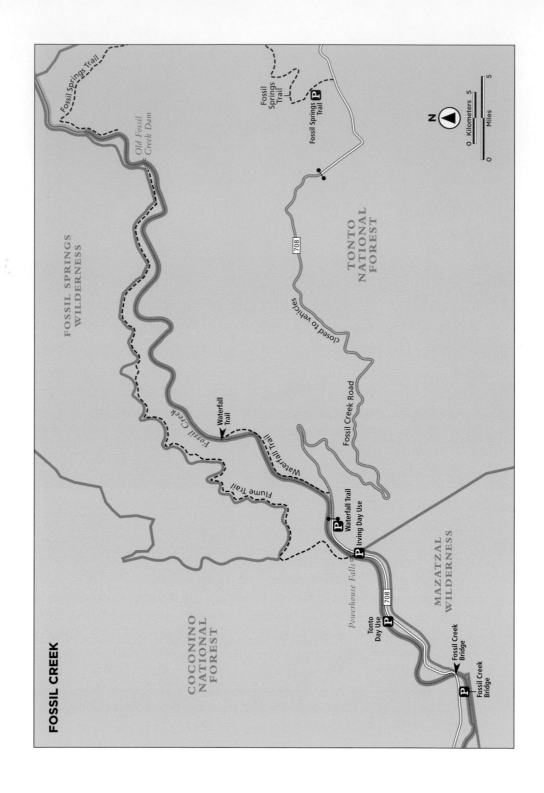

FOSSIL CREEK

align usage with capacity. Now, all visitors must acquire a permit to spend the day along Fossil Creek, the number of which is limited each day.

Additionally, new management plans consider limiting the types of "water play" allowed at some locations, such as the waterfall near the put-in for this run. This would greatly affect the boating opportunities in this special place. Paddling is an ancient, healthy, sustainable, immersive way for the public to experience the recreational, scenic, and other values of Fossil Creek. It should be recognized as one of the activities that define the recreational Outstandingly Remarkable Value in the management plan, and should be protected and enhanced under the plan. You simply cannot find boating like this anywhere else in the country.

The closure of Fossil Creek Road between the Waterfall trailhead and Fossil Springs parking area further limits historic paddling opportunities. The parking permit season also limits the ability to take advantage of higher flows from unexpected storms. Last-minute permits are rarely available, even if the resource is prime for paddling and poor for swimming and lounging.

While Fossil Creek's future paddling regulations are in flux, we cannot dispute the importance and value of experiencing this river as a boater. Floating under cottonwood canopies, watching schools of native roundtail chub and Sonoran sucker swim in deep pools, or curving down a travertine chute to boof a small ledge makes paddling Fossil Creek worth every second.

The old Fossil Creek Dam, located a little over 2 miles upstream from the Waterfall Trail access site, used to divert nearly the entire creek's volume into a flume. Originally constructed in 1913, the Irving Power Plant and downstream Childs Power Plant were the first hydroelectric facilities in the state of Arizona. Arizona Public Service decommissioned the dam in 2005, and the river once again became free-flowing. Wild and Scenic designation followed in 2009.

PADDLER'S NOTES

A day-use parking permit is required April 1 to October 1 for any of the nine parking areas along Fossil Creek. US Forest Service staff checks for permits before you reach the parking areas. You can reserve these online at Recreation.gov. If you're hoping for a weekend paddle, consider reserving your permits a month in advance. River managers are considering revisions to the permit system, so check the Coconino and Tonto National Forest websites for updates or give the hotline a call (928-226-4611). Fossil Creek Road may not be open in the off-season or during monsoon rains in the summer, giving you another reason to call. During the permit season, camping is not permitted along Fossil Creek. Childs Dispersed Camping Area can be found by following the rough Childs Power Road over the ridge to the Verde River.

With the creek flowing near a road for the majority of this section, many paddlers pick apart the run or take multiple laps on some rapids. Because you may not get your top choice for a parking area, it is often easiest to bring one vehicle to the creek and walk or hitch your shuttle. Most kayakers walk the mile up the Waterfall Trail to begin their paddle.

We recommend this run for kayakers and not rafters, as the low-volume flow makes the drops too narrow and shallow for wider crafts. Navigating over travertine ledges requires a supplementary set of kayaking skills, especially with such a low-volume run. Your boat may need to go on edge to prevent a sandpaper stop over the rough ledges that would abruptly change your line as well as scrape your boat.

The run begins with Fossil Creek Waterfall's 20-foot plunge into a magical pool below. From there, scout drops and ledges from shore or the trail. Powerhouse Falls near the former Irving Power Plant have several options; be sure to scout here. Take out at the bridge or any of the other parking areas along the way.

DIRECTIONS TO TAKEOUT
From Camp Verde, take AZ 260 east out of town. In 7 miles, turn right onto Fossil Creek Road/FR 708. While you'll reach the Fossil Creek Bridge parking area in 15 miles; expect to take up to an hour on this dirt road. Best to call the Coconino National Forest Service's Fossil Creek Hotline, (928) 226-4611, to ask if that route is open prior to your paddle.

DIRECTIONS TO PUT-IN
From the Fossil Creek Bridge river access site, continue up Fossil Creek Road to the Waterfall Trail parking area for the farthest upstream road access point. You may need to just drop boats here and go park in the lot that your permit dictates. From the parking lot, hike your boat up one mile to the first waterfall of the run.

NEARBY ATTRACTIONS
Sections of the Wild and Scenic Verde River can be reached from the confluence of Fossil Creek. Add a river trip along this run if flows allow. We also recommend hiking up to the actual springs on Fossil Creek.

23

RIO GRANDE

Section name	Upper Box, Orilla Verde, and Racecourse
Distance	Upper Box: 6.5 miles; Orilla Verde: 6.5 miles; Racecourse: 4.5 miles
Flow range	400–3,000 cfs
Season and source of water	Spring; snowmelt
Gauge location	Cerro, USGS #08263500; Taos Junction Bridge, USGS #08276500
Time required	1 day
Classification	*Wild* and *Scenic*
Difficulty	Upper Box: V–V+; Orilla Verde: I–II; Racecourse: III
Managing agency	Bureau of Land Management Taos Field Office; Rio Grande del Norte National Monument
Permit required?	Yes
Shuttle type	Vehicle
Outstandingly Remarkable Values	Culture, history, fisheries, wildlife, geology, recreation, scenery
Why paddle this section?	A paddling option for everyone; deep gorge chasm with extreme whitewater; diverse desert landscape with a tranquil float; colorful history of early inhabitants and settlers

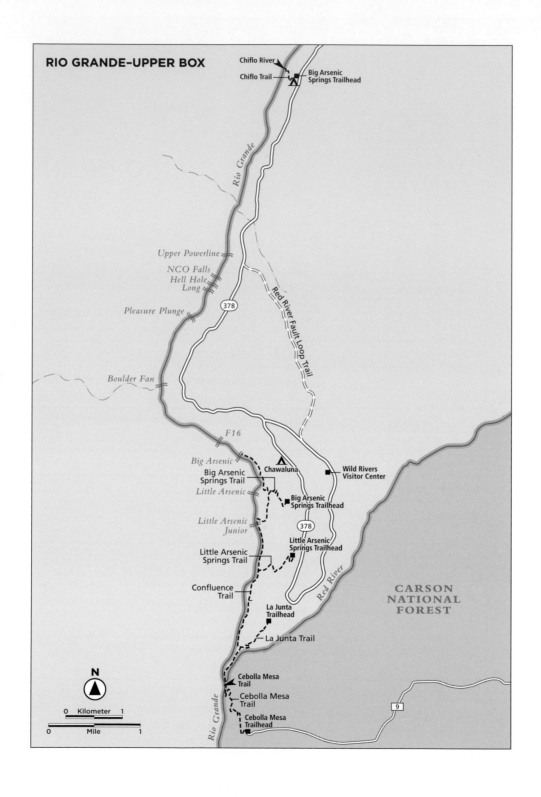

RIO GRANDE–UPPER BOX

Chiflo River
Chiflo Trail
Big Arsenic
Springs Trailhead

Rio Grande

Upper Powerline
NCO Falls
Hell Hole
Long

Pleasure Plunge

378

Red River Fault Loop Trail

Boulder Fan

F16

Big Arsenic
Big Arsenic
Springs Trail

Chawaluna

Wild Rivers
Visitor Center

Little Arsenic

Big Arsenic
Springs Trailhead

Little Arsenic
Junior

378

Little Arsenic
Springs Trailhead

Little Arsenic
Springs Trail

Confluence
Trail

Red River

CARSON
NATIONAL
FOREST

La Junta
Trailhead

La Junta Trail

Cebolla Mesa
Trail

Rio Grande

Cebolla Mesa
Trail

9

Cebolla Mesa
Trailhead

N

0   Kilometer   1

0   Mile   1

Bring a lunch because you'll want to enjoy the whitewater in the Taos Box all day. ADAM ELLIOTT

RIVER DESCRIPTION

With a whitewater culture infused with rich and colorful New Mexican flavor, the Rio Grande ushers paddlers through a geological and archaeological story unlike any other in the nation. From the state border and flowing south, the river steeply descends into a whitewater maelstrom known as the Taos Box at the bottom of the Rio Grande Gorge. The tumult recedes to allow a gentle float through the Orilla Verde's lush riparian zone, with cottonwood and willow trees that transition into a diverse juniper-scrub landscape. Finally, enjoy a classic intermediate paddler's challenge on the lower Racecourse stretch, where surf spots and wave trains entertain boaters until the leaves begin to change in the Sangre de Cristo mountains near Taos.

The Rio Grande is the third longest river in North America at 1,900 miles, and flows from Colorado through New Mexico and into Texas, where, as the border with Mexico, it empties into the Gulf of Mexico. The characteristics of New Mexico's Rio Grande River differ greatly from Texas's Rio Grande, but Wild and Scenic designations exist in both regions. This description focuses on the upper river through New Mexico.

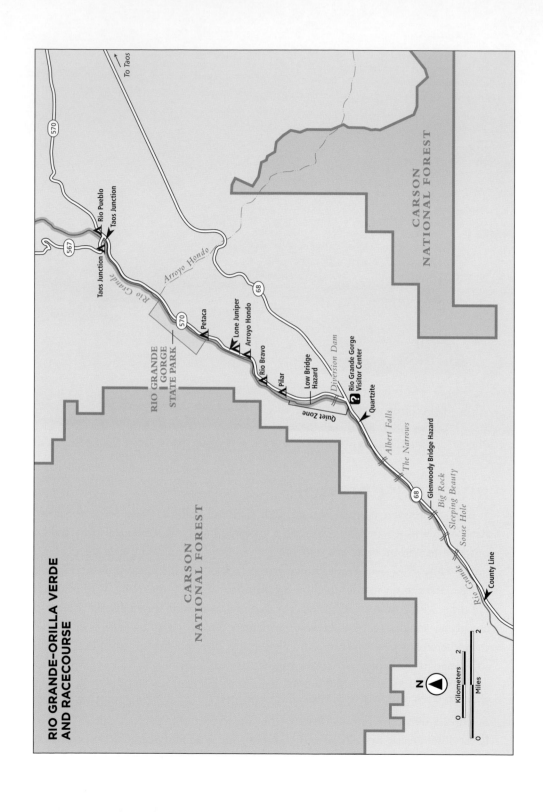

RIO GRANDE–ORILLA VERDE
AND RACECOURSE

N

Kilometers
0   2

Miles
0   2

To Taos

570

567

Rio Pueblo
Taos Junction

Taos Junction

567

Arroyo Hondo

Rio Grande

570

Petaca

Lone Juniper
Arroyo Hondo

Rio Bravo

Pilar

Low Bridge
Hazard

68

Diversion Dam

Quiet Zone

Rio Grande Gorge
Visitor Center

Quartzite

Albert Falls

The Narrows

Glenwoody Bridge Hazard

Big Rock

Sleeping Beauty

Souse Hole

68

Rio Grande

County Line

RIO GRANDE
GORGE
STATE PARK

CARSON
NATIONAL FOREST

CARSON
NATIONAL FOREST

Unlike the many stories of a river carving its way across a landscape to form a canyon, the Rio Grande in New Mexico found a canyon and commandeered it. The hijacked valley was created by the thinning and faulting of the earth's crust rather than the erosion and incision caused by the power of water moving downhill. This occurred as two tectonic plates separated to make way for lava as it pushed through the crust into volcanoes. The deep chasm became known as the Rio Grande Rift. Small streams routed into this now gaping fracture and carved a downhill path to become the mighty Rio Grande. The river deserves the geologic Outstandingly Remarkable Value, especially when viewing the massive schism pulling apart the landscape from the drive along NM 68 from Pilar to Taos.

The history of human use of the river is equally dynamic. Evidence of the 10,000 years of human habitation, from hunter-gatherers to Puebloans to Athabascans to Hispanic settlers, wins this river the cultural and historic Outstandingly Remarkable Values.

If you think desert environments are hot, bleak, and dusty, you will be proved terribly wrong in the Rio Grande Valley. New Mexico's flora and fauna rank among the most diverse in any state. From the alpine conifer zone found in Taos's Sangre de Cristo mountains to the river's riparian wetlands, you'll find thick forests, cacti blooms, rare birds, large mammals, and more.

This river's vibrant story helped gain Wild and Scenic designation as one of the original eight rivers, with 55.7 miles designated in 1968. In 1994, another 12.5 miles were added to the system. The total 68.2-mile stretch begins at the Colorado border and extends downstream, including 4 miles of the Red River, a major tributary. In 2013, the Rio Grande del Norte National Monument was established to further protect the surrounding landscape for its cultural legacy and scientific values.

PADDLER'S NOTES

The 800-foot deep Rio Grande Gorge provides extraordinary whitewater for experts and novices alike. Known as the "Taos Box" section, the steep upper reaches of this gorge are split into the Upper and Lower Box. We'll focus on the Upper Box here, as well as stretches of the river below the Lower Box that range from beginner to intermediate in difficulty. Most local outfitters commercially raft the Lower Box's class III–IV rapids, and can provide more information if you're interested.

Plan to be at the top of your game if you have the Upper Taos Box section of the Rio Grande in your sights. The run should only be attempted by experts no matter the flow levels. Sharp and angulated basalt rocks broke off the canyon walls to form the rapids, and countless sieves are found throughout the run. You'll start the paddle by hiking to the river on the Chiflo Trail. The whitewater intensity grows quickly, starting with Powerline Rapid, a mile-long class V–V+ rapid, with NCO Falls, Hell Hole, Long rapid, and Pleasure Plunge not far downstream. We highly recommend scouting these due to the presence of sieves and the difficulty of boat-scouting. Enjoy a brief mile or so of calmer flow before Boulder Fan, F16, and the mandatory scout at Big Arsenic Falls. Birds of prey and big horned sheep are frequently seen in the box. Keep your eyes open for more than just the whitewater.

Little Arsenic rapids follow, covering almost the entire next mile. Take out by hiking out of the canyon on river left on Little Arsenic Springs Trail. Or continue downstream for another mile of class III–IV to hike out on the Cebolla Mesa Trail, on river left just after the confluence with Red River.

Seeking a more tranquil day on the river? The Orilla Verde stretch of class I–II winds through a more open canyon landscape with plentiful time to take in the surrounding desert canyon environment. Pull over and check out some of the archaeological remains along the river, including rock art and ruins, or look for playful river otters and the bright flowers of cacti.

While floating through the village of Pilar, keep your voices down. A mandatory quiet zone here helps local residents not be reminded of tourists every hour throughout busy summer days. A low bridge spans the river just downstream from Pilar, which you'll want to pull over to scout. A series of class II rapids signals your takeout at the Quartzite access site on river left.

Continue from the Quartzite river access site to float the class III Racecourse section of the Rio Grande. The rapids here are just right, not too mellow and not too extreme. Most rapids are easily scouted, from either shoreline or during your shuttle drive thanks to the adjacent road. Albert Falls, named for Albert Einstein by nearby boaters from Los Alamos, is the first class III drop. A short section of class II waves connects Albert Falls with the beginning of the Narrows, a long corridor of class III waves and holes with little recovery time between. After passing underneath the low Glenwoody Bridge, you'll reach Big Rock Rapid. Most boaters take this one on the right, avoiding massive boulders and the "toilet bowl" hydraulic they form.

Take your lunch at Sleeping Beauty rapid, where a great wave can entertain kayakers for hours. At most flows, Souse Hole may be the biggest rapid on the run. A steeper drop and larger wave can flip rafts and certainly roll a kayak. Take out at the County Line access on river left about a mile downstream.

A fantastic compilation of river maps and geologic descriptions can be found in *The Rio Grande: A River Guide to the Geology and Landscapes of Northern New Mexico* by Paul Bauer. Pages are waterproof, and more information on rapids and access locations will help you craft your schedule to suit your needs.

DIRECTIONS TO TAKEOUT

From Santa Fe, take US 84 west, heading north out of town. This changes into US 285 northbound. In Española stay straight on US 68. In 24 miles you'll pass County

Looking upstream into the Taos Box from the Rio Grande Gorge Bridge, 565 feet above the river. ADAM ELLIOTT

Line access, the takeout for the Racecourse section. In another 4.5 miles, Quartzite access will be on the left. If you're headed to the Upper Taos Box, continue toward Taos on US 68. In 15 miles turn left on NM 240 east to avoid Taos town traffic. In 2.3 miles, turn right to stay on NM 240 east, then turn left onto Blueberry Hill Road in 0.3 mile. In about 5 miles turn right onto US 64, then left onto NM 522 northbound. In a little over 15 miles turn left on FR 9 to the Cebolla Mesa Campground.

DIRECTIONS TO PUT-IN
The put-in for the Racecourse section is Quartzite, just 4 miles north of the takeout. To reach the Taos Junction Bridge put-in for Orilla Verde from Quartzite, turn left onto NM 570 and drive for 6 miles to the boat ramp. For the Upper Box put-in, head back to NM 522 northbound, turn left, and drive for 7.5 miles through Questa. Turn left onto NM 387 toward Cerro. This changes into NM 378; in 5 miles you'll arrive at the Chiflo trailhead.

NEARBY ATTRACTIONS
Take time to see as much of the deep Rio Grande Gorge as you can while in the area. Head to the Wild River Recreation Area, located 30 miles north of Taos, and hike

5 TIPS FOR KEEPING FOOD FRESH ON THE RIVER

A delicious meal in the backcountry can taste better than one from any five-star restaurant—if your ingredients haven't spoiled. Follow these simple tips to keep your food fresh while floating your next Wild and Scenic river.

1. **Know your produce varieties.** Some fruits and vegetables naturally last longer than others. For example, romaine lettuce stays fresher longer than other varietals. Blueberries last longer than strawberries. Tomatoes, apples, and oranges are great for longer trips, especially if you follow the next tip. And root veggies are the champions of food storage. Also, remember that canned fruit works well in pancakes.

2. **Store fruits and veggies prone to bruising in your pots, pans, or hard boxes.** Avocados, tomatoes, and blueberries all keep longer if they are protected from the jostling that occurs in any watercraft and out of the sun. This even works in lightweight self-support kayak or canoe trips with a few pots but no coolers or boxes.

3. **Ditch the ziplocks.** Store lettuce and other fragile veggies in brown paper bags or clean used cereal bags. Produce needs to breathe and the paper bags or open cereal bags maintain better airflow and prevent too much moisture from building up to cause produce to "sweat."

4. **Store non-cooler vegetables and eggs as low as possible within your kayak, canoe, or raft.** Most Wild and Scenic rivers flow at fairly cold temperatures. If your veggies are below the waterline of the boat, the river will keep them cool as you float.

5. **Make a mental (or actual) map of stored food locations.** On group trips, designate one person who accesses cooler food to minimize the time that cooler lid stays open. On self-support trips, pack longer-lasting root vegetables deeper in your boat so they stay in the cool water as much as possible. Keep food you'll want sooner easily accessible.

Don't skimp on bringing the greens for multi-day trips! ADAM ELLIOTT

850 feet down into the gorge to see some of the class V whitewater of the Upper Box. Or simply stop in the parking areas on US 64 and walk across the Rio Grande Gorge Bridge, 10 miles west of Taos, to peer down into the abyss. The Orilla Verde Recreation Area offers many riverside campgrounds and other hiking options as well.

24

VIRGIN RIVER

Section name	Temple of Sinawava to Court of the Patriarchs
Distance	5 miles
Flow range	150–600 cfs
Season and source of water	Early spring, snowmelt; summer, monsoon floods
Gauge name and location	Springdale, USGS #09405500
Time required	Half day
Classification	*Recreational*
Difficulty	II
Managing agency	Zion National Park
Permit required?	Yes, acquired at park visitor center
Shuttle type	Vehicle or shuttle bus
Outstandingly Remarkable Values	Culture, fisheries, geology, recreation, scenery, wildlife
Why paddle this section?	A zero-crowd Zion Canyon experience; rich riparian vegetation and blue water contrast brightly colored rocks; a serene float through an iconic national park

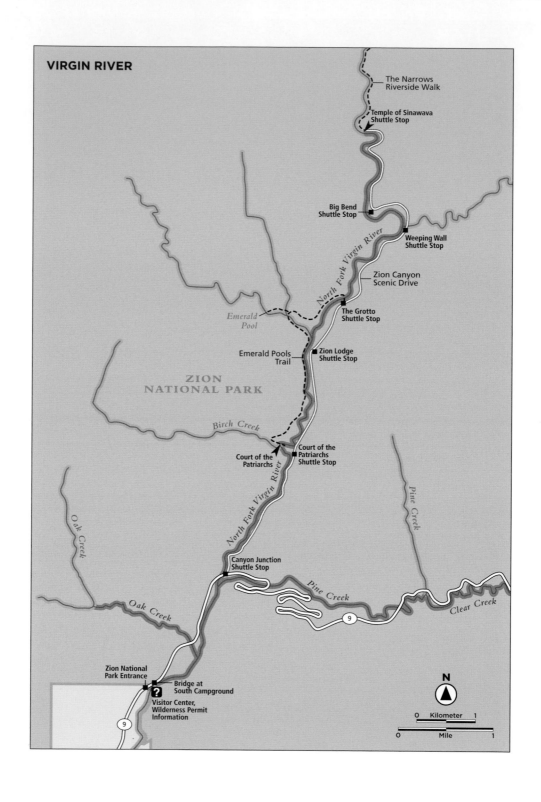

Susan is dwarfed by riverside cottonwood and the Great White Throne in the distance.
ADAM ELLIOTT

RIVER DESCRIPTION

The Virgin River carved one of America's most iconic canyons: Zion. To float this river is to travel the path that carved a landscape of infinite rock hues, Navajo sandstone cliffs, hanging waterfalls, and towering monoliths. Along with the seeps and springs dripping over carved canyon walls, the river supports a lush riparian corridor in this region of the Colorado Plateau. For this reason, the river and spectacular geologic features are truly a grand oasis for a weary traveler in the Southwest.

It may sound as if the Wild and Scenic designation of the Virgin River includes just one waterway, but it actually encompasses thirty-eight separate streams and tributaries in three different drainages. Designation covers 169.3 total river miles and is the only Wild and Scenic river system in Utah. Four native fish species swim in the Virgin's cool waters, including the Virgin spinedace, found only in this system. Periodic disturbance from flooding, carving new meanders, and frequent sediment loads make the Virgin a high-functioning ecological paradise for plants and wildlife.

Upstream of the put-in the river has chiseled the sandstone cliffs to form The Narrows. Hikers and backpackers know this section of river better than river runners: The hike is one of the most popular in the country. While rapids may be classed as III and IV, the remote nature of the run and high consequences demand solid class V paddling skills. Boaters have encountered serious hazards requiring search and rescue extraction. The 100-foot tall canyon walls make it nearly impossible for help to reach the river. However, if you have the skills, this may be the most memorable day (or days) you ever experience in your boat. If the risk is too great, inquire about a backpacking permit to hike up the river when water levels drop. On all sections of the Virgin River a whitewater-worthy watercraft is required (sorry inner tubers).

PADDLER'S NOTES

All paddlers must acquire a permit at the wilderness booth in the Zion National Park Visitor Center the day before or the day they wish to paddle. Water levels must be between 150–600 cubic feet per second (cfs) for the permit to be issued. This booth rarely has the long lines seen at the normal information booth and rangers are equally knowledgeable.

For the first 5 miles of the Virgin River, from Temple of Sinawava to Court of the Patriarchs, the river sweeps in wide meanders forming class I and II riffles. At high flows, these riffles may feel like class III, with the possibility of wood around every corner. The park maintains the river as a wilderness area and therefore does not clear wood out of the channel. Be sure to scout what you cannot see, even at lower flows. We found clear lines but some logs blocking other channels.

The peaceful float through this typically crowded park helped us absorb the sounds, smells, and colors of the landscape. We heard the river bubble over cobbles. We stared at delicate stone spires. We found deer sipping from the clear, blue water where no other tourist could be seen. When we did pass hikers as they splashed the refreshing river water over their sweaty skin, they inevitable expressed jealousy of our chosen form of recreation. Take out at Court of the Patriarchs to keep the day mellow, or continue downstream to get into some whitewater. You'll arrive at a horizon line underneath a footbridge that will indicate it is time to pull over. Any of the shuttle stops upstream can be used as takeouts as well.

Below Court of the Patriarchs, the action picks up into class IV, pushing into class V at higher flows. The series of rapids below here are known as Satan's Staircase. An obvious horizon line underneath a pedestrian bridge leads into the first drop, Corral Falls, likely named after the stables nearby and formed by an old diversion dam. Below here boulder gardens, holes, and technical lines fill the channel and a steep bank prevents easy road access. Takeout is at the bridge near South Campground and the Visitor Center.

DIRECTIONS TO TAKEOUT

The Zion National Park entrance is in Springdale. The lowest takeout option is near the bridge at South Campground, near the visitor center. This is also where you'll leave a vehicle if taking out upstream, because no parking areas exist along the shuttle route. Parking at the visitor center fills up almost immediately after the park opens in the morning.

DIRECTIONS TO PUT-IN

At the same time you acquire your backcountry permit to float the river, inquire about a special parking permit that will allow you to park at the Temple lot. This is necessary after about mid-March, when the Floor of the Valley Road closes to public vehicles. Park at the Temple lot and use the shuttle when your run is complete to retrieve your vehicle. If you brought your playboat (or any boat shorter than the width of the bus), according to a ranger you could strap it to the front of the bus, where the bikes go, preventing you from having to set shuttle at all. Of course, packrafts and other inflatables may be simply carried on board.

NEARBY ATTRACTIONS

The hiking, climbing, wildlife viewing, trekking, biking, and more throughout Zion National Park entices visitors from across the globe. You'll find low-gradient hiking paths riverside that allow for a dip in the Emerald Pools formed by the Virgin River, or you can opt for the more thrilling hiking option along the ridgeline to Angel's Landing. Permits for backpacking and camping in the backcountry should be reserved months in advance, although several spots are left open for walk-ins each day. The town of Springdale provides any services you may need, including ice cream—a popular treat on hot Utah summer days.

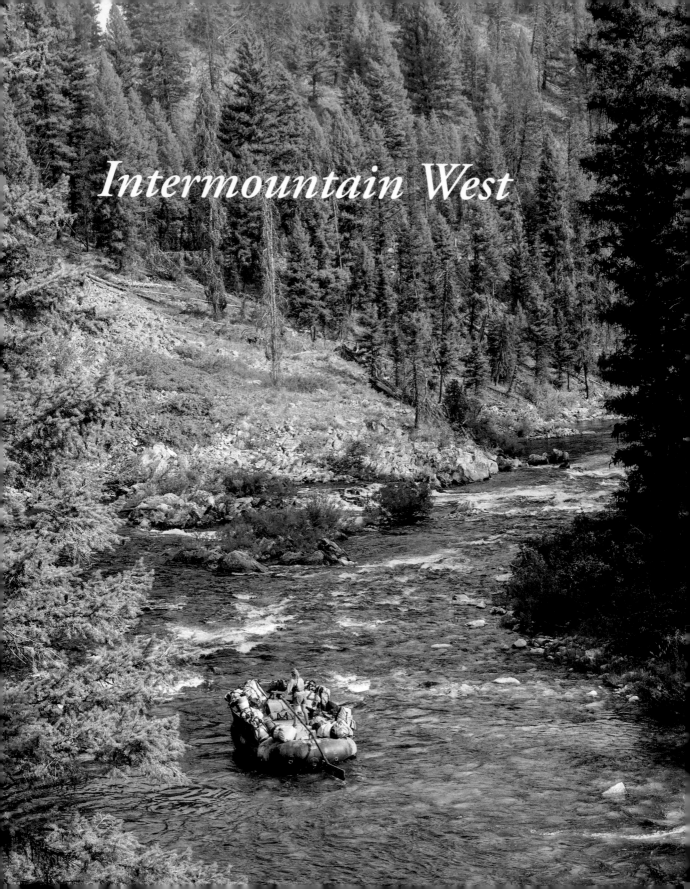

Intermountain West

25

MIDDLE FORK FLATHEAD RIVER

Section name	Schafer Meadows to Bear Creek; Bear Creek to West Glacier
Distance	Above Bear Creek: 26 miles; below Bear Creek: 31.5 miles
Flow range	1,000–20,000 cfs
Season and source of water	Mid-May to mid-July; snowmelt
Gauge location	West Glacier, USGS #12358500
Time required	1–6 days
Classification	*Wild* and *Recreational*
Difficulty	III (IV)
Managing agency	Glacier National Park and Flathead National Forest
Permit required?	No
Shuttle type	Flight, horse pack, or hike in and vehicle
Outstandingly Remarkable Values	Fisheries, geology, history, recreation, scenery, wildlife, paleontology, water quality, botany
Why paddle this section?	Snorkel-worthy water clarity; deep wilderness; ultimate Montana experience; great fishing

Opposite: Gear boat driver Audrey Gehlhausen launches early to let the current take her down. ADAM ELLIOTT

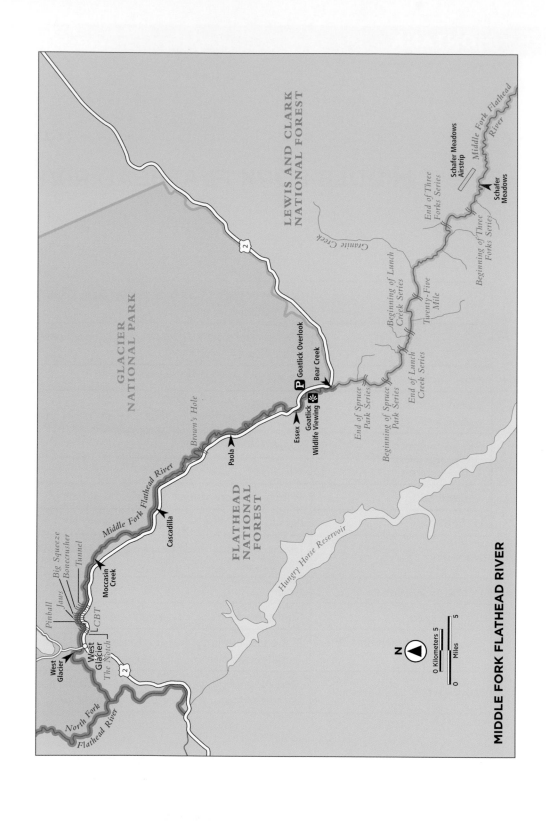

MIDDLE FORK FLATHEAD RIVER

RIVER DESCRIPTION

Floating the Middle Fork Flathead River below Schafer Meadows transports paddlers into the heart of Montana's legendary wilderness and wild river territory. Flathead National Forest's Great Bear Wilderness Area and Bob Marshall Wilderness (the "Bob," as it is known by its fans) completely encompass the *Wild* reaches of the upper river. Few roads or access points in this reach make bear sightings just as likely as fellow river runner sightings. The lower *Recreational* section of the Middle Fork Flathead borders Glacier National Park's southern edge and entertains visitors with great whitewater, tranquil pools, and epic mountain scenery.

The list of Outstandingly Remarkable Values for this river seems never-ending, and for good reason. Few river systems in the country can match the high quality of the Flatheads, whether the Middle, North, or South Fork. First, the water quality produces indescribable hues of blue, turquoise, and green. We felt as though we had discovered a new rainbow consisting of the Flathead's blue and turquoise hues and the kaleidoscope of rocks on display in the clear, shallow pools. It is purely mesmerizing, particularly when your boat gains speed moving toward a rapid and the polychromatic river bed races quicker beneath the glassy surface. High-quality fishing can be found here as well. Bring your fly rod (and your Montana fishing license) to partake in the aquatic bounty. Westslope cutthroat trout call the Flathead home, indicating great water quality found in few other Western rivers.

While the Flathead's designation did not come until 1976, its roots extend to the National Wild & Scenic Rivers Act's origin. Frank and John Craighead, two brothers who grew up on the East Coast but extensively explored, studied, and eventually lived near the rivers and wild areas of Idaho and Montana, first suggested the idea for the Wild & Scenic Rivers Act in the late 1950s. They fought directly to keep the proposed Spruce Park Dam off the Middle Fork Flathead. From this fight, they claimed that our nation needed a specific conservation program to protect the rivers that lacked development. Eventually, Congressman Stewart Udall, later Secretary of Interior and champion of the Wild & Scenic Rivers system, asked Frank Craighead to draft a report on a river classification system in 1958. This would later become the genesis of river classifications as *Wild*, *Scenic*, and *Recreational*. It was the Middle Fork Flathead's wild character that inspired this action.

Despite the contribution that the forks of the Flathead River made to the formulation of the Wild & Scenic Rivers Act, no new designations have taken place in Montana since then. That will hopefully change soon, with widespread citizen support for new river protections throughout the state. Take a look at the future Wild and Scenic river descriptions in this book for more information.

PADDLER'S NOTES

We've broken the river descriptions into two sections: the *Wild* reach and the *Recreational* reach. While these two sections can be linked, the access into the *Wild* reach makes logistics a little trickier. Neither section requires a permit to float but be mindful of the regulations and get serious with your bear-bag hanging or bring canisters.

While 46.6 miles of the upper reaches are designated as *Wild*, paddlers typically only float the final 26 miles downstream of Schafer Meadows. Because you'll be flying into Schafer Meadows in a small commuter plane, you'll begin to feel the distance between you and civilization before even arriving at the river. Other access options include packing gear onto horses or your own back and trekking in on Granite Creek Trail to float 18 miles of the *Wild* section. We opted to hike in with packrafts for our trip, a cheaper option and better later in the season when flows drop.

In several places on the run, rapids are known as series and span up to a few miles. You won't necessarily find continuous rapids for miles, but they are stacked very close together and often worth a scout.

Three Forks Series comes into play just a few miles downstream of Schafer Meadows. These drops, slots, and waves can morph into class IV action, but with breaks in between. Twenty-Five Mile rapids come just a few miles downstream from Granite Creek. Two distinct rapids make up this series, with the first being full of small maneuvers at low water making it more difficult to navigate than at high water.

Lunch Creek Series may be the longer series, but is less steep than the others. Plan to spend some time in Spruce Park Series, just a few miles before the beginning of the *Recreational* section. The first rapid contains undercut rocks and will likely be the most difficult in the series. Scout from the left. The rest of this series descends through one of the more spectacular gorges on the river, with narrow channels created out of blockish chunks of cliff wall.

So many great camp spots line this stretch that naming a few would be a disservice to them all. We enjoyed camping on gravel bars during lower water, while some groves of trees can be found for shade.

The *Recreational* classification extends for 31.5 miles along US 2 downstream of the Bear Creek access. Multiday or single-day trips with just as much great scenery and whitewater, and minimal shuttle frustrations, make this section more popular.

Start the day as far upstream as Bear Creek, at the boundary of the wilderness area. Downstream from here, the river meanders away from the road enough to feel as though civilization must exist in a faraway land. Between the Bear Creek and Essex access locations, you'll get a front-seat view of goats enjoying the salt seeps at river level in the Goatlick area. Only the goats can reside between these two access locations, so plan on camping below Essex.

Bring a snorkel and mask, because these pools are deep! Susan paddles through one of the more interesting fishing spots along the Middle Fork Flathead. ADAM ELLIOTT

Except for Brown's Hole, a class III hit, the river remains mostly class II all the way to the Cascadilla access location at river mile 30.5. Take out here, or plan on continuing all the way to West Glacier access, another 14 miles. River users can only put in at Moccasin creek access due to the popularity of the lower river. Between Cascadilla and Moccasin Creek, the river widens and becomes braided into sinuous channels between newly formed cobble bars in a reach called Nyack Flats. The river's free-flowing nature may be most obvious in this reach, with new channels cutting through cobble bars and logjams damming smaller channels to initiate island formation. Scout the channels when in doubt to be sure a logjam won't thwart your descent.

If you're looking for more whitewater and a shorter day on the river, start at Moccasin and take out at West Glacier. These 7 miles provide great pool-drop class III rapids that get spicier as the water level gets higher, and push into the class IV difficulty range. This section can often be paddled into late summer.

Before any trip into the Flathead watershed, grab a copy of the *Three Forks of the Flathead Float Guide*, published by the Forest Service.

BEARS ON WILDERNESS RIVERS

Bear sightings can add a thrilling twist to your boating stories around the campfire—if all goes well. Keep these tips in mind to stay safe in bear country while paddling.

1. **Hang a bear bag like you mean it.** Don't skimp on the distances between the tree, ground, and bag. Get that bag 10 feet off the ground and at least 4 feet from any vertical support, like a tree. Using multiple throw-ropes and your pin kit's carabiners and pulleys can make the process easy. If boat capacity allows, bring bear canisters.

2. **Pack away everything with a scent.** Include everything that smells in your hanging bear bag. This could be toothpaste and toothbrushes, lip balm and lotions, utensils and dishes. And take your last swig from your whiskey flask. It has to go in there too.

3. **Carry bear spray.** Don't bury that can of bear spray in your overnight bag during the day. Even floating around a blind corner could be the time you get too close for comfort to a bear. Carry the canister in an

Hiking through bear country mandates carrying bear spray at the ready. We also sang songs and called out ahead to greet the bears. ADAM ELLIOTT

DIRECTIONS TO TAKEOUT

From Kalispell, take US 2 east toward Glacier National Park. Just after passing the entrance to the park you will begin to follow the Middle Fork Flathead. Turn left onto the Going to the Sun Road in West Glacier and another immediate left onto Riverbend Drive to reach the West Glacier access point. Or take out at any of the river accessible place while floating and at camp. Check regulations because bear spray is not always allowed in national parks and other locations, such as within Yosemite, where only black bears are present.

4. **Camp away from your kitchen.** Set up your tent at least 100 yards away from cooking and food storage areas. These smells stick around even after you clean up using those Leave No Trace practices you've been practicing.

5. **Always be Bear Aware, even in campgrounds.** Bears love the fast-food options at many campgrounds. Encounters are not limited to backcountry river trips through remote wilderness. They can happen in the front country too. Store your food in bear-safe containers in campgrounds with known populations.

Bear-safe food storage can be accomplished by hanging one horizontal rope between two trees and hanging a second rope to a food bag from a carabiner. The bag of food needs to be 10-plus feet off the ground, 4-plus feet away from the nearest tree, and 5-plus feet under the point of hanging. ADAM ELLIOTT

access locations along this road for the *Recreational* section. The Bear Creek access point is the first takeout option when floating the *Wild* stretch.

DIRECTIONS TO PUT-IN

Logistics for traveling to the put-in for the *Wild* reach depend on where you are starting your river trip. If you've opted to charter a flight to Schafer Meadows, you'll

The Great Bear Wilderness has some beautiful geology hidden among the pines. We spotted this broken slope of sedimentary rock high above the Middle Fork Flathead River. ADAM ELLIOTT

likely meet the plane in Kalispell and hire a shuttle driver to leave your car at one of the access points along US 2. If you are looking to hike in with your equipment, we suggest entering on the Granite Creek trail. To reach the trailhead, continue driving on US 2 past the Bear Creek access. Make a hard right on Skyland Road (FR 5282) about 10.5 miles after Bear Creek. You should see a mileage sign to Granite Creek Trailhead along this road. In 8 miles, veer right onto a dirt road, where you see another sign pointing you to the trailhead. You'll dead-end at the trailhead in a mile. Any of the US 2 access locations work for starting a float on the *Recreational* reach.

NEARBY ATTRACTIONS

Glacier National Park shouldn't be missed. Even if you only have one extra day in the area, take the park's shuttle bus on a tour of glacial peaks and lakes that will leave you breathless. For additional paddling or fishing options, take a look at the Wild and Scenic North or South Fork Flathead Rivers. Or stop along Flathead Lake on your way back to Missoula to paddle or swim in the largest natural freshwater lake west of the Mississippi.

26

MIDDLE FORK SALMON RIVER

Section name	Boundary Creek to Cache Bar
Distance	96 miles
Flow range	700–10,000 cfs (1.7–6 feet)
Season and source of water	Late spring and summer; snowmelt
Gauge location	Middle Fork Lodge near Yellowpine, USGS #13309220
Time required	5–7 days
Classification	*Wild*
Difficulty	III–IV
Managing agency	Salmon–Challis National Forest
Permit required?	Yes
Shuttle type	Vehicle
Outstandingly Remarkable Values	Culture, fisheries, geology, history, recreation, scenery, wildlife, botany, traditional cultural use, water quality
Why paddle this section?	Most iconic multiday river trip in America; continuous and fun whitewater; hot springs galore, unbelievable scenery

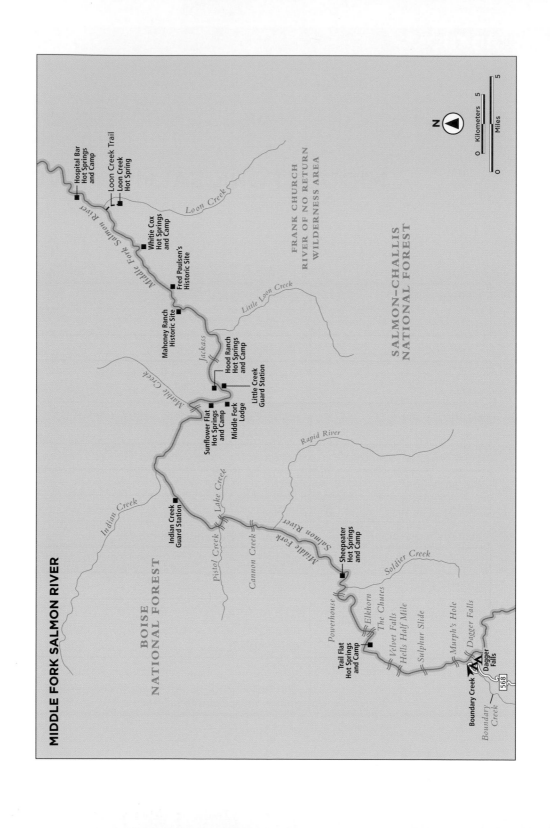

MIDDLE FORK SALMON RIVER

BOISE NATIONAL FOREST

SALMON–CHALLIS NATIONAL FOREST

FRANK CHURCH RIVER OF NO RETURN WILDERNESS AREA

Hospital Bar Hot Springs and Camp

Loon Creek Trail

Loon Creek Hot Spring

Whitie Cox Hot Springs and Camp

Fred Paulsen's Historic Site

Mahoney Ranch Historic Site

Hood Ranch Hot Springs and Camp

Little Creek Guard Station

Sunflower Flat Hot Springs and Camp

Middle Fork Lodge

Indian Creek Guard Station

Sheepeater Hot Springs and Camp

Trail Flat Hot Springs and Camp

Powerhouse

Elkhorn

The Chutes

Velvet Falls

Hells Half Mile

Sulphur Slide

Murph's Hole

Dagger Falls

Boundary Creek

568

Middle Fork Salmon River

Loon Creek

Little Loon Creek

Jackass

Marble Creek

Indian Creek

Lake Creek

Pistol Creek

Cannon Creek

Middle Fork Salmon River

Rapid River

Soldier Creek

Boundary Creek

N

Kilometers 0 5

Miles 0 5

RIVER DESCRIPTION

The Middle Fork Salmon River may be the most beloved multiday river trip anywhere in the world. The river flows freely through pristine mountains of the Intermountain West in Idaho's renowned Frank Church–River of No Return Wilderness. Green shades of water and steady gradient create rapids exciting enough to fire your adrenaline, but manageable for most intermediate rafters and kayakers at average flows. Wildlife frequent the shorelines and skies, both of which we recommend observing from multiple riverside hot springs. Spending six days on this stretch of this Wild and Scenic river should be a goal for every river runner.

The Middle Fork originates northwest of Stanley, and north of the Sawtooth Mountains at the confluence of Marsh and Bear Valley Creeks. The river then cuts through the center of the largest contiguous wilderness area in the Lower 48, the Frank Church–River of No Return Wilderness.

Native American tribes within the region referred to the people of the Middle Fork canyons as the Mountain Sheepeaters. Bands of these nomadic people left behind the earliest evidence of human habitation in this remote mountain region. However, earlier cultures likely inhabited the region as far back as 12,000 years ago. The Sheepeaters relied heavily on bighorn sheep for protein from meat, clothing from hides, and tools from horns. They likely utilized the rugged topography to hunt the wild beasts, herding groups toward steep cliffs or using a perch above a common watering hole at the river bottom to hunt. You'll enjoy watching herds of bighorn sheep as they adeptly maneuver across the mountain landscape and traverse the forested hillsides.

While no fish bones have been found in archaeological sites, heaps of river mussel shells can be seen at many. The Sheepeaters raked the bottom of the river for the mussels and steamed them in ovens. Pictographs also allude to habits and lifestyles of early inhabitants. However, archaeologists can't conclude exactly why early inhabitants painted the images upon the rocks.

The entire 96 miles of river pass by with very little evidence of man. Only a few ranches and outposts remain, mostly from the ore and gold mining days. These historical cabins, along with several airstrips, were grandfathered into the wilderness, which was championed by Idaho Senator Frank Church.

The depth of wilderness surrounding this river makes it ideal for spotting rare wildlife. For example, on a hike along the Middle Fork Trail downstream from Boundary Creek launch, I (Susan) ran into what was likely a mountain lion within fifteen minutes of walking. Luckily, my dog's growling caused the animal to slink back into the woods, and I decided a trail run would better suit the return trip back to Boundary Creek.

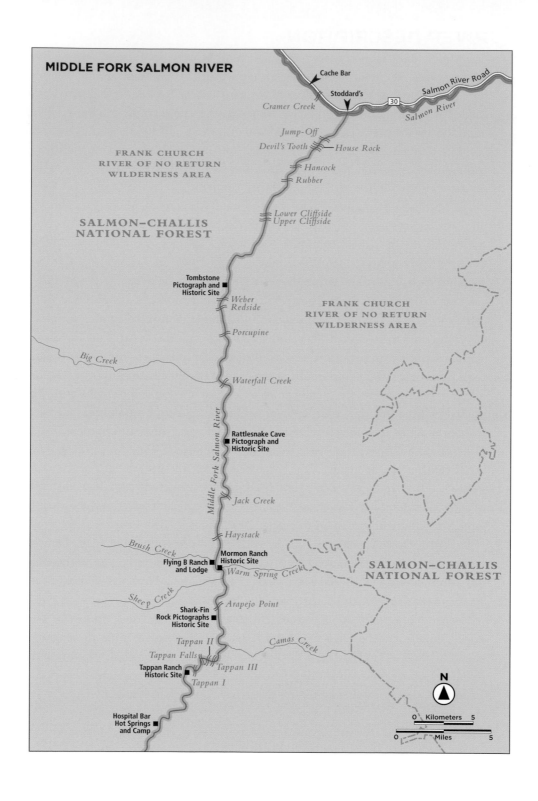

MIDDLE FORK SALMON RIVER

Cache Bar
Stoddard's
Cramer Creek
Salmon River Road
30
Salmon River

FRANK CHURCH
RIVER OF NO RETURN
WILDERNESS AREA

Jump-Off
Devil's Tooth
House Rock
Hancock
Rubber

SALMON–CHALLIS
NATIONAL FOREST

Lower Cliffside
Upper Cliffside

Tombstone
Pictograph and
Historic Site
Weber
Redside

FRANK CHURCH
RIVER OF NO RETURN
WILDERNESS AREA

Porcupine

Big Creek

Waterfall Creek

Middle Fork Salmon River

Rattlesnake Cave
Pictograph and
Historic Site

Jack Creek

Haystack

Brush Creek

Mormon Ranch
Historic Site
Flying B Ranch
and Lodge
Warm Spring Creek

SALMON–CHALLIS
NATIONAL FOREST

Sheep Creek

Arapejo Point

Shark-Fin
Rock Pictographs
Historic Site

Tappan II
Tappan Falls
Tappan Ranch
Historic Site
Tappan III
Tappan I

Camas Creek

N

Hospital Bar
Hot Springs
and Camp

0   Kilometers   5

0   Miles   5

PADDLER'S NOTES

Obtaining a private permit for this run is a bit like drawing a king and an ace in a game of blackjack. Apply for your permit through the Four Rivers Lottery system between December 1 and January 31 for a launch date in the next summer. Each of the four rivers in the lottery make for an incredible Wild and Scenic trip, so go ahead and request a permit for all of them to up your chances.

Flows on this river can range from 700 cubic feet per second (cfs) to 10,000 cfs for the average boater. However, most river runners familiar with the Middle Fork will tell you to launch at Boundary Creek with rafts if the gauge reads at least 1,000 cfs. Below that, you'd be better off flying into Indian Creek rather than pushing loaded rafts over the shallow rapids. Ice and snow on roads and on the river prevent boaters from accessing this run from November through late May. Kayakers can launch on Marsh or Bear Valley Creeks in the early season, if the road to Boundary Creek has too much snow.

Rangers lead a round-robin draft to assign campsites at your pretrip meeting the morning of your launch, based on all trip leaders' preferences for a launch that day. Bartering is common.

With over 300 named rapids in the 96 miles of whitewater on the Middle Fork Salmon, it would be silly to name and describe them all here. However, we'll touch on some of the classics, and trust you'll pick up a copy of *Middle Fork of the Salmon River: A Comprehensive Guide* for the run to get you through the rest.

From the Boundary Creek launch, the gradient starts steep, with nearly continuous whitewater for 26 miles. Just assume all class III rapids could end with a flip at higher flows. Within the first mile, you'll encounter Murph's Hole, a class III feature that can dish out some action from the get-go. Velvet Falls, at river mile 5.2, has a longer lead-in and often surprises rafts who haven't set themselves up to run the smoother left line over the main drop. At river mile 11.4 you'll enter the longer Powerhouse rapid, often broken into three sections.

Enjoy a few miles of smaller rapids and pleasant drifting before Lake Creek enters from river right. Forest fires and the subsequent floods in 2011 moved the debris that formed Lake Creek rapid at river mile 21.5. More debris flows have changed the rapid since then, as well as downstream Pistol Creek rapid. One of the rapids mentioned in more carnage stories, Pistol Creek, just half a mile downstream from Lake Creek, sends rafters around a bend between vertical rock walls on both sides of the river. Most parties scout this one from a perch river right and upstream.

Indian Creek Airfield and Guard Station, at river mile 25.2, may be the beginning of your late-summer, low-water trip. A pricey case of beer purchased here can bring a lot of joy to a self-support kayak trip, like the one I (Susan) took back in early May 2010, before permit season started.

Fires have scorched, burnt, and given shape to this landscape. ADAM ELLIOTT

The next two rapids both occur at right-hand bends in the river. First up is Marble Creek rapid at river mile 32.3, followed by Jackass rapid at river mile 37.7.

The Tappan rapids, a series of class III drops, start at river mile 57.6 and continue for about a mile. Tappan Falls, located in the middle of the series, should be scouted. Starting at mile 78, canyon walls rise up on either side of the river for a section known as the Impassible Canyon. The Middle Fork Trail that follows the river on the left turns to follow Big Creek out of the canyon before the topography drops off here.

You're back into rapids by river mile 81.8, with Redside and Weber rapids, both with fun hydraulics and short drops. Cliffside rapids (upper and lower) await you at river mile 87.8. Those impassable canyon walls will feel tight when the river's current sends you careening toward them here. Rubber, Hancock, Devil's Tooth, and Jump-Off rapids occur between river mile 90 and 94. All are ranked class III.

Nearly every campsite on the Middle Fork Salmon has spectacular views of the river and great places to lounge. A few campsites really top the charts, however, due to the hot springs and hiking. Sunflower Flat camp may be one of the more popular spots due to the presence of both hot springs pools and a shower (and, unfortunately, plenty of poison ivy). We also love the camp at Loon Creek. The hot springs here can be found about a mile up the trail that follows the creek. A tub made from hewn timbers sits next to the creek and can fit ten people comfortably. Note where all the hot springs can be found as you float. Even if you can't camp at them all, stopping for a midmorning soak brings a little luxury to your wilderness experience.

While many established trails exist, some of the best exploration is off-trail. For instance, from Marble Creek camp, follow the trail along the creek upstream to start, then zigzag off-trail and upslope to the saddle for excellent views of camp and the downstream horseshoe river bend. Be sure you remember how to get back down, especially if you head off-trail. A wealth of good waterfall hikes can be found in the Impassible Canyon, such as Parrott's Grotto, Redwall/Gold Creek, or Waterfall Creek.

Bring your fly rod if you know that native westslope cutthroat will taunt you otherwise. Idaho Fish and Game only permits catch-and-release with single barbless and baitless hooks on this stretch, but we hear the fishery is one of the finest in the West and worth every cast.

DIRECTIONS TO TAKEOUT

From Salmon, drive north on US 93 toward North Fork. Turn left at the North Fork convenience store onto Salmon River Road/FR 30. Stay on this road for 40.7 miles as it meanders along the Main Salmon River until you get to Cache Bar.

DIRECTIONS TO PUT-IN

Boundary Creek launch site can be reached by driving west on ID 21 South for 21 miles from Stanley. Turn right onto Bear Valley Road/FR 579. You will see brown signs for Boundary Creek Boat Launch. Stay on FR 579 for just under 10 miles. Turn right onto FR 568. Again, there should be signs. In a little over 10 miles you'll reach Boundary Creek campground and launch.

NEARBY ATTRACTIONS

Stanley is a great town to hang out in before or after your trip, but may not have all the necessities you need. Day stretches of the Salmon River can be run, and hiking near Redfish Lake is highly recommended. Of course, you'll want to swim in the lake after as well.

MAIN SALMON RIVER

Section name	Corn Creek to Carey Creek
Distance	81 miles
Flow range	2,000–30,000 cfs
Season and source of water	Spring through summer; snowmelt
Gauge location	Whitebird, USGS #13317000
Time required	5–6 days
Classification	*Wild*
Difficulty	II–III
Managing agency	Salmon–Challis National Forest
Permit required?	Yes
Shuttle type	Vehicle / hire a shuttle
Outstandingly Remarkable Values	Culture, fisheries, geology, history, recreation, scenery, wildlife, botany, traditional cultural use, water quality
Why paddle this section?	Large sandy beaches; beginner to intermediate whitewater; deep wilderness; great early explorer and homesteader storytelling

RIVER DESCRIPTION

If you are a fan of the beach lifestyle but want to get your mountain time in on vacations as well, the Main Salmon River should be at the top of your river list. Fields of soft, white sand surrounded by towering ponderosa pine and Douglas fir trees line the river's rugged shoreline as it cuts through the Lower 48's largest wilderness area,

If you boat the rivers of central Idaho during fire season, cherish the wonderful sunsets.
SUSAN ELLIOTT

Idaho's famed Frank Church–River of No Return Wilderness. Rapids thrill, but rarely scare, and invite beginning, intermediate, and expert paddlers to find their excitement for the day.

They called the Main Salmon River the River of No Return. While it has been hard to trace the origin of this foreboding nickname, it is possible to understand why. William Clark, half of the intrepid Lewis and Clark duo, accompanied a member of the local Shoshone tribe into the Main Salmon's canyon despite forewarning from the tribes that passage would be impossible. The Shoshone and their descendants likely had known this because they'd lived and traveled over 10,000 years in the area's rugged terrain. Upon looking down at what we believe was Pine Creek rapid, Clark affirmed the impossibility of navigating the river and backtracked to find another route to the Pacific.

Today, that same Salmon River flows equally unrestrained thanks to the 1980 Wilderness and Wild and Scenic River designations. Luckily, today's river equipment and hydrological prediction methods make trips into this formerly impassable canyon quite enjoyable and smooth.

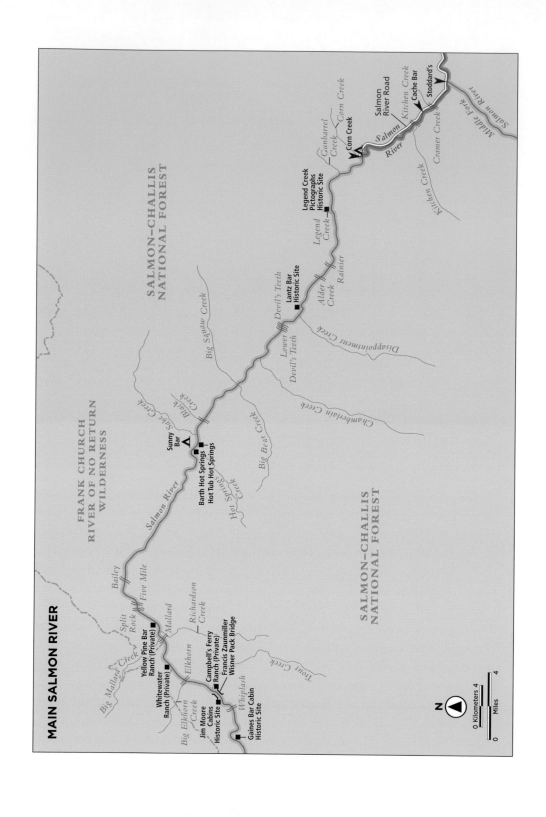

MAIN SALMON RIVER

FRANK CHURCH
RIVER OF NO RETURN
WILDERNESS

SALMON–CHALLIS
NATIONAL FOREST

SALMON–CHALLIS
NATIONAL FOREST

Big Mallard Creek

Split Rock

Big Mallard Creek

Bailey

Five Mile

Yellow Pine Bar Ranch (Private)

Mallard

Whitewater Ranch (Private)

Elkhorn

Big Elkhorn Creek

Jim Moore Cabins Historic Site

Campbell's Ferry Ranch (Private)

Francis Zaunmiller Wisner Pack Bridge

Whiplash

Gaines Bar Cabin Historic Site

Richardson Creek

Trout Creek

Salmon River

Sabe Creek

Black Creek

Sunny Bar

Barth Hot Springs
Hot Tub Hot Springs

Hot Springs Creek

Big Bear Creek

Big Squaw Creek

Chamberlain Creek

Disappointment Creek

Devil's Teeth

Lower Devil's Teeth

Lantz Bar Historic Site

Alder Creek

Rainier

Legend Creek

Legend Creek Pictographs Historic Site

Gunbarrel Creek

Corn Creek

Corn Creek

Salmon River Road

Salmon River

Kitchen Creek

Cache Bar

Stoddard's

Cramer Creek

Kitchen Creek

Middle Fork Salmon River

N

0 Kilometers 4
0 Miles 4

The Main Salmon River cuts west to east across the middle of Idaho, through a nearly impenetrable block of designated wilderness and national forest areas. The Frank Church–River of No Return Wilderness encompasses most of the watersheds draining the south side of the river. This vast and primitive area won protection thanks to the dedication of Idaho's Senator Frank Church. This champion congressman linked several primitive areas through novel legislation. On the north side of the Main Salmon River, the Selway–Bitterroot Wilderness also feeds water to the Wild and Scenic Selway, Lochsa, and Middle Fork Clearwater Rivers.

By the mid-1850s, intrepid explorers began running long, wooden boats called scows down the Main Salmon River in search of gold and fortune. Many built cabins and ranches on bars and flats, creating a tenacious community of homesteaders like Buckskin Bill, Jim Moore, and Polly Bemis. The living was not easy then. Caretakers and residents live with more conveniences today, such as electricity from hydropower and weekly mail delivery via aircraft. Stopping at the small museums along the river and listening to the stories told by these residents makes a Main Salmon trip unlike any other. One can only imagine a life among these deep rock walls, with the company of bears, bighorn sheep, moose, cougars, and elk, and minimal contact with the outside world.

PADDLER'S NOTES

If you want to gather your friends and all the gear necessary to do this trip, you'll need to score a permit first. This is no easy task for launch dates between June 20 and September 7. Apply through the Forest Service's Four Rivers Lottery and Permit Reservation System. You'll see that you can also request permits for the Middle Fork Salmon, Hells Canyon of the Snake River, and the Selway River as a part of this system—all four designated Wild and Scenic. Outside of the busy summer season, permits for the Main are unlimited although the river could be frozen or inaccessible due to snow.

Early summer trips can have epic high water on the Main, thanks to the undammed nature of the run and the Middle Fork Salmon dumping in upstream. Mid-July usually provides more relaxed trips with plenty of water. By late August, the river gets pretty low. You'll also encounter jet boats out there, a rare sight for a wilderness river. Their use was grandfathered into the wilderness designation. Rules of the river state that non-motorized crafts have the downstream right of way, but know that jet boats can't stop everywhere and greatly appreciate when you pass quickly.

If you've won a permit and gathered your own crew for a trip, you'll want to arrive at Corn Creek the night before your scheduled launch day. Once you have a permit, hire a shuttle service to take your vehicle from the put-in to the takeout; there are several companies that shuttle around Idaho's many rivers. The quickest route around the

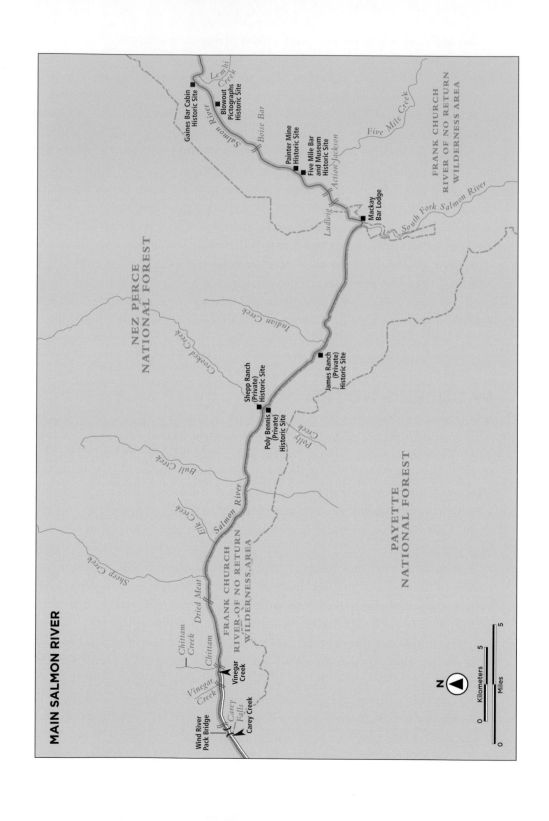

MAIN SALMON RIVER

Frank Church Wilderness takes a full day of driving. River campsite reservations and the mandatory Forest Service briefing take place at the ranger station on the morning of your launch. To prevent large groups from overrunning small campsites, each site carries a small, medium, or large group designation. The system allows you to spend more time relaxing on the water rather than rushing to claim a camp. However, you won't be able to reserve every night of your trip. Remember to look at the group size for each camp and chat with other trips to avoid any conflict.

While you'll need to review all the regulations, a few of note are provided here. All soapy or used water (dishes, bathing, teeth brushing, etc.) should be dumped above the high-water line and not into the river. This applies to the hot springs as well, so bring a bucket and plan to bathe away from the actual springs. Campfires should always be contained in a fire pan. And, as usual, all waste should be transported out, including human and dog waste. Of course, avoid dealing with all of this and book a trip with one of the many outfitters who run the Main Salmon River.

Class II–III rapids fill your first and last two days on the water, while the middle of your trip may feel more mellow. Class I-II rapids lend perfectly to hopping on that stand-up paddle board and even taking a few intentional and refreshing swims. Rainier and Alder Creek rapids kick off the trip with fun waves and some surf spots. The biggest rapid on the run will be Black Creek rapid at river mile 20.7, formed by a side canyon debris flow in 2011. Scout on river left.

Several hikes on both sides of the river surround Frank Lantz's homestead site at river mile 10.9, making the camps around here a great option for the eager explorers. A trail leads from both Upper and Lower Lantz Bar Camps. The homestead no longer has caretakers, but the story of Lantz's tenacity to live along the Salmon River epitomizes the type of hearty characters who committed themselves to living in the wild.

A shift in the canyon's geology starts below Big Squaw Creek, near Black Creek rapid. The Idaho Batholith formation creates rounded, black, and bulbous rock walls. This band of granite runs north to south across Idaho and only pops up for a few miles along the Salmon River.

Perhaps you took a particularly wet and rowdy route through Black Creek rapid. You'll especially love what's around the corner. On river left, pull over at mile 22.3 for the best riverside hot spring tub in all of Idaho (yes, we believe that). Hot Tub hot springs sits perched a few hundred feet up the small side channel. The water is clear, hot, and oh-so-relaxing in the deep pool that sits around ten people comfortably. Drain the tub after your session and use the provided scrub brushes to give the pool a quick wipe down. Think of the hot spring karma it will bring. Don't forget to plug up the pool to begin filling it for the next group.

We loved Sunny Bar Camp, on river right just downstream from the hot springs. Not a traditional camp on the Main Salmon due to lack of a large beach, Sunny Bar

KIDS' ACTIVITIES ON THE RIVER

Bringing the kids along on river trips introduces a new kind of joy and wonder to days spent on the water. The river inspires limitless outdoor discoveries for curious and creative young minds. After many family river trips with young and old kids, we found these pointers can help you guide your kiddos in building a connection to the natural world. You'll quickly see that river trips help disguise learning opportunities as play.

1. **It all starts with good trip preparation.** If kids are sunburned, cold, or dehydrated, they won't be happy no matter how fun the activity may be. Help older kids learn to manage self-care practices on their own, such as applying sunscreen, wearing personal flotation devices (PFDs), and drinking plenty of water. All kids should learn that these essential activities will allow them to play longer and harder all day.

2. **Direct kids to a microenvironment.** A single pool, a tiny side stream, a colorful rock pile: All provide ample opportunity for discovery. Kids can manipulate these environments to see how nature responds. As natural scientists, children want to poke and prod their environments to learn about the world. These spots become mini-outdoor laboratories to know and understand the bigger world.

3. **Prepare an activity kit for kids to record their experiences.** Some items you may want to include are:

   - A field journal with a daily log
   - Watercolor paints and brushes
   - Pens and pencils
   - Plastic collection jar
   - A map
   - Sponge

is in a forested ponderosa pine grove that offers ample shade and still plenty of room for games.

If you're keen to see how early homesteaders lived in this rugged terrain, plan stops at Jim Moore's place, Campbell's Ferry, and Five Mile Bar. Buckskin Bill's outpost at Five Mile Bar features a museum of his gun-building craft and an homage to his reclusiveness.

The whitewater kicks back up on your last day with Dried Meat, Chittam, and Vinegar rapids—all class III fun with big-water-style waves and hydraulics. Camping on river right on your last night can be hot on long summer days. Take your time on the water by adding swimming stops and stopping to enjoy shady nooks for lunch.

4. **Guide kids in observation games.** Find a bug and brainstorm what the bug is doing and how its body works. Listen to animal sounds and talk about where the animals might live. Look at a rapid and discuss what happens when the river hits a rock or a downed tree. These are especially great games for sitting on a boat with high-energy children.

5. **Just let kids be wild.** Ultimately, kids don't need much to entertain themselves on river trips. Games arise out of thin air. Sticks, rocks, and sand become tools for building. And buckets, ropes, and chairs make great obstacle courses. Letting kids' minds wander will produce magical results that stimulate their innate senses of wonder and nourish their connections with the Earth.

6. **Bring a pirate flag!**

When kids can have independence on the river, they learn to make their own decisions, evaluate risks, and lead others, among many other essential skills.
ADAM ELLIOTT

Jet boaters use Vinegar Creek boat ramp more than raft trips. Float down to Carey Creek to give them their space and decrease your vehicle miles.

Any multiday river trip deserves your investment in a specific mile-by-mile waterproof guidebook. The Main Salmon's version of this is *Idaho's Salmon River: A River Runner's Guide to the River of No Return, Corn Creek to Carey Creek,* by Eric and Allison Newell.

The calm stretches along the Main Salmon River invite the paddler's eyes to explore the incredible mountain scenery. SUSAN ELLIOTT

DIRECTIONS TO TAKEOUT

From the riverside town of Riggins, take FR 1614 as it follows the Salmon River upstream. Drive for 18.2 miles before reaching French Creek Road. Turn left here to continue on FR 103 upstream to the Carey Creek river access site.

DIRECTIONS TO PUT-IN

From Salmon, drive north on US 93 toward North Fork. Turn left at the North Fork convenience store onto Salmon River Road/FR 30. Stay on this road for 46 miles as it meanders along the Main Salmon River to Corn Creek.

NEARBY ATTRACTIONS

Taking a commuter flight over the wilderness area to either your put-in or takeout is a fantastic way to see a different perspective of this vast territory. Most commercial trips have guests take at least one flight before or after their trip. Whitewater is everywhere in Idaho. Consider checking out another Wild and Scenic river from this book while you are there.

28

JARBIDGE RIVER

Section name	Murphy Hot Springs to Bruneau River
Distance	31.5 miles
Flow range	700–2,500 cfs
Season and source of water	Spring; snowmelt
Gauge location	Bruneau River at Hot Springs, USGS #13168500
Time required	4–5 days with Bruneau River
Classification	*Wild*
Difficulty	III–IV (V)
Managing agency	Bureau of Land Management, Boise District
Permit required?	Yes; Aquatic Invasive Species (AIS) permit
Shuttle type	Vehicle (four-wheel drive if floating Jarbidge River only)
Outstandingly Remarkable Values	Culture, ecology, fisheries and aquatic species, geology, recreation, scenery, wildlife
Why paddle this section?	Remote self-support trip through Idaho's little explored but richly rewarding desert canyon country

RIVER DESCRIPTION

The Jarbidge River in southwestern Idaho's forgotten canyonlands becomes an annual pilgrimage for the boaters who have taken the time to explore it. Typically run as a four- or five-day self-support kayak trip, the river is filled with technical class III rock

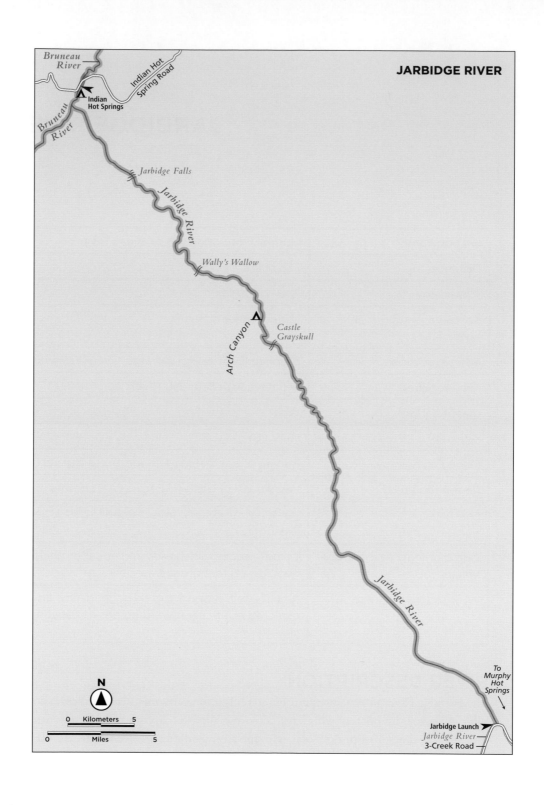

JARBIDGE RIVER

Bruneau River

Indian Hot Spring Road

Indian Hot Springs

Bruneau River

Jarbidge Falls

Jarbidge River

Wally's Wallow

Arch Canyon

Castle Grayskull

Jarbidge River

To Murphy Hot Springs

Jarbidge Launch

Jarbidge River

3-Creek Road

N

0   Kilometers   5

0   Miles   5

A paddler is about to make the crux move at Jarbidge Falls. ADAM ELLIOTT

gardens, remote and scenic pools through twisting canyons, and several classic class IV–V rapids. A big portage (or two) keep the river in the advanced boater class.

Driving to the put-in, past the rundown vacation village of Murphy Hot Springs, you get the sense that the world has mostly forgotten this part of the state. Yet, for anglers and seasonal kayakers, it is a little slice of paradise to drop into the shaded canyons below the rimrocks and rolling sage fields full of cattle. Geologic activity from the nearby Yellowstone hotspot created bulbous outcrops and steep cliff walls, colored in every shade of red, orange, and yellow. The green riparian zone entices paddlers into small camping spots beneath the monoliths, steep side canyons, and deep gorges.

The Bureau of Land Management had created a fantastic guidebook for the Jarbidge, Bruneau, and Owyhee Rivers. Detailed topographic river maps are printed on waterproof paper for the boater's convenience. However, as of 2017 a new edition was in printing and old copies were hard to find. It is worth calling the BLM's Boise office (208-384-3300) to inquire if new copies are available. The BLM guide shows countless unnamed class III rapids throughout the Jarbidge. Therefore, more attention will be given here to class IV and V rapids, or significant portages.

PADDLER'S NOTES

Most paddlers take on the Jarbidge and the Bruneau in one trip. Just downstream from the put-in, the main Jarbidge starts off as a low-volume, almost continuous class II stream with a fishing trail on river right. After a few miles, however, its true character starts to emerge as you cut deeper into the igneous canyons. The cliffs soon rise high on either side, in steps of rusty-looking rhyolite, a volcanic formation similar to basalt that never reached open air in the molten lava stage. Instead, the lava cooled very slowly underground, and developed large crystalline structures of quartz and feldspar.

There are a few camps right off the bat on river right, but there are many more after the first unnamed class IV rapid, around mile 10.5. Keep your eyes open for owls, peregrine falcons, and other birds of prey. On our four-day trip, we saw two different fights between peregrine and great horned owls. From miles 10 to 15 there are no rapids to speak of, but the current keeps up nicely as it winds through a tight canyon.

At mile 16.5 paddlers will encounter an "odd feeling," with a flat section of river and dead trees standing in the water. In 2009, a massive rockslide buried Sevy Falls rapid and created a new class V rapid called Castle Grayskull, also known as Tonsmeire Falls or Barker Falls. At low flow, the rapid becomes "manky," or full of nasty rocks. This actually makes the rapid a bit easier to run. At higher water, a massive hole forms along the river-left bank, backed up by a rock jumble with wood in it. A portage on river right is the chosen route for 99 percent of paddlers.

Most of the rapids on the river are boat-scoutable. The three exceptions are Castle Grayskull (Barker's), Wally's Wallow, and Jarbidge Falls. All three are portageable. Wally's Wallow, at river mile 21.5, requires two significant changes in direction, with undercut boulders and a woody pour-over to avoid. Seasoned boaters will not find this very difficult at lower flows. Jarbidge Falls, at river mile 26.3, however, is a significant rapid requiring some hard paddling and tight lines. When scouting the rapid on river right, you'll need to ferry back across to river left for the better portage. Don't forget to scout the ferry, and don't miss it!

A handful of class III rapids follow Jarbidge Falls, then the river mellows out before the confluence with the Wild and Scenic Bruneau River at mile 29.5.

Just downstream from the confluence at mile 30, a great camp for multiple groups is on river left, along with the excruciatingly hot Indian Hot Springs. A tub exists that sometimes has a plastic sheet for a liner. With some patience and a several buckets of cold river water, you can control the temperature of the hot springs in the tub.

While it is possible to take out when the Jarbidge enters the Bruneau River (or put-in for just the Bruneau), access is abusive to even four-wheel-drive rigs. Instead, continue paddling down the Bruneau River for another few days and take out below. Take a look at the river description in this book for more details on that run.

DIRECTIONS TO TAKEOUT

From Bruneau, drive southeast on Hot Springs Road for 8 miles. The road will change name, becoming the Clover–3 Creek Road, and veer uphill to the left as it leaves the river. Keep heading uphill on the Clover–3 Creek Road, and follow it for a total of 40.4 miles, just past the crossing of Clover Creek. Turn right here on Indian Hot Springs Road and be ready to travel a rugged four-wheel-drive road 16 more miles down to the river.

DIRECTIONS TO PUT-IN

From the takeout road at the intersection of Indian Hot Springs Road and Clover–3 Creek Road, drive south for 30 miles, then turn right on 3 Creek Road. Follow 3 Creek Road west for 10 miles, past Murphy Hot Springs, down to the Jarbidge launch site at the confluence of the east and west forks of the Jarbidge.

NEARBY ATTRACTIONS

For photographers and birders, both Bruneau Dunes State Park and the Snake River Birds of Prey Natural Conservation Area provide lots of opportunities to take photos of birds and beautiful landscapes. Also, driving to the Bruneau Canyon Overlook should not be missed. The view into the canyon complements the views from the bottom of the canyon in a way that will make you feel the breadth of the Wild and Scenic Jarbidge and Bruneau Rivers.

BRUNEAU RIVER

Section name	Indian Hot Springs to south of Bruneau
Distance paddled	40 miles
Flow range	700–2,500 cfs
Season and source of water	Spring; snowmelt
Gauge location	Bruneau River at Hot Springs, USGS #13168500
Time required	2–3 days
Classification	*Wild*
Difficulty	III–IV
Managing agency	Bureau of Land Management, Boise district
Permit required?	Yes; Aquatic Invasive Species (AIS) permit
Shuttle type	Vehicle
Outstandingly Remarkable Values	Culture, ecology, fisheries and aquatic species, geology, recreation, scenery, wildlife
Why paddle this section?	Remote wilderness through canyonlands; great whitewater and wildlife

RIVER DESCRIPTION

Paddlers seek the Bruneau River for an equally dramatic canyon experience as the upstream Jarbidge section, but without the portages. Bigger flows change the character of class III and IV rapids that most rafters prefer and kayakers love. When low flows turn the Jarbidge into one long rock garden, paddlers can still enjoy the Bruneau River.

The road and river access point at Indian Hot Springs. ADAM ELLIOTT

For many of us, the Jarbidge–Bruneau River wilderness is a quirky, overlooked landscape in southwestern Idaho, south of the mighty Snake, north of Nevada, and just east of Oregon. Sagebrush fills the rolling landscape with little outcroppings of rimrock and plenty of roaming antelope and cattle. Lots of cattle. Boise is the capital of this region and the state, and represents the bourgeois to the surrounding proletariat. Drive south from Boise for thirty minutes—leave the strip malls and car dealerships behind—and you can taste the early twentieth-century landscape. Drive another thirty minutes and you might find your pickup truck surrounded by 300 head of cattle, with a few young cowboys callin' to the dogies.

The Bruneau River slices from south to north through this rolling cattle country plateau, originating in the Jarbidge Mountains of northern Nevada. Most of the watershed, including the East and West Forks of the Bruneau, the Jarbidge, and Sheep Creek originate in the Bruneau–Jarbidge Rivers Wilderness Area, and were inducted into the Wild and Scenic Rivers system during the Omnibus Public Land Management Act of 2009. There is much to explore here, and even our four-day self-support kayak trip felt a week too short.

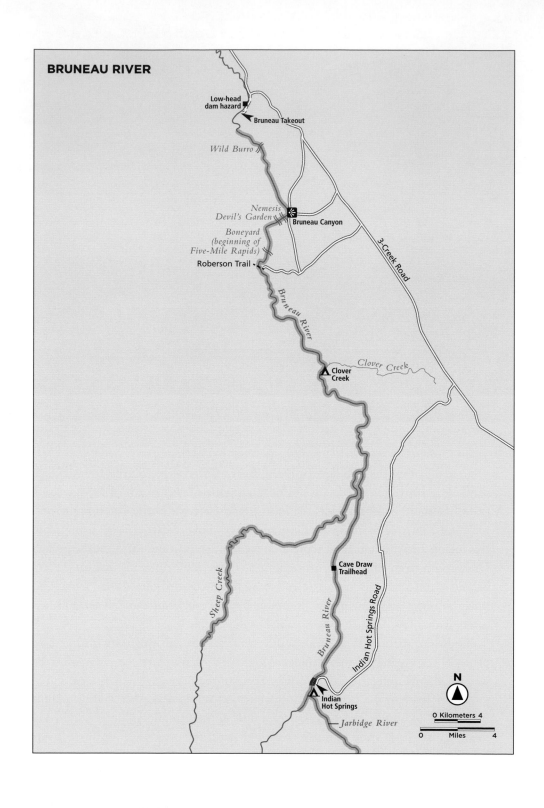

BRUNEAU RIVER

Low-head dam hazard

Bruneau Takeout

Wild Burro

Nemesis
Devil's Garden

Bruneau Canyon

Boneyard
(beginning of
Five-Mile Rapids)

Roberson Trail

3-Creek Road

Bruneau River

Clover Creek

Clover
Creek

Sheep Creek

Cave Draw
Trailhead

Indian Hot Springs Road

Bruneau River

Indian
Hot Springs

Jarbidge River

N

0 Kilometers 4

0   Miles   4

Our initial sight of the lower Bruneau Gorge was from the Bruneau River Overlook, 12 miles from the takeout. We arrived late at night and awoke with the frosty, bright dawn to gaze down into the still shadowed, reddish-brown gorge, with the white-speckled river coursing 1,200 feet below. This is a great place to camp before your trip.

PADDLER'S NOTES

At river mile 29.5, the Bruneau almost doubles in flow volume with the addition of the Jarbidge River, which enters just upstream from the put-in at Indian Hot Springs. The flow could accommodate up to a 16-foot raft at higher water, and certainly smaller rafts at every other level. Indian Hot Springs is little more than an old tub with very hot water, a hose, and a big field for camping. It is, however, an idyllic and remote scene.

The first whitewater below the confluence, the class III Cave rapid feels big and pushy if you have just paddled on the Jarbidge, but has a fun S-turn crux move from right to left. There are several other class III rapids in the next 11 miles. At mile 43, Sheep Creek joins in from river left, where someone could potentially exit the canyon. A trail can be found on the north side of the Sheep Creek canyon about a half-mile up from the confluence with the Bruneau. Alternatively, this may be a great place to explore on foot before making camp across the river.

Too many class III rapids to describe fill the Bruneau, along with some excellent camping spots. It is more fun to discover them all for yourself. Commercial trips with Barker River Expeditions (Barkerriver.com) offer opportunities for less-experienced paddlers to see the river, or an easy way for advanced paddlers to preserve their own vehicles.

At mile 37.7, there is an excellent hike up Cave Draw on river left. Follow the drainage up the canyon for less than a mile to a series of caves and arches. Explore to your heart's content. Bring a camera and expect to spend a bit of time just hanging out. For a great final camp Clover Creek, on river right at mile 52, is a great place to spread out, climb, and relax by the fire.

At mile 59.6, Roberson Trail crosses the river, with routes out via both the east and west sides of the canyon. The route is often used by locals for a daily run down to the normal takeout. They need to get splashed after wading through the poison oak on the trail.

Mile 61, class IV Boneyard rapid, marks the beginning of Five-Mile Rapids, a nearly continuous section of class III and IV whitewater that can be read-and-run. However, a swim or flip in this section could be very dangerous. Devil's Garden and Nemesis are two class IV rapids near the end of the 5-mile section, making it important to stay alert and scout when eddies are available. The Bruneau Canyon Overlook is situated directly over the end of Five-Mile Rapids.

After mile 65, there are a handful of class II rapids with one more class IV rapid, Wild Burro, at mile 68. The takeout is at mile 71.5 on river right. Don't miss it; just downstream is a river-wide low-head dam.

A kayaker plays in the final few miles of Bruneau Canyon. The overlook is up to the right in this picture. ADAM ELLIOTT

DIRECTIONS TO TAKEOUT

From Bruneau, drive southeast on Hot Springs Road. In 8 miles, head straight through an open gate onto private land instead of bending to the left where the road turns into Clover–3 Creek Road. The large parking area is about 1 mile away, and has an interpretive sign down by the river that shows a map of both the Jarbidge and Bruneau Wild and Scenic River canyons.

DIRECTIONS TO PUT-IN

From Bruneau, drive southeast on Hot Springs Road for 8 miles. The road will change name, becoming the Clover–3 Creek Road, and veer uphill. Keep heading uphill and follow the road for a total of 40.4 miles, just past the crossing of Clover Creek. Turn right here on Indian Hot Springs Road and drive 16 more miles down to the river.

NEARBY ATTRACTIONS

With packrafts, inflatable kayaks, or other small craft, the West Fork of the Bruneau, Sheep Creek, or even Clover Creek through the East Fork Bruneau Canyon is worth exploring for experienced paddlers. For backcountry skiers, the Jarbidge Mountains would make for some fine spring skiing before a paddle on the snowmelt. Nearby Bruneau Dunes State Park and the Snake River Birds of Natural Conservation Prey Area provide great wildlife viewing as well.

LOCHSA RIVER

Section name	Fish Creek to Split Creek
Distance	9 miles
Flow range	1,500–25,000 cfs
Season and source of water	Spring; rain and snowmelt
Gauge location	Lowell, USGS #13337000
Time required	Half day to full day
Classification	*Recreational*
Difficulty	III–IV
Managing agency	Nez Perce-Clearwater National Forest
Permit required?	No
Shuttle type	Vehicle, hitchhiking, bike
Outstandingly Remarkable Values	Fisheries, history, recreation, scenery, wildlife, botany, traditional cultural use, water quality
Why paddle this section?	Fantastic big-water surf in a deep forested canyon; roadside access but still in a remote setting

RIVER DESCRIPTION

Boaters in Montana and Idaho know the Lochsa River as their local spring and summer big-water paradise. Rafters and kayakers—even surfers and stand-up paddleboarders—camp along US 12 to spend hours surfing Pipeline wave and days lapping the river between Fish Creek and Split Creek. The wild mountains of the northern Rockies

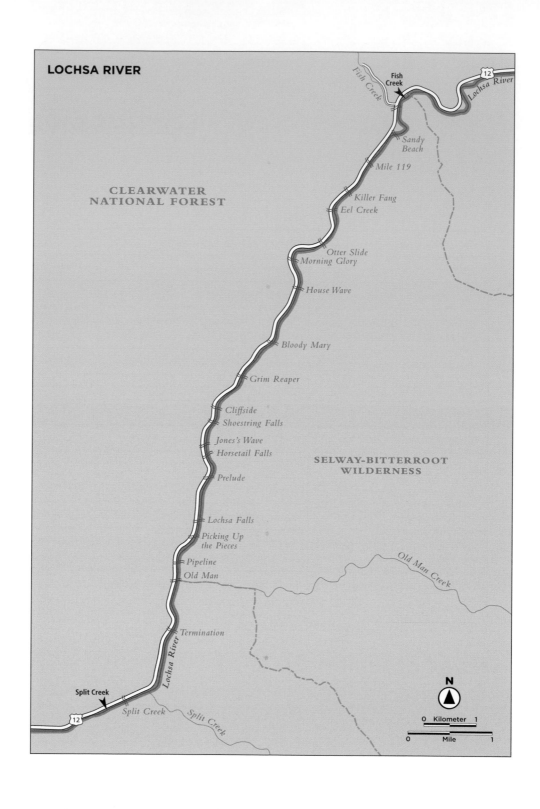

LOCHSA RIVER

Fish Creek

Fish Creek

Lochsa River

12

Sandy Beach

Mile 119

CLEARWATER
NATIONAL FOREST

Killer Fang
Eel Creek

Otter Slide
Morning Glory

House Wave

Bloody Mary

Grim Reaper

Cliffside
Shoestring Falls

Jones's Wave
Horsetail Falls

SELWAY-BITTERROOT
WILDERNESS

Prelude

Lochsa Falls

Picking Up
the Pieces

Old Man Creek

Pipeline
Old Man

Termination

N

Split Creek

Lochsa River

12

Split Creek

Split Creek

0   Kilometer   1

0   Mile   1

surround big-river features around every bend. The Lochsa stands as a favorite river for everyone who has floated it.

Bundled into the original Wild & Scenic Rivers Act under the Middle Fork Clearwater designation, the Lochsa and nearby Selway Rivers have been protected since 1968. Early descents by intrepid river runners, such as Oz Hawksley, helped bring this river to the awareness of politicians as the first batch of Wild and Scenic rivers formed. Today, the Lochsa's roadside access deep within national forest land make paddling different sections easy while maintaining a wild feel.

The Lochsa and Middle Fork Clearwater River's exceptional scenic beauty and cultural significance were recently jeopardized by Exxon Mobil. The company sought to use US 12 to transport Korean-manufactured megaloads carrying tar sands refinery equipment to Canada. With two Wild and Scenic rivers running along the road, the shipments would have created an "industrial corridor" and threatened the Outstandingly Remarkable Values protected by law for each of the rivers, according to a study conducted by the Forest Service.

"These rivers anchor cathedral-like forests that inspire awe, reflection, and reverence," noted Kevin Lewis, executive director of Idaho Rivers United. "They are recreational Edens for fishermen, campers, hikers, hunters, bicyclists, history buffs, whitewater kayakers, and rafters. Massive loads of industrial equipment do not belong here." Luckily, in early 2017, stakeholders reached a settlement with the Forest Service to restrict the megaloads and uphold the historic uses of US 12.

PADDLER'S NOTES

The rapids between Fish Creek and Split Creek along the Lochsa River contend as some of the highest quality and quantity in the West. Spaced just enough apart to catch your breath (although not at high flows—expect a freight train for that), most rapids have multiple lines, so you can pick your flavor of challenge for the day. Generally, these are class III rapids, according to locals. Depending on your comfort in big water, they may all feel more like class IV. If you're lucky, you will run into a Montana or Idaho local boater who feels right at home among the chaos of lateral waves, surprise hydraulics, and boily runouts. Scout when you can't see or haven't met your local guide yet, and be prepared to hit your combat roll. Remember, you can always read and run better from the tops of waves!

At Lochsa Falls, around 6 miles from Fish Creek, you'll be joined by spectators from the road. This one can dish out some carnage. Look for a green tongue into the "V" on the right and avoid the large pour-over ledge on the left. Pipeline wave downstream also attracts an audience, as well as park-and-play boaters and surfers. Your surf session will be worth the wait if a line has formed. Consider adding a day to your trip to get more rides in here.

Matt Rusher soul-surfing Pipeline on the Lochsa. DAVE GARDNER

Many of the other rapids have both big lines and sneak lines at average flows. More boulders at low flows please technical boaters, while high water draws out the more advanced paddlers looking to run nine miles of continuous class IV-IV+.

DIRECTIONS TO TAKEOUT
Many roads lead to the Lochsa, so whether coming in over Lolo Pass or up the Clearwater, continue on US 12 to mile 111.4.

DIRECTIONS TO PUT-IN
Head upstream on US 12 for 8.8 miles to the Fish Creek access site at mile 120.2. Some paddlers put in 2.5 miles farther upstream at Wilderness Gateway to extend the run.

NEARBY ATTRACTIONS
Camping at Wilderness Gateway keeps you close to the whitewater for easy laps on the Lochsa. Be sure to look into the trails leading to multiple hot springs in the area. Also, if you've done your homework and applied for a Selway permit early (and won one), you should certainly add a day to your itinerary to float the Lochsa, or at least paddle the unpermitted stretch below Selway Falls.

SELWAY RIVER

Section name	Paradise to Selway Falls
Distance	47 miles
Flow range	700–30,000 cfs
Season and source of water	Summer; snowmelt
Gauge location	Lowell, USGS #13336500
Time required	2–5 days
Classification	*Wild*
Difficulty	III–IV
Managing agency	Selway-Bitterroot National Forest
Permit required?	Yes; Aquatic Invasive Species (AIS) permit required from May 15 to Jul 31
Shuttle type	Vehicle
Outstandingly Remarkable Values	Fisheries, history, recreation, scenery, wildlife, botany, traditional cultural use, water quality
Why paddle this section?	A treasured river with a difficult permit to score; big whitewater protected for over fifty years

RIVER DESCRIPTION

Paddlers place the Selway River multiday trip on the highest pedestal of dream white-water adventures. The lucid water bubbles over boulders and around rocky bends, fish swarm in deep pools, mountain peaks climb from shorelines, and old-growth forests

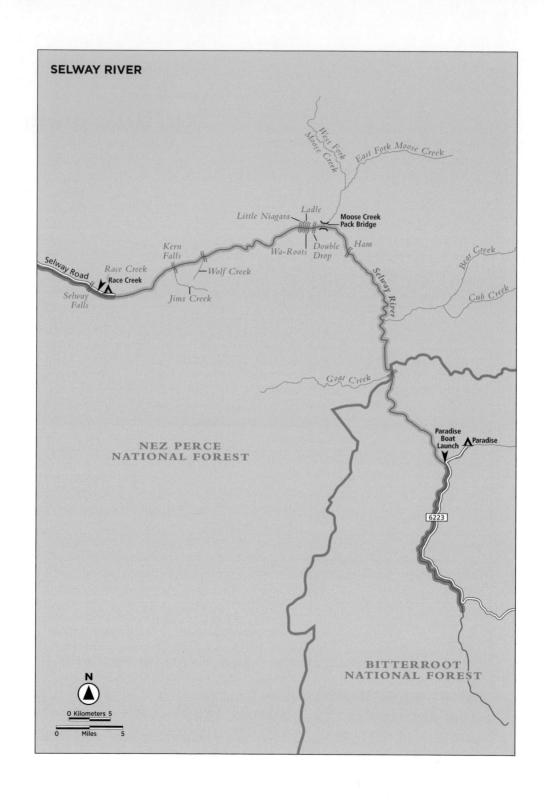

SELWAY RIVER

West Fork Moose Creek

East Fork Moose Creek

Little Niagara   *Ladle*
**Moose Creek
Pack Bridge**

*Kern
Falls*

Wa-Roots   *Double
Drop*   *Ham*

Selway Road

Race Creek
Race Creek

Wolf Creek

Bear Creek

Selway River

Cub Creek

*Selway
Falls*

Jims Creek

Goat Creek

NEZ PERCE
NATIONAL FOREST

Paradise
Boat
Launch   ▲Paradise

6223

N

0 Kilometers 5

0   Miles   5

BITTERROOT
NATIONAL FOREST

Ladle rapid during a high-water self-support trip during the pre-permit season. DAVE GARDNER

blanket the landscape. And we haven't even mentioned the whitewater yet. Class III and IV rapids fill the 47 miles from Paradise Campground to Selway Falls. Early-season trips find sections of continuous class IV+ action that requires navigation through sets of raft-surfing hydraulics and air-catching waves. Later-season trips require technical whitewater maneuvering, still class IV, with more mild stretches allowing you time to take in the display of Idaho's finest wilderness terrain.

Oz Hawksley, a river conservation pioneer native to Missouri's Ozarks and influential in the protection of many Western rivers, made the first descent of the Selway in 1960 as an official AWA-sponsored trip (now American Whitewater). He made the journey with four other adventurers (one being his thirteen-year-old son) in an army surplus raft with a homemade frame and a decked Grumman canoe with custom skirt covers. They expected to take on whitewater based on reading profile charts of the elevation changes, but knew little about the level of difficulty.

The Selway, as a portion of the original Middle Fork Clearwater 1968 designation, is one of the longer rivers in the Wild and Scenic system that is protected from source to mouth. The Selway–Bitterroot Wilderness Area envelops the river, promoting the feeling of complete solitude in the wild. Only a few airstrips and a lodge remind you of civilization.

The designated wilderness here sits next to the Frank Church–River of No Return Wilderness to the south, which is the largest expanse of wilderness in the Lower 48. Sightings of bear, wolves, elk, moose, mountain lions, and more large mammals are reported every year as they move about this wild territory. Old-growth trees still stand strong, and a rich and healthy ecosystem continues to thrive. Hence, it is not surprising that the Selway boasts so many Outstandingly Remarkable Values.

PADDLER'S NOTES

Trip planning can begin when you or a friend scores a coveted Selway River permit (or you book a commercial trip). Apply in the Four Rivers Lottery at Recreation.gov in December and January for the following summer's trip dates. In the old days paddlers referenced flows based on the staff gauge at Paradise that measured the river in feet. These days the real-time USGS gauge near Lowell, near the takeout, is the reference point for trip planning. The Forest Service has published a handy conversion table providing an estimate of the stage height at Paradise based on the flow at Lowell. At flows above 10,000 cubic feet per second (cfs) at Lowell, 3.3 feet at Paradise, things get meaty.

At 500 miles, the shuttle route is long. Hiring a shuttle is worth it. The drive to Paradise Campground and boat launch over Nez Perce Pass can be deep in snow until late spring, often only getting plowed a few days before permit season begins (May 15–Jul 31). Early season nonpermit trips can require heavy-duty four-wheel drive if this is the case. When flows hold out, post-season trips can be a decent low-water option.

Class III dominates the first half of the trip, with Goat Creek and Ham rapids standing out as more difficult class IV action. Goat Creek rapid, at mile 11.5, involves zigging and zagging around large boulders at most flow levels. Ham rapid waits at river mile 23, and contains two bigger drops with massive boulders.

Oz Hawksley often recounted a trip in 1961, when a raft pinned on a boulder and "dump-trucked" (dumped bags and boxes into the river), including that night's ham dinner. They returned the following week and used a dive mask and fins to recover the prized ham, leading to extra portions of ham for the group that night at dinner. They dubbed the rapid Lost Ham, shortened to Ham rapid today.

Keep an eye out for the Moose Creek pack bridge at river mile 27. The tributary on river right, Moose Creek, adds a significant amount of water to the run, and

"KEEP YOUR RIVERS FLOWING AS THEY WILL, AND YOU WILL CONTINUE TO KNOW THE MOST IMPORTANT OF ALL FREEDOMS— THE BOUNDLESS SCOPE OF THE HUMAN MIND TO CONTEMPLATE WONDERS, AND TO BEGIN TO UNDERSTAND THEIR MEANING."

— David Brower as quoted in Oregon Rivers *by Larry Olson and John Daniel*

Downstream from Double Drop, kayakers take in the full majesty of the Selway River canyon. DAVE GARDNER

the class IV action quickly picks up just downstream with Double Drop, Wa-Poots (or Wa-Roots), Ladle, and Little Niagara rapids. These come in quick succession between river miles 27 and 30, and can feel like one long and difficult rapid at higher flows. Many boaters refer to Ladle as the hardest drop on the run. Boaters find sneak routes or big lines all over the rapid depending on the water level. Best to scout a lot in these few miles of big water.

Downstream, class II-III continues, with Wolf Creek rapid and Jims Creek standing out as closer to class IV. Different flow levels dictate very different lines in these rapids, and in all rapids on the Selway. Be sure to scout and reference the *Guide to the Selway River* by RiverMaps.

The entire length of this river contains some of the best riverside wilderness camping in the West. You won't find much until river mile 10, but beyond there you'll float past camps that boast sandy beaches, still-water pools for swimming and fishing, giant cedars and ponderosa pines, large boulders, and animal tracks from the locals.

The takeout on river right will be just after Race Creek campground. Selway Falls is a little over a mile downstream. Stop at the falls on your way out to see the chaos of sieves and boulders that rarely sees the paddle strokes of boaters.

Self-support kayakers paddle the runout of the center line at Ladle. DAVE GARDNER

DIRECTIONS TO TAKEOUT
From US 12 in Idaho, turn at road mile 96.9 onto Selway Road. Selway Falls and Race Creek river access are located about 18 miles upstream.

DIRECTIONS TO PUT-IN
From Darby, Montana, turn right onto MT 143/West Fork Road. Turn right onto Nez Perce Road in 14 miles. This turns into Magruder Corridor Road as you cross into Idaho. Take this road for about 46 miles to its end at Paradise Campground and boat launch.

NEARBY ATTRACTIONS
Idaho is a Wild and Scenic mecca. Definitely spend a day paddling the Lochsa after your Selway trip. Great whitewater can be found just upstream from the confluence. Before your trip, you'll be closer to the Salmon watersheds. If you can line up permits, try to add a Main or Middle Fork Salmon trip to your itinerary. Of course, hiking, camping, and fishing spots abound throughout this entire region.

32

CACHE LA POUDRE RIVER

Section name	Narrows; Stevens Gulch to Bridges Takeout (BTO)
Distance	3.5 miles; 6.3 miles
Flow range	300–3,000 cfs or 1–5.5 feet
Season and source of water	Spring and summer; snowmelt
Gauge location	At the mouth near Fort Collins, DWR gauge ID CLAFTCCO0 (cfs); visual at Pineview Rapid (feet)
Time required	Half day to full day
Classification	*Recreational*
Difficulty	IV–V+; III–IV
Managing agency	Arapaho & Roosevelt National Forests
Permit required?	No
Shuttle type	Vehicle, hitchhiking
Outstandingly Remarkable Values	Recreation, scenery, hydrology, water quality
Why paddle this section?	Range of difficulty to suite every paddler's needs; great downriver play features; riverside campgrounds

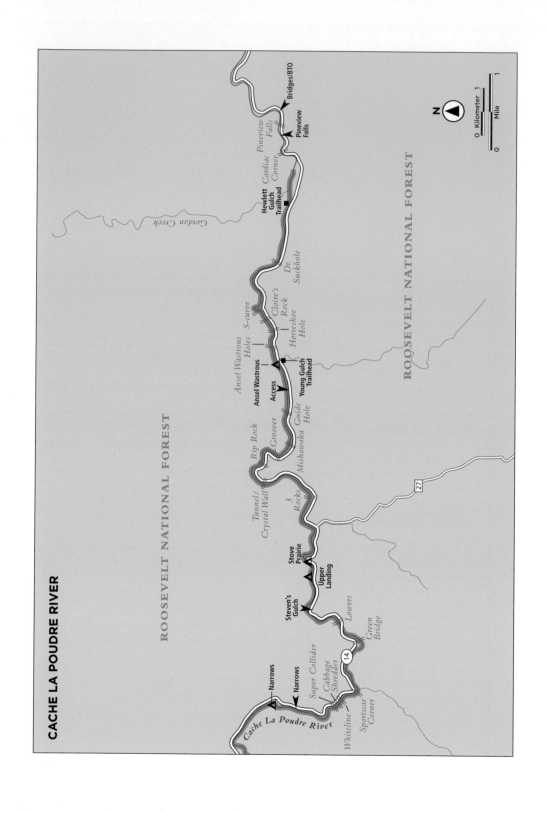

CACHE LA POUDRE RIVER

From Mishiwaka Inn to Poudre Park is likely the most popular section, but convenient road access allows for fun extensions of the run. ADAM ELLIOTT

RIVER DESCRIPTION

The chaotic upper Cache la Poudre River polishes canyon walls and crashes along rough and tumbled talus slopes. As the gradient decreases, the river valley steadily opens to reveal forested and rocky slopes interspersed with floodplain terraces. You'll likely find fishing lines cast in the current and kids playing in the pools along the gentler stretches, as well as campgrounds and picnic areas. This river is loved.

The Cache La Poudre River, or simply the Poudre, flows from Colorado's Rocky Mountain National Park into towns and cities along Colorado's Front Range. Boaters find the gamut of whitewater options here. Class V headwaters transition to class IV drops with class III fun in between. Sections below the designated reach and closer to town offer gentler floats for beginner paddlers or lazy Sunday afternoons.

Colorado's only Wild and Scenic river, the Poudre has 38 miles of *Recreational* classified river miles and over 9 miles of *Wild*. The South Fork Poudre has even more designated miles, protecting a greater portion of the watershed. However, eight upstream reservoirs and eight diversions from other watersheds supplement the natural flow in the Poudre River's Wild and Scenic sections. The 1986 designation was aimed at striking a balance between conservation and future water development on other reaches.

Fishermen love the Poudre as much as boaters. The river supports healthy rainbow, brown, and brook trout populations, much of which have been introduced. The newcomer trout species nearly pushed out the native greenback cutthroat trout populations entirely. Now on the threatened species list, they have been reintroduced in streams in the Poudre watershed where migration barriers prevent nonnative species from taking over the neighborhood.

PADDLER'S NOTES

The Narrows section of the Poudre is a classic class V reach of whitewater for the expert kayaker. The Upper Narrows was first run in the early 1980s in an oar frame raft. Today, paddlers place this section in the class V–V+ category. Kayakers generally prefer to paddle this reach when the Pineview foot gauge reads between 1.5 and 4 feet. The Middle Narrows is also popular to lap up to and above 3.5–4 feet. Many kayakers will continue to paddle this advanced reach when flows drop even lower, and venture into the maelstrom at higher water too.

While the Narrows only stretches a little under 3 miles, kayakers often pick and choose the section they'll attempt. The road alongside makes for easy scouting on the way to the put-in. The upper stretch has three big class IV–V rapids at most flows: Super Collider, Cabbage Shredder, and Whiteline. These three rapids require precise boofing over ledges and tight maneuvers around pin rocks. Cliff walls rise steeply, and the echoes of whitewater increase the intimidation factor.

Below Whiteline the Middle Narrows mellows into class IV. The lower Narrows is known for the class V action under the CO 14 bridge. The thrashing spectacle of thunderous flow in the upper reaches of the Poudre deserves a view, even if you plan to stand comfortably on hard ground to take it in.

From Stevens Gulch downstream to Pineview Falls, the difficulty eases slightly to class III, with several spicy class IV spots. Split Rock, or 3 Rocks, rapid kicks off the show, followed by Tunnel and Mishawaka rapids, all fitting into the class III+/IV range at most flow levels but becoming continuous IV+ at high water. Some boaters take out before the Mishawaka Inn on CO 14, or put in here, to pick the run apart into upper and lower sections. Generally, class III can be found below Hewlett Gorge trailhead to Poudre Park.

Cardiac Corner rapid will kick up the difficulty before boaters descend into Pineview Falls, a stacked class IV rapid that can be punishing if you are not on your game. Try boofing or splatting the massive rock on river left near the bottom of the rapid. Bridges Takeout (BTO) is around 3 miles downstream. A wave here attracts local park-and-play kayakers.

Susan blasts through another wave train on the only Wild and Scenic river in Colorado.
ADAM ELLIOTT

DIRECTIONS TO TAKEOUT

Head northwest out of Fort Collins to get on US 287 northbound. Soon after you see the river on your left, turn left onto CO 14 westbound. You'll reach the BTO above Pineview Falls in a little over 9 miles. Takeout for the Narrows reach is easiest at the Stevens Gulch river access point.

DIRECTIONS TO PUT-IN

Stevens Gulch access is 8 miles up the canyon on CO 14 from BTO. For the Narrows, drive another 2.7 miles and look for the pullout on the left before Narrows Campground.

NEARBY ATTRACTIONS

Spend a few days in this canyon. Between the plentiful campgrounds, trails, and river sections, you won't get bored. Fort Collins certainly has a great assortment of fun activities, such as hanging out on the lawn with a cold beverage after a New Belgium Brewery tour.

33

SNAKE RIVER

Section name	Grand Teton National Park; Alpine Canyon
Distance	In Grand Teton National Park: 20 miles; Alpine Canyon: 8 miles
Flow range	300–10,000 cfs; 1,800–20,000 cfs
Season and source of water	Spring and summer; snowmelt and Jackson Dam releases
Gauge location	Near Alpine, USGS #13022500
Time required	1 day
Classification	*Scenic* and *Recreational*
Difficulty	Grand Teton National Park: I–II; Alpine Canyon: III–IV
Managing agency	Grand Teton National Park; Bridger–Teton National Forest
Permit required?	Yes; a permit is required Pacific Creek to Moose Landing, and an Aquatic Invasive Species (AIS) permit is required for both sections.
Shuttle type	Vehicle
Outstandingly Remarkable Values	Within the national park: culture, fisheries, geology, recreation, scenery, wildlife, ecology; within Alpine Canyon: recreation, scenery, wildlife.
Why paddle this section?	A floating view of the Grand Teton range; fantastic big wave and big canyon whitewater trip

A canoe trip on the Snake River in Grand Teton National Park may be the best way to view sunset over the Grand Tetons. WILL TAGGART

RIVER DESCRIPTION

The Wild and Scenic Snake River's main stem can be either a tranquil float through one of America's most stunning mountain valleys or a wild ride down one of the most popular whitewater day trips in the country. These two sections embody the high caliber of protected rivers in the system. Between them, nearly every Outstandingly Remarkable Value has been found, and the two distinct experiences provide for a well-rounded paddling adventure. From gazing up at the peaks of the Teton range while gently floating the meanders within the national park to charging into the surging Lunch Counter surf wave, you won't be disappointed with any day on the Snake River.

The Snake River Headwaters designation includes both of these reaches, as well as twelve more tributaries. This watershed-style designation makes a whole lot of ecological sense. "The main stem is only as good as its tributaries," notes Aaron Pruzan,

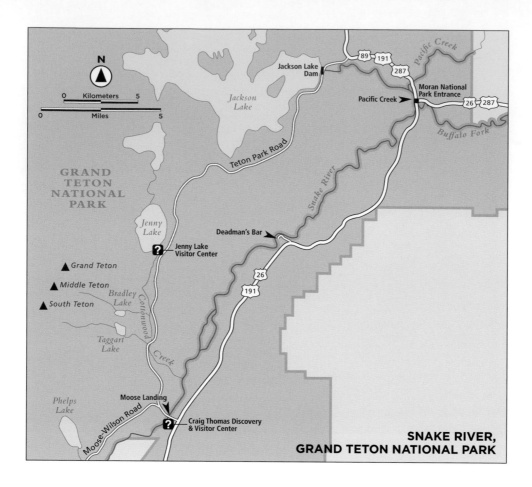

Map labels:
N
Kilometers 0 — 5
Miles 0 — 5
Jackson Lake
Jackson Lake Dam
89 191
287
Pacific Creek
Moran National Park Entrance
26 287
Buffalo Fork
GRAND TETON NATIONAL PARK
Teton Park Road
Snake River
Jenny Lake
Jenny Lake Visitor Center
Deadman's Bar
Grand Teton
Middle Teton
South Teton
Bradley Lake
Taggart Lake
Cottonwood Creek
26
191
Phelps Lake
Moose Landing
Moose-Wilson Road
Craig Thomas Discovery & Visitor Center
SNAKE RIVER, GRAND TETON NATIONAL PARK

a local paddle sports shop owner and one of the core proponents for protecting the Snake River Headwaters. If upstream tributaries remain vulnerable to development or pollution, the main stem river will feel the negative impacts even if it is protected. Along with taking the time to slowly educate and build support for protecting these rivers and streams as Wild and Scenic, Pruzan attributes the watershed protection concept to taking this designation across the finish line.

While paddlers enjoy floating on the Snake River through Grand Teton National Park, other rivers within the park are not open to boaters. In Yellowstone National Park just north of here, all rivers are off-limits to paddlers, even those with a Wild and Scenic designation and a recreational Outstandingly Remarkable Value. While backpackers can explore the backcountry, paddlers are denied this experience. Yellowstone is the only national park to explicitly ban paddling on all waterways.

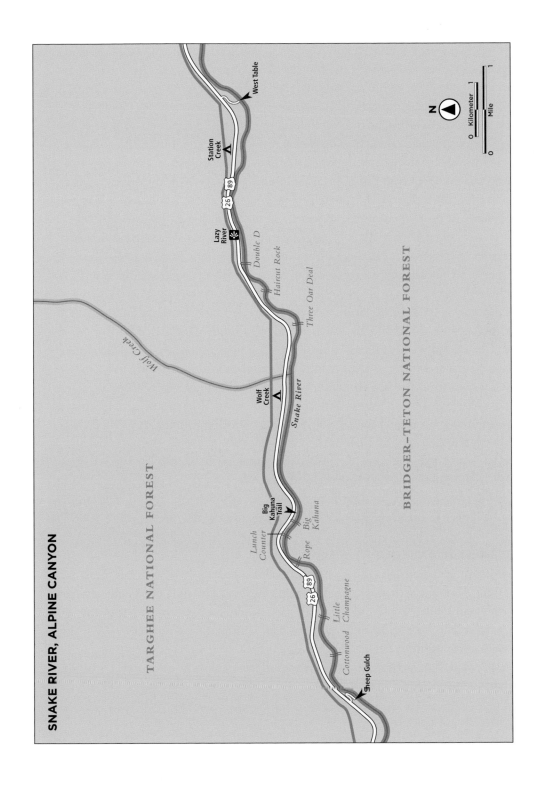

SNAKE RIVER, ALPINE CANYON

TARGHEE NATIONAL FOREST

BRIDGER–TETON NATIONAL FOREST

West Table

Station Creek

Lazy River

Double D

Haircut Rock

Three Oar Deal

Wolf Creek

Wolf Creek

Snake River

Big Kahuna Trail

Lunch Counter

Big Kahuna

Rope

Little Champagne

Cottonwood

Sheep Gulch

N

0 Kilometer 1

0 Mile 1

PADDLER'S NOTES

The gauge listed here is best for the Alpine Canyon section. The Snake River gauge near the Moran entrance station, within the national park, is closer to the upstream section. Boatable flows within the national park begin as low as 300 cubic feet per second (cfs), and with class I–II rapids, it is possible that flows upwards of 10,000 cfs may still be appropriate for beginners. You'll need to purchase your permit to float at one of the park's visitor centers. To boat anywhere in Wyoming, you must also purchase an Aquatic Invasive Species permit, typically sold at the same location as any river permit.

While this stretch of river can be great for beginners, it has a very dynamic character. Logjams can shift, and braided channels can complicate navigation. Start with a good map, follow the deepest channel, and watch out for these changing features.

The views along the Snake River through Grand Teton National Park are unmatched. The Tetons themselves feel as though they rise from the right bank. Be sure to scout your takeout when setting shuttle so you don't miss it while you are gawking at these incredible views.

For Alpine Canyon, prime flows for surfing can be found between 6,000–12,000 cfs. Flows as high as 40,000 cfs can be paddled, although normal surf spots wash out and new high-water features emerge. At these high flows, beware of dangerous hydraulics such as Three Oar Deal, which become class V.

You'll encounter a few class III rapids in the first few miles of Alpine Canyon, along with lots of big, swirly eddy lines and smaller surf waves. The two most well-known rapids occur about 5 miles into the run. First, you'll hit Big Kahuna wave—a favorite one for raft guides to drench their guests and potentially get some swimmers.

The popular Lunch Counter wave is just downstream. Expect to see spectators on the river-right rocks, as well as kayakers and surfers lapping the wave. A great parking area makes park-and-play possible here. A few more rapids fill the next 2 miles to the takeout at Sheep Gulch.

DIRECTIONS TO TAKEOUT

Moose Landing is about 12 miles north of Jackson on US 191/26 north. Turn left onto Teton Park Road to reach the Landing, on river right near the Craig Thomas Discovery and Visitor Center, where you'll want to purchase your float permit. If you want to take out (or put-in) at Deadman's Bar, continue north on US 191/26 for another 9 miles and turn left on Deadman's Bar Road to reach the access point at the end of the road. For Alpine Canyon, drive south from Hoback Junction for 12 miles on US 89/26 to reach West Table access.

Rafters and kayakers enjoy Snake River's Alpine Canyon all summer long. WILL TAGGART

DIRECTIONS TO PUT-IN

Continue driving north on US 191/26 from Deadman's Bar Road. In 9 miles enter the national park through Moran entrance. Pacific Creek launch area is located on the left just after the entrance. For Alpine Canyon, continue on US 89/26 for 7.4 miles to reach Sheep Gulch access.

NEARBY ATTRACTIONS

Your float permit for paddling the Snake River within the national park is also good for most of the lakes. Add an evening float on Jackson or Jenny Lakes while you are in the area. Don't forget paddling opportunities on the tributaries of the Snake as well, such as Granite Creek and Hoback River.

34

GRANITE CREEK

Section name	Above Hoback River confluence
Distance	2–8 miles
Flow range	Estimated 200–1,000 + cfs
Season and source of water	Spring and summer; snowmelt
Gauge location	None
Time required	1 day
Classification	*Wild* and *Scenic*
Difficulty	II–III
Managing agency	Bridger–Teton National Forest
Permit required?	No
Shuttle type	Vehicle
Outstandingly Remarkable Values	Geology, recreation, scenery, ecology, wildlife, culture, fisheries
Why paddle this section?	Access to Greater Yellowstone area without the crowds; clear stream with continuous but moderate whitewater; great link with Hoback and Snake Rivers downstream

RIVER DESCRIPTION

Beginning in the alpine majesty of Wyoming's Bridger–Teton National Forest, the glacial blue water of Granite Creek flows direct from its snowy source. The small but navigable creek tumbles over sagebrush grasslands covered in colorful wildflowers for much of the earlier paddling season. The southern end of the Gros Ventre mountain

The road to Granite Creek can be helpful when scouting the lower class III rapids.
ADAM ELLIOTT

range towers in the background. Snow fills valleys on north faces even into July each year. You'll find yourself floating backward to take in this breathtaking backdrop.

Protection for this gem waterway came as part of the Snake River Headwaters watershed designation in 2009. While only listed as one designation, thirteen distinct rivers and creeks throughout the Greater Yellowstone Ecosystem were included. As of 2018, Yellowstone and Grand Teton National Parks consider paddling an illegal form of human-powered recreation, except for the Snake River below Jackson Dam. Thus, many of these designated reaches are off-limits to boaters. Groups like American Whitewater have been working with other national parks, such as Yosemite, to demonstrate that a river serves much like a trail for backcountry explorers, and paddlers often leave less impact than footprints. Perhaps someday the rest of the Snake River Headwaters designations will be open to paddling as a result of this work.

The upper section of Granite, above the hot springs, carries a *Wild* designation. Flows likely wouldn't support paddling during most years here but may provide adequate

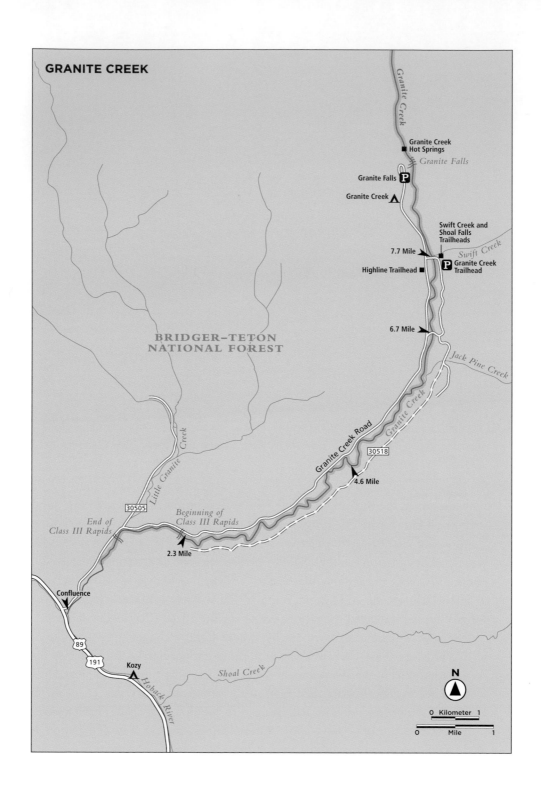

GRANITE CREEK

Granite Creek

Granite Creek
Hot Springs

Granite Falls

Granite Falls **P**

Granite Creek ▲

Swift Creek and
Shoal Falls
Trailheads

7.7 Mile ▸ ■ *Swift Creek*

Highline Trailhead ■ **P** Granite Creek
Trailhead

6.7 Mile ▸

Jack Pine Creek

**BRIDGER–TETON
NATIONAL FOREST**

Granite Creek Road *Granite Creek*

30518

4.6 Mile ▸

Little Granite Creek

30505

*End of
Class III Rapids*

*Beginning of
Class III Rapids*

2.3 Mile ▸

Confluence ▾

89

191

Kozy ▲

Hoback River

Shoal Creek

N ▲

0 Kilometer 1

0 Mile 1

flows for exploratory missions at peak snowmelt runoff. Lower downstream, the designation changes to *Scenic* as the road meanders closer to the river in some locations. The last mile before the Hoback River confluence was left out of the designation.

The scenery Outstandingly Remarkable Value couldn't be more obvious. The landscape ranges from occasional meandering wetlands to steep talus slopes, rich conifer forests, and ample wildflower fields. The diversity of the recreation value comes in multiple forms, from the hot springs upstream, to horse packing and hiking, to winter backcountry snowmobile tours. The cultural value comes from Granite Hot Springs's concrete pool and log bathhouse, built in the 1930s by the Civilian Conservation Corps. These facilities created recreation opportunities within the forest that increased in popularity after World War II. Finally, the mixture of ecological zones, varying geologic strata, and extensive intact wilderness surrounding the river provide a base for the geologic, ecological, fisheries, and wildlife values for this river.

PADDLER'S NOTES

The upper stretches of Granite Creek bend and meander through wildflower fields at a steady class II pace. Generally, the creek can be run mid-May through early July, depending on the snowpack for that year. Make up your mind by looking at the creek as it flows into the Hoback River. If it looks decently floatable here, you will likely have enough water upstream for a great day.

The final 3 miles before the confluence with the Hoback increase in difficulty to include continuous class III rapids. While the technical maneuvers may not be too tricky, they come quick and don't let up for at least a mile. A swim here would at least result in some serious bruising and likely lost equipment. Luckily, this lower section is easily scouted from the road on the way up, and can be portaged on the right. On your drive to the put-in, pull over about 1 mile from the confluence and take a look at the rapids for at least a mile upstream from there. Always keep an eye out for wood while floating.

For a grand Wild and Scenic experience, and a bigger day of paddling, float a lower stretch of Granite Creek and continue into the designated Hoback River. After 13 miles on the Hoback, you'll reach your third designated river for the day, the great Snake River. Granite Creek may only flow at a few hundred cubic feet per second, but you'll be on thousands by the time you hit the Snake. This may be one of the few locations in the country where it is possible to paddle three distinct Wild and Scenic rivers in one day.

DIRECTIONS TO TAKEOUT

From the roundabout in Hoback Junction, take the second ramp onto US 189/191 eastbound to follow the Hoback River upstream. After 11 miles, turn left on Granite Creek Road (FR 30500). The first takeout option is the confluence parking area to the

Near the confluence with the Hoback River, Granite Creek has wide open skies and a meandering yet swift flow. ADAM ELLIOTT

right. The creek remains accessible by road in multiple locations, allowing for different takeouts depending on your goals.

DIRECTIONS TO PUT-IN

Continue driving up Granite Creek on FR 30500 until you find a desirable spot to start your day. The run can be started as high as Granite Falls parking lot, just at the base of the falls.

NEARBY ATTRACTIONS

We left this valley ashamed that we had only planned a day trip. Between Granite Creek Campground and the many riverside dispersed camping options, the opportunities to settle into the incredible landscape were everywhere. A view of Granite Falls at the top of the road complements a soak in the developed hot springs, especially after a day hiking from the Granite Creek Trailhead. If your sights are even grander, don't forget the town of Jackson to the northwest, and both Grand Teton National Park and Yellowstone National Park farther north.

HOBACK RIVER

Section name	Granite Creek Confluence to Snake River
Distance	13.5 miles
Flow range	1,000–5,000+ cfs
Season and source of water	Spring and summer; snowmelt
Gauge location	None
Time required	1 day
Classification	*Recreational*
Difficulty	III
Managing agency	Bridger–Teton National Forest
Permit required?	No
Shuttle type	Vehicle
Outstandingly Remarkable Values	Scenery, recreation, culture, ecology, wildlife
Why paddle this section?	Reliable flows into summer; easy access with classic Wyoming scenery; multiple sections possible

RIVER DESCRIPTION

The Hoback River in the Greater Yellowstone area offers a range of whitewater in its 10-mile designated Wild and Scenic reach, with more great river upstream. The river originates in the Wyoming Range and eventually turns west before emptying into the great Snake River. A staple for local paddlers, this run flows until late summer most

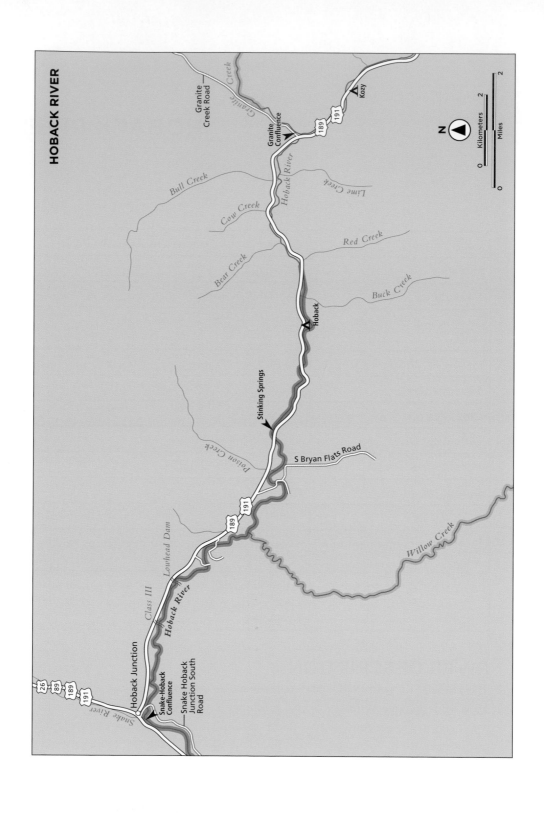

Geologic features on river right along the Hoback River display incredible hues of orange, red, and yellow. Adam Elliott

years, and even into early autumn when a particularly heavy snowfall has blessed the mountain headwaters.

The Hoback is one of thirteen stretches of river included in the single Snake River Headwaters Wild and Scenic designation; flip to the description for nearby Granite Creek on page 196 for more background info.

The geologic features through Hoback Canyon tower along the riverside in spectacular orange, yellow, and red hues. After Granite Creek empties into the Hoback, the river flows through the canyon, slicing through the Wyoming Thrust Belt geologic formation. The belt formed more than sixty-five million years ago due to compressional forces, and spans from the Arctic to Mexico. The best cross-sectional example of this feature, however, can be seen from the seat of your boat along the Hoback River. Other conglomerate and dolomite cliffs, flatiron peaks, and even a stinking

THE SCIENCE OF FREE-FLOWING RIVERS

Free-flowing rivers are the circulatory system of our landscapes. River systems deliver water, sediment, wood, and nutrients from the upper to the lower watershed, and biota from the oceans back up into the watershed. Fragmentation of a watershed, such as with the construction of a dam, levee, weir, embankment, and so on, curtails vital processes, similar to causing a stroke within the human circulatory system. Create enough blockages or strokes within the human brain, and eventually a person will not survive. Same goes for rivers.

Our free-flowing rivers do a lot of work for us and for the broader landscape. Leif Embertson of Natural Systems Design, an environmental science and engineering firm focused on river restoration, describes four river processes essential to healthy ecosystems and communities:

1. **Movement and purification of water.** The amount and timing of a river's flow drives landscape formation, provides aquatic and riparian habitats, and increases our resilience to climate change. For example, water from a free-flowing river spills into floodplains to create rich wetland habitat, which reduces downstream flooding risks and risks from extreme droughts. By altering the timing and amount of water through either flood storage dams or water withdrawals, a river likely won't reach the floodplain. This can then reduce groundwater recharge, resulting in higher stream temperatures, lower summertime stream flow, and an increase in downstream vulnerability to drought.

2. **Sediment transport.** Landscape erosion from steep tributaries in the upper watershed releases sediment into the river. That sediment moves downstream to create floodplains and coastal estuaries. Downstream river deltas and coastal estuaries also work to protect cities and inland areas from flooding during severe storms. Fragmentations disrupt the flow of sediment, which can cause channels to deepen and disconnect from floodplains. Finer sediment, like sand, never reaches the ocean. Estuaries begin to shrink, and critical habitats for invertebrate and fish populations disappear.

3. **Transport of wood.** Trees eroded from the upper watershed are transported to the middle and lower watershed, creating stable logjams. While they are a hazard to paddlers, these logjams help create the complex mosaic of side channel and floodplain habitats that lead to a more diverse ecosystem. Just as with sediment, dams and reservoirs keep wood from moving downstream. Without wood, these complex habitats cannot form.

4. **Transport of nutrients.** In a free-flowing river, nutrients like iron, nitrogen, phosphorus, and so on, float downstream to enrich riparian and floodplain habitats. In some regions, like the Pacific Northwest, marine-derived nutrients even travel upstream, with spawning salmon, from the ocean to the upper watershed. Fragmentation that blocks fish migration can dramatically reduce the availability of nutrients needed to support healthy riparian forests and food sources for invertebrates, insects, fish, and wildlife.

The interaction of these processes created every river on the planet. The unique geology, flow regime, climate, and vegetation communities in each watershed create a diverse variety of river structure and interconnected habitats. If we fragment every river, we could disrupt all these natural processes and ultimately create simplified environments with less biodiversity and decreased resilience to climatic and human impacts.

Looking down into the newly freed White Salmon River canyon and Condit Dam after a hole was blown in the base of the dam to drain the reservoir in preparation for a full dam removal. ADAM ELLIOTT

Susan launches her packraft over one of the many waves on the Hoback River. ADAM ELLIOTT

hot springs seep (you'll smell it before you see it as you float) provide great geologic diversity that add to the geologic Outstandingly Remarkable Value.

The designation notes the value of fisheries to the Hoback system due to the presence of cutthroat trout and at least ten native species that were historically present in the Greater Yellowstone ecosystem. Diverse habitat and connectivity to the Snake River ecosystem provide ample opportunity for countless other species to flourish as well.

PADDLER'S NOTES

Steady class I–II water characterize most of the Wild and Scenic Hoback River, with some class III feel in bigger waves and eddy lines at higher water. The wide channel allows for easy maneuvering around waves and rocks at most flows. Higher water makes even the mellower stretches feel pushy, however.

A total of nine bridges span the wide Hoback River through this reach. Abutments catch large wood and other debris floating downstream, creating potential hazards for paddlers. Choose a route wisely at these locations. The landscape continues to produce slides and avalanches that can also change the character of the river each year.

> "ANY RIVER IS REALLY THE SUMMATION OF THE WHOLE VALLEY. TO THINK OF IT AS NOTHING BUT WATER IS TO IGNORE THE GREATER PART."
> —*Hal Borland,* This Hill, This Valley

DIRECTIONS TO TAKEOUT

The lowest takeout on the Hoback is at the confluence with the Snake in Hoback Junction. You will want to park somewhere near the roundabout. When you get off the river, on the right just before floating into the Snake, carry boats up to the road and send the driver to fetch the car. No public parking currently exists right at the river, but the walk isn't bad.

DIRECTIONS TO PUT-IN

From Hoback Junction, drive 11 miles up US 189/191 eastbound to reach Granite Creek flowing in on the left. Turn up Granite Creek Road to park at the confluence. Other access locations along the Hoback can be used to shorten your paddle as well.

NEARBY ATTRACTIONS

Read through the description of Granite Creek on page 196, and add that onto your paddle if there is enough water. Or just drive up Granite Creek Road for great camping and hot springs at the base of the Gros Ventre Range. The Snake River downstream of the Hoback confluence offers a great mellow float trip, followed by one of the classic whitewater stretches through Alpine Canyon.

Midwest

36

ELEVEN POINT RIVER

Section name	Greer Crossing to Riverton
Distance	19 miles
Flow range	400–4,000 cfs
Season and source of water	Year-round; spring-fed
Gauge location	Bradley, USGS #07071500
Time required	1–3 days
Classification	*Scenic*
Difficulty	I–II
Managing agency	Mark Twain National Forest
Permit required?	No
Shuttle type	Vehicle
Outstandingly Remarkable Values	Fisheries, geology, history, recreation, scenery, wildlife
Why paddle this section?	Gentle multiday beginner paddling; lots of exploration potential up tributaries and springs; a rich Ozark landscape journey

Opposite: Smith Falls is the tallest and most magnificent of the travertine falls along the Niobrara, and is just a short walk from the river. ADAM ELLIOTT

"THERE'S NOTHING...ABSOLUTELY NOTHING...HALF SO MUCH WORTH DOING AS SIMPLY MESSING AROUND IN BOATS."

—Kenneth Grahame, The Wind in the Willows

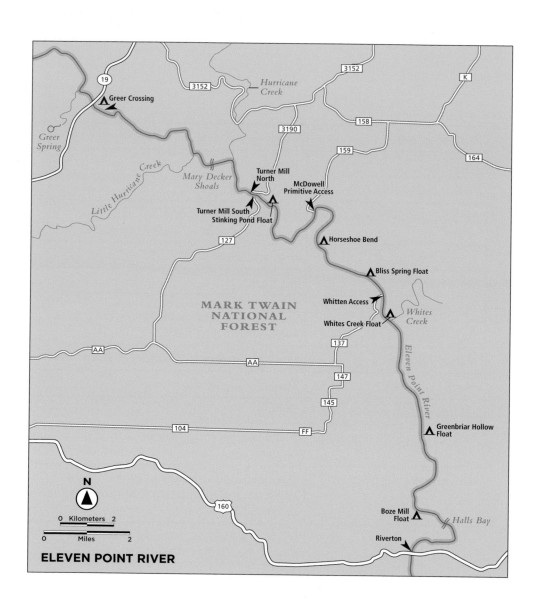

ELEVEN POINT RIVER

Canoes were made for the Eleven Point. KYLEE ALLEN

RIVER DESCRIPTION

A classic Midwest canoe journey and a favorite in the region, the Eleven Point River beckons paddlers to spend several days, swim in clear pools up spring-fed tributaries, or rest in shady alcoves under dipping branches. Sometimes, the thick and green canopy seems to connect overhead, creating a forest tunnel. The Eleven Point River epitomizes the Ozark landscape, with too many plant and animal species to list, fascinating geologic formations such as caves, bluffs, and springs, and a history of deserted boomtowns.

Clearly, the river deserves protection. It was identified and chosen as one of the eight original Wild and Scenic rivers in 1968. Forty-four miles were classified as *Scenic* that year. While access locations make a day trip possible, seven riverside float-in camps and dispersed camping along cobble bars allow paddlers to sink into the river's rhythm for several days.

The river's water originates primarily from springs that seep from dolomite bluffs or rise from underground aquifers. The clear water stays cool throughout the year and

The Eleven Point River holds many treasures just around the corner, or just under the surface. Bring a rod and bring a Civil War history book. KYLEE ALLEN

rarely drops to a level too low to float. Greer Spring ranks as the world's tenth largest spring, and contributes half of the river's flow for downstream reaches. The colder temperature alters fish habitat downstream, and provides 6 miles of blue-ribbon trout corridor. Special fishing regulations apply here.

Evidence and stories of early mills, many constructed prior to the American Civil War, create a foggy historic account of early Eleven Point River usage. Exploring up the side tributaries to their spring sources often reveals physical evidence, such as left-over turbines, waterwheels, or foundations. The Confederate army used many of these mill sites as recruiting locations and staging areas during the war.

PADDLER'S NOTES

Boat rentals and shuttles can be found in both Alton and Riverton. Lands surrounding the river are about half public and half private, which means you'll want to know before you go exploring. Eleven access points reach the river throughout the entire designated reach, many with boat ramps and vault toilets. While you won't find rapids above a class II difficulty, boaters should always be on the lookout for root wads and other snags, which can easily tip a canoe.

This trip along the Eleven Point River begins just downstream of Greer Spring. The springwater enters on river right, and begins to emerge from the ground just a mile up from the confluence. Take a walk to this source on your way to the put-in. The trailhead can be found along MO 19 to the west, before you reach the river from Alton. Resist the urge to swim or wade in the spring; it is prohibited.

In nearly 3 miles, Little Hurricane Creek enters on the right. This signals that you'll reach Mary Decker Shoals, a class II riffle, in the next mile. Loggers manipulated the boulders in the riverbed to facilitate transport of timber downstream. Today, those boulders form chutes to spice up your paddle.

Five miles in, you'll pass Turner Mill river access site on both sides of the river (north and south). Turner Mill Springs flows into the Eleven Point on the left. Paddle up a ways and continue on foot to explore this miniature riparian forest. Less than a mile downstream from these access points is the first float camp, Stinking Pond. Look for the 20-foot bluff on the left and you'll find the spot.

More float-in camps can be found every few miles beyond Turner Mill Springs. Be sure to check out the karst rock formations up Whites Creek whether you stay at that camp or not. At Boze Mill camp (one of the most popular), you'll find more remnants of early mill days. A deep swimming hole will be your reward for taking the detour up the creek. You'll navigate a final riffle, the Halls Bay rapids, before reaching your takeout in Riverton.

Download the US Forest Service's *Eleven Point Scenic River Travel Guide* for river mileage and site descriptions for a more in-depth float guide.

DIRECTIONS TO TAKEOUT
From Alton, take US 160 east for 13 miles out of town. After crossing the river, turn left to head toward the boat ramp at Riverton, located on river left upstream of the bridge.

DIRECTIONS TO PUT-IN
Head back to Alton and turn right on MO 19 northbound. In 9.3 miles you'll cross the river using Greer Bridge (backtrack slightly to find the trail to Greer Spring). You can access the river from Greer Crossing Recreation Area, on the right just beyond the bridge.

NEARBY ATTRACTIONS
The Mark Twain National Forest, Missouri's first national forest, offers more trails, lakes, and campgrounds to continue your Ozark adventure. If you are keen to see more of the wildlands, caves, springs, hollows, waterfalls, and more, plan a long hike on a section of the Ozark Trail—or traverse the entire 140 miles of the trail.

37

NIOBRARA RIVER

Section name	Cornell Bridge to Rocky Ford
Distance	22 miles
Flow range	450–1,200 cfs
Season and source of water	Spring, summer, early autumn; groundwater flow and rainfall
Gauge location	Sparks, USGS #06461500
Time required	1–3 days
Classification	*Scenic*
Difficulty	I–II
Managing agency	National Park Service, Niobrara National Scenic River
Permit required?	No
Shuttle type	Vehicle
Outstandingly Remarkable Values	Fisheries, geology, recreation, paleontology, scenery, wildlife
Why paddle this section?	An unexpected tropical Eden environment; tributary waterfalls galore; gentle beginner paddling

The sandy cliffs along the Niobrara are bursting with springs. Everywhere you look there is another trickle or full waterfall. ADAM ELLIOTT

RIVER DESCRIPTION

Hidden in Nebraska's rolling prairie landscape, the Niobrara River boasts a jungle-like atmosphere with friendly, beginner paddling opportunities. While floating the Niobrara, a concert of birdcall and insect chirps fill every moment of the day and echo off tall sandy cliffs. The orchestra of wildlife lives among a diverse number of plant species that create a thick, lush canopy over side-stream waterfalls. With numerous private campgrounds, the Niobrara invites boaters to float multiple sections, and to pitch a tent along the way to fully immerse in the special character of this unique Midwestern river.

The *Scenic* designation begins at Borman Bridge, about 5 miles upstream of Cornell Bridge, and extends for 76 miles downstream. Most paddlers explore the first half or first third of this section, as the river becomes more braided downstream of Norden Bridge. This description details the 22 miles downstream of Cornell Bridge. However,

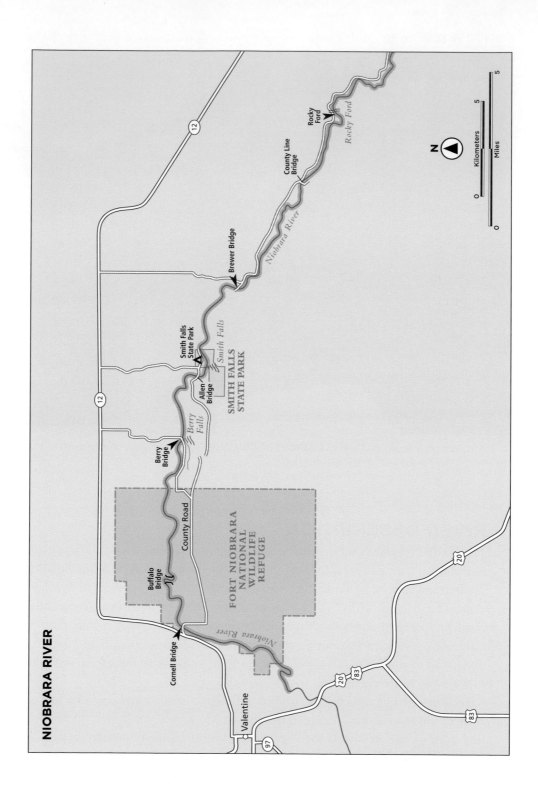

higher flows in the spring make the lower section manageable with very few other paddlers to share the waterway.

This Midwestern river supports an exceptional and surprising amount of biological diversity, lending to the wildlife Outstandingly Remarkable Value. Ecosystems from the north, south, east, and west converge along the Niobrara to support a multitude of plant and animal species not typically seen in the Midwest. Over millions of years, many species were captured in this pocket of temperate and moist climate as the surrounding land turned to grassland and prairie.

Besides an incredible array of plant life, you'll be amazed at the number of migratory birds using the verdant corridor for feeding and nesting. On our first day canoeing the Niobrara, we stopped paddling to watch the flight of a great blue heron. The bird swooped in slow motion close enough to our canoe that we could see the intricate coloring of the blue- and grey-tinted wings and white breast. The habitats along the river also support whooping cranes, eagles, peregrine falcons, and more. Paleontologists have discovered eighty new species of extinct animals in the rich fossil record of the Niobrara river corridor.

As if the biological diversity were not enough, the display of colorful bands in the eroded sediments along towering cliff walls provide dynamic scenic views throughout your float. Like beaches pasted to canyon walls, the sandy sediment deposited by marine seas, streams, wind, and volcanoes over the past ninety-eight million years has been eroded by millennia of forceful river currents. Each distinct layer provides specific fossil evidence and contributes differently to the perpetual spring flows and seeps into the river.

PADDLER'S NOTES

Groundwater releases water slowly to provide great flows that attract paddlers and tubers all summer long. Boaters looking for a longer and wilder experience should plan a trip all the way to Meadville Bridge in the spring. Equipment rentals and shuttles can be found everywhere in Valentine. Much of the riverside property is owned by private campgrounds, which offer these services in addition to overnight accommodations, such as tent camping or cabins. Many access sites are private, but if you hire a shuttle driver, you'll gain access to most of them.

Smith Falls State Park, 15 miles from Cornell Bridge, is the campground for paddlers, in our opinion. Nearly every river runner will stop here to take a stroll up to Nebraska's tallest waterfall, Smith Falls, at 63 feet. As crowds diminish in the evening and early morning, campers may enjoy the falls and additional hiking opportunities in a more intimate setting. Take the time to hike the nature trail downstream of the falls on river right. You'll gain some elevation and view the river corridor from the canopy

CANOE TRIPPING WITH DOGS

Wallace loves his life jacket. We snap that piece of floatation around his furry neck as his tail ferociously wags from side to side. Our five-year-old shepherd-mutt has learned to love river trips as much as we do, or at least we assume he does.

Of course, this didn't happen by luck. We learned a few lessons the hard way. We now know that he doesn't like *every* aspect of the canoe trip. And after several outings, we've learned how to help him get the most out of our days on the water while also behaving like the obedient best friend we know he can be.

We planned two multiday trips without Wallace ever having sniffed a canoe before. The moment we pushed off at Cornell Bridge onto the Niobrara with Wallace between us in the canoe, the boat began to rock. Wallace would look over the left gunwale, then the right, then back to the left. Each time he moved, the canoe tilted several inches. And he moved a lot. The primary stability was shot, and we had to quickly get comfortable trusting in the secondary stability. As we paddled near the riverbanks, Wallace would also begin to whine excitedly, likely with the thought of finding sticks and playing fetch. At first, it seemed annoying, but the river has a way of stripping away frustrations, and we soon grew to love his voice.

We found the more Wallace played at camp, the calmer he would be in the canoe. Thus, we chucked sticks all morning, and even brought one on board for a chew toy. After enough land-based play, Wallace would drift off to sleep on our sleeping pad in the bottom of the boat. We exchanged silent thumbs-up and took too many photos of our sleeping baby, like two weary but excited parents at naptime. Then a beaver tail would slap and the canoe would nearly capsize with the abrupt surge of an awakened dog.

On our final night canoeing the Saint Croix River, we spent the evening chopping and sautéing over our camp stove as Wallace disappeared into the woods to explore smells—and luckily not roll in them. Wallace returned ready to eat and promptly hit the sack after a full, exhausting day. While we maintained an astute vigilance on hikes for three-leaved, rash-inducing poison ivy plants, we became lax on our last night at camp. That night we all happily slipped our tired bodies into sleeping bags and smiled ourselves off to sleep. A few days later, Adam found strips of rash on his arms and torso in the exact locations you might expect after making contact while spooning your dog. Next time, bedtime baths may be in order.

Bringing Wallace on the river opens our eyes to simple pleasures and the bliss of the present moment. His company may require us to shift plans or carry extra equipment, but it is always worth it.

Susan attempts to keep Wallace between her feet to prevent him from rocking the canoe on the Niobrara River.
Adam Elliott

perspective. Regardless of where you choose to camp, call the campground offices to get information rather than relying on websites.

As you progress downstream, bridges make great markers for how far you've traveled. Within the first 10 miles, you'll float through the Fort Niobrara National Wildlife Refuge. Trails lead from the river up to the refuge's visitor center on river right. Beware of poison ivy anytime you step onto the shore. Keep your eyes peeled for the many waterfalls flowing into the Niobrara as you float. Some are hidden a short distance up side streams.

Be sure to take out above Rocky Ford rapid on river left. The class III rapid should not be attempted by beginning canoeists or tubers. Download the National Park Service's map for the Niobrara to see river mileage, locations of waterfalls, and more. Stop in the park service visitor center in Valentine for more information.

DIRECTIONS TO TAKEOUT

If you shuttle yourself, you can park at Rocky Ford Outfitters for a small fee. From Valentine, take NE 12 eastbound out of town. Stay on this road for 27.8 miles, keeping track of your mileage because your next right turn is not marked well or named. If you hit Norden, you've gone too far. Once you turn right off NE 12 toward Rocky Ford, travel 6 miles to where the road meets the river. Turn right to drive upstream for 1.5 miles to the takeout.

DIRECTIONS TO PUT-IN

From Rocky Ford, make your way back to NE 12 and head west, back toward Valentine. In about 24 miles turn left into the Cornell Bridge river access parking lot. This is a public access site, but there is a fee to launch on the river from here.

NEARBY ATTRACTIONS

Stop into the Niobrara National Scenic River Visitor Center in Valentine while you are in town. A short video and plenty of interpretation materials will make your paddle much richer. If you are keen to float another river while in the region, look into the designated reach of the Missouri River upstream of the Niobrara confluence.

SAINT CROIX RIVER

Section name	Thayer's Landing to Nevers Dam Landing
Distance	54.5 miles
Flow range	1,000–5,000 cfs
Season and source of water	Spring, summer, and autumn; rainfall
Gauge location	Danbury, USGS #05333500
Time required	1–6 days
Classification	*Scenic* and *Recreational*
Difficulty	I–II
Managing agency	National Park Service, Saint Croix National Scenic Riverway
Permit required?	No
Shuttle type	Vehicle
Outstandingly Remarkable Values	Culture, recreation, scenery, aquatic, riparian
Why paddle this section?	Large and scenic river with a wilderness feel; great campsites only accessible by paddling

RIVER DESCRIPTION

Wooded hillsides, thickly forested islands, and 60-foot sandstone bluffs along some sections inspire paddlers to sink into the Saint Croix River's free-flowing corridor.

Susan keeps a keen eye out for turtles along the banks of the Saint Croix. ADAM ELLIOTT

Your canoe will slice through the glassy water beneath towering hardwood and coniferous trees, and between large islands. Turtles slip into the water with a "plunk," and beavers slap their tails as you float nearby. Sunrise draws fog into the river valley for picturesque and tranquil views during your first paddle strokes each morning. With easy camping options, a variety of wildlife to view, and mellow currents, this river trip may be one of the best multiday canoe journeys in the country.

Wisconsin's Senator Gaylord Nelson can be credited with inserting the Saint Croix and its major tributary, the Namekagon River, into the original Wild & Scenic Rivers Act in 1968. Today, a total of 252 miles of the Saint Croix and Namekagon are included in the Wild and Scenic Rivers system as a mix of *Scenic* and *Recreational* river segments. Located near the twin cities of Minneapolis and St. Paul, the Saint Croix River serves as an indispensable resource for recreation. Yet, with so many miles to choose from, river users often see few others while paddling, especially on the upper reaches described here.

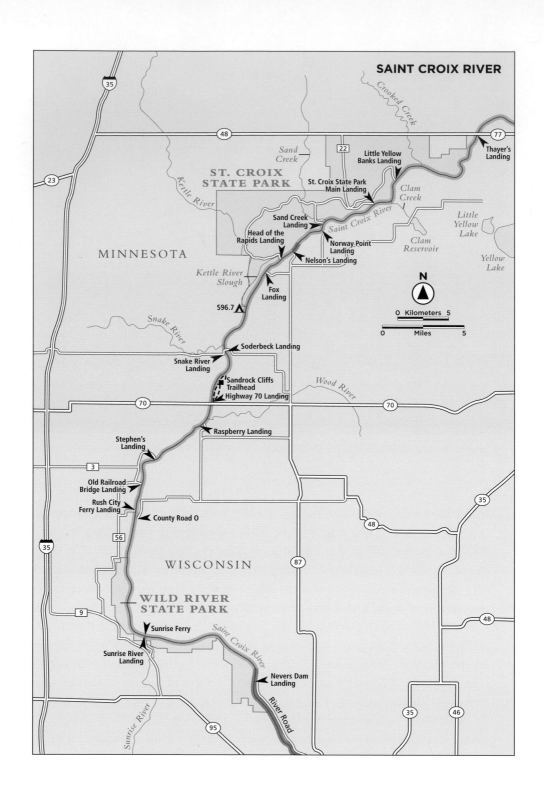

SAINT CROIX RIVER

Crooked Creek

35

48

23

Sand Creek

22

77

Thayer's Landing

Little Yellow Banks Landing

ST. CROIX STATE PARK

St. Croix State Park Main Landing

Kettle River

Clam Creek

Sand Creek Landing

Saint Croix River

MINNESOTA

Head of the Rapids Landing

Norway Point Landing

Little Yellow Lake

Nelson's Landing

Clam Reservoir

Yellow Lake

Kettle River Slough

Fox Landing

N

S96.7

Kilometers

Snake River

Miles

Soderbeck Landing

Snake River Landing

Sandrock Cliffs Trailhead

Wood River

Highway 70 Landing

70

70

Raspberry Landing

Stephen's Landing

3

Old Railroad Bridge Landing

35

Rush City Ferry Landing

County Road O

48

56

87

WISCONSIN

35

WILD RIVER STATE PARK

9

48

Sunrise Ferry

Saint Croix River

Sunrise River Landing

Nevers Dam Landing

35

46

Sunrise River

95

River Road

The Kettle River tumbles fast and turbulent into the calmer St. Croix river at St. Croix State Park. ADAM ELLIOTT

The river designation protects the water and a small slice of land on either side of the Saint Croix, but both Minnesota and Wisconsin have augmented this by placing large state parks and forests or protected wildlife areas along the corridor. This extension of wild public lands greatly enhances and strengthens the riparian ecosystem. For instance, Minnesota's St. Croix State Park, the largest in the state, extends along the river-right bank for the first 22 miles of your float downstream from Thayer's Landing. Hiking trails and historic buildings built by the Civilian Conservation Corps can be found within the park.

For thousands of years the river's steady power and gentle gradients made transportation and movement possible for Native peoples. By the early 1800s, the fur trade brought in European settlers who sought to trade with the Natives for beaver, prized for their luxurious pelts. Within several decades, hunting nearly depleted the beaver population for the demanding European markets. Settlers then began using the river's flow to transport vast numbers of logs to downstream mills. Men called "river pigs" would drive the logs downstream by hopping from log to log and shuffling them to prevent jams. Naturally, the job cost many men their lives. By the early 1900s, much of the valuable trees were gone and the logging industry began to decline.

Today, fishermen enjoy the river's populations of smallmouth bass, walleye, northern pike, large muskie, and sturgeon, while other wildlife enthusiasts find the diversity of bird species captivating. Ecological communities converge to attract more species, while the orientation of the river north to south invites migratory stopovers as birds travel this important flyway to southern climates for the winter or northern climates for the summer.

PADDLER'S NOTES

The Saint Croix can be broken into many different sections. We enjoyed this upper stretch as a wilder experience along the designated *Scenic* portion of the river. Downstream of Nevers Dam Landing, the river transitions to a *Recreational* river with more river users.

Whatever section you plan on paddling, take a few days to do it. Campsites along the river are some of the best-maintained river-accessed camps we've seen. Most include a picnic table, fire ring, pit toilet, and cleared area to pitch your tent with a great view of the river. Best of all, only paddlers can access these sites, adding to the wild feel of the river trip.

Between Nelson's Landing and S96.7 campsite, a slight increase in gradient produces more class II riffle potential. We enjoyed paddling on the right side of the large island, known as the Kettle River Slough. A trail leads up the Kettle River on river left for several miles (river right of the Saint Croix), with benches along the way to take in the view.

Downstream of the Kettle River, the Saint Croix widens significantly to feel like a new river. Islands continue to split the river corridor into narrow channels, enticing paddlers to explore. The still and glassy water on a clear day in this reach can turn each stroke into a meditative movement.

Our favorite riverside hiking option led us to the top of shaded sandstone cliffs along a smaller channel via the Sandrock Cliff trails. About 5 miles of trails provide a few different loop options. Then, we canoed downstream and took the smaller left channel to float past the base of these picturesque and crumbling cliff walls.

Finally, experienced paddlers and campers should consider planning a nighttime float on this river. As the sun sets, the river shines in new and brilliant colors. Your senses heighten as you begin to distinguish new sounds and the feeling of every stroke. Of course, be sure you have a planned campsite to land at and a powerful flashlight to find it.

An evening paddle on the first day of our float was one of the major highlights of this trip.
ADAM ELLIOTT

DIRECTIONS TO TAKEOUT
From Taylors Falls, cross to the Wisconsin side of the Saint Croix and turn left onto WI 87 north. In 2.9 miles turn left onto River Road. Nevers Dam Landing is on the left in 8 miles.

DIRECTIONS TO PUT-IN
Thayer's Landing is located just 3.6 miles west of Danbury, Wisconsin, on WI 77. This road is MN 48 if arriving from the Minnesota side.

NEARBY ATTRACTIONS
Stop into Minnesota's Interstate State Park, near Taylors Falls, to see the highest concentration of glacial potholes found in the world along the shores of the Saint Croix. These giant tunnels, caves, and abysses were formed by powerful river currents from the glacial Lake Duluth, which carved into the hard basalt cliffs. The section of cliffs along the river is equally spectacular.

WOLF RIVER

Section name	Section IV: Otter Slide to Big Smokey Falls
Distance	6 miles
Flow range	250–1,000 cfs
Season and source of water	Spring, summer, and fall; rainfall
Gauge location	Langlade, USGS #04074950
Time required	1 day
Classification	*Scenic*
Difficulty	III–IV
Managing agency	Menominee Indian Tribe, National Park Service
Permit required?	Yes
Shuttle type	Included in permit
Outstandingly Remarkable Values	None identified
Why paddle this section?	Remote; great variety of rapids mixed with calm pools; granite rock features and a tight bedrock gorge with lush riparian zones

RIVER DESCRIPTION

The Wolf River has served as a paddler's hub for generations of Midwestern boaters. At the top of the Wild and Scenic Section IV, the Wolf River bends away from the road to propel paddlers on a tour of a lush riparian corridor interspersed with several classic class III–IV rapids, surf waves, and drops. While the rapids and falls within the

Adam takes the conservative left line at Lower Delles rapid. Susan Elliott

designated reach provide enough reason to hop in a raft or kayak, the miles of easier whitewater and tranquil floating upstream turn this river valley into a perfect weekend destination rather than just a quick day trip.

The Wolf River's diverse scenery makes the shorter Section IV visually stimulating for the entire duration. Orange-tinted, clear water complements the green color palette of the rich forest ecosystem. Maple, basswood, beech, aspen, and birch mingle with conifers such as spruce, balsam fir, cedar, and pine. Calm pools between bedrock rapids increase aquatic diversity, as seen in the population of floating lotus flowers and reeds.

Back in 1968, President Lyndon Johnson signed 24 miles of the Wolf River into the Wild and Scenic River system, billing it as an "Eastern river" because it is technically located east of the Mississippi (by just a hair). While the National Park Service is listed as the federal agency with oversight over the river's Wild and Scenic status, the entire designated reach flows through Menominee Indian Reservation land. Therefore, the tribe manages the river and regulates all access to Section IV.

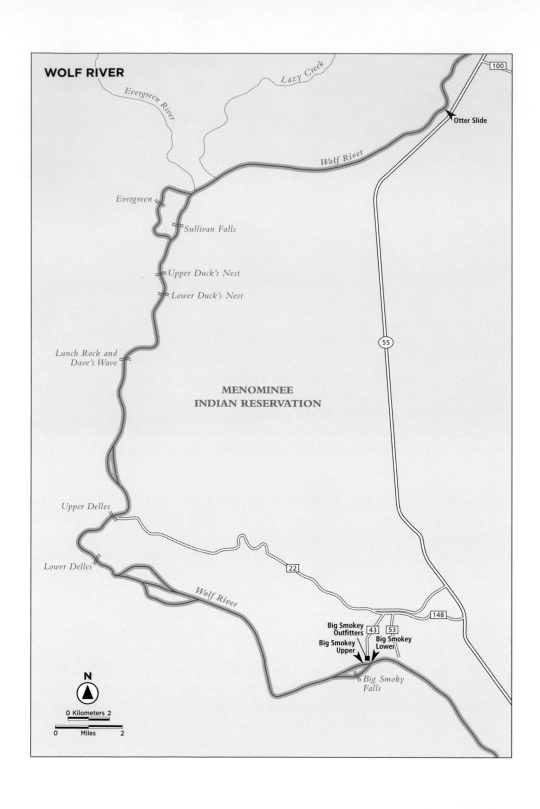

WOLF RIVER

Lazy Creek

Evergreen River

Wolf River

100

Otter Slide

Evergreen

Sullivan Falls

Upper Duck's Nest

Lower Duck's Nest

55

*Lunch Rock and
Dave's Wave*

**MENOMINEE
INDIAN RESERVATION**

Upper Delles

22

Lower Delles

Wolf River

148

Big Smokey
Outfitters

43   53

Big Smokey
Upper

Big Smokey
Lower

*Big Smoky
Falls*

N

0 Kilometers 2

0   Miles   2

Originally, the tribe did not allow the public to use this stretch of the river. This may have been due to turmoil in the 1960s, and having had their tribal status stripped in 1961. Although President Johnson signed the Wolf into protection, he denied the Menominees' appeal to reinstate tribal status. In 1973, President Richard Nixon provided the requested federal recognition of the reservation lands and the local economy began to improve. The tribe operates Big Smokey Outfitters located at the breathtaking Big Smokey Falls.

PADDLER'S NOTES

While 6 miles may seem short, don't skimp on time in this spectacular river corridor. If you can, carry that boat back up to run some of the rapids a few times. Sit on the warm bedrock shelves by the river and eat a sandwich. Surf those waves. You'll miss being so far away from the road once you return to your car. Purchase your float permit and shuttle at Big Smokey Outfitters or Shotgun Eddy's. Contact them via their Facebook pages to be sure they are open before you arrive.

A mile and a half from Otter Slide launch area, the river splits around an island. To the right, a bony class II rapid awaits, while river left drops over the class III, 6-foot Sullivan Falls. Boaters can scout, portage, or lap the falls from the trail on the left. If the concession stand is open here, consider buying something for good karma.

Next, a short stretch of moving water takes you into Upper and Lower Duck's Nest rapids, both class III with the option to eddy-out in between. In Lower Duck's Nest, the channel narrows into a fun wave train that ends with a surf spot called Dave's Wave. Stop for lunch and even a sunny nap on the large sloping slab of bedrock on river left about three-quarters of a mile downstream.

Enjoy the mile of flat water before the next set of rapids. The water lilies are particularly magnificent, and are rarely seen on whitewater rivers anywhere. Upper Delles rapid, a class III narrow wave train, can be recognized by the bedrock wall on the left that pinches the river. The river bends to the left over a short ledge and puts you at the top of Lower Delles rapid.

To reach the culminating rapid of the run, you'll first have to pay by paddling 2 miles of flat water. Big Smokey Falls, class III–IV, can be recognized by the sign for a footbridge to the left, and falls to the right. It is possible to take out on the left channel before the nasty (unrunnable) sieve on that side of the island. Most kayakers and rafters take the right channel to the falls and scout high from the right bank. Take out on the left at Big Smokey Falls Outfitters, in the pool below the falls.

It's important for all paddlers to remember that you are a guest on the reservation and maintaining goodwill is important. Be courteous to those renting rafts from the tribe and help out when you can. Remember that the majority of those renting rafts on this river are inexperienced and may not be boating in control—be prepared to help with a rescue. Past conflicts between rafters and kayakers have threatened access.

DIRECTIONS TO TAKEOUT

From the small town of Langlade, head south on WI 55. Drive 14.5 miles and turn right onto Dells Road toward Big Smokey Outfitters. In 0.4 mile, turn left onto Big Smokey Falls Road to reach the falls and outfitters' base. During busy weekends they will often designate a specific area for kayaker parking.

DIRECTIONS TO PUT-IN

The Otter Slide put-in is 2.8 miles north of Big Smokey Outfitters on WI 55. However, you won't need to drive your vehicle here because a shuttle is included with the mandatory permit you'll purchase from the outfitter.

NEARBY ATTRACTIONS

The Nicolet National Forests borders the Menominee reservation. Campgrounds, mountain biking, hiking trails, and more will extend your adventure. Of course, spend time on the upstream sections of the Wolf River as well. Shuttles can be hired at Bear Paw Outdoor Center, (715) 882-3502.

Bear Paw Outdoor Adventure Resort has a terrific tree and kayak sculpture, and excellent pizza and beer for apres paddle. Susan Elliott

Opposite: A group of paddlers enjoy a warm fall day on the Chattooga. Leland Davis

East

40

CHATTOOGA RIVER

Section name	Section IV
Distance	8 miles
Flow range	0.9–2.5 feet
Season and source of water	Year-round; rainfall and groundwater
Gauge location	Near Clayton, USGS #02177000
Time required	1 day
Classification	*Wild*
Difficulty	III–IV+
Managing agency	Francis Marion and Sumter National Forests
Permit required?	Yes, self-registered
Shuttle type	Vehicle
Outstandingly Remarkable Values	Geology, history, recreation, scenery
Why paddle this section?	Classic Appalachian whitewater steeped in legend and history; great boofs and rock slides throughout

RIVER DESCRIPTION

Legends float among the paddling community of the whitewater found on the Chattooga River's Section IV. The rapids here have furnished paddlers with campfire stories

Katie Abercrombie and Asia Greer slaying Jawbone Falls on the Chattooga.
JOHN ABERCROMBIE

for generations. Nonpaddling visitors multiplied in the early 1970s with the movie *Deliverance*, filmed on the rocky banks and tumultuous rapids of the Chattooga River. The whitewater and deep, rugged mountain landscape continues to attract adventurers today, leaving every one of them with a Chattooga River story to tell.

The climate in the region resembles that of the wet Pacific Northwest, with up to 80 inches of rain each year. The Gulf of Mexico's moisture-rich air creates extensively diverse habitats. Those habitats were threatened by early white settlers logging the land with particularly damaging methods for the environment. In the early twentieth century, the US Forest Service began purchasing these overcut private lands to control soil erosion, and established the now extensive national forest in the Chattooga watershed.

Designated in 1974, the Chattooga is the Southeast's longest free-flowing waterway. The river was studied to determine eligibility in 1963, over a decade prior to actual designation. While it did not make the first batch of Wild and Scenic rivers, it was the first river protected after 1968.

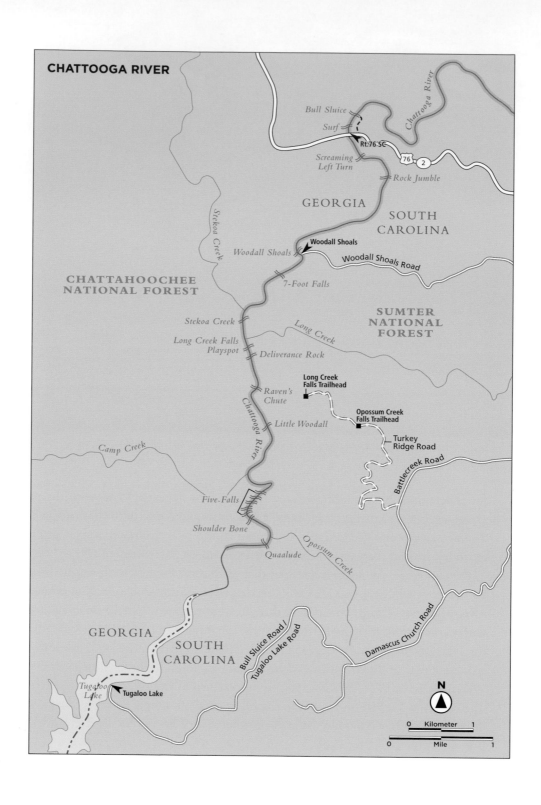

CHATTOOGA RIVER

Bull Sluice

Surf

Rt. 76 SC

76 2

Screaming
Left Turn

Rock Jumble

Chattooga River

GEORGIA

SOUTH
CAROLINA

Stekoa Creek

Woodall Shoals   Woodall Shoals

CHATTAHOOCHEE
NATIONAL FOREST

Woodall Shoals Road

7-Foot Falls

SUMTER
NATIONAL
FOREST

Stekoa Creek

Long Creek

Long Creek Falls
Playspot

Deliverance Rock

Long Creek
Falls Trailhead

Raven's
Chute

Opossum Creek
Falls Trailhead

Chattooga River

Little Woodall

Turkey
Ridge Road

Camp Creek

Battlecreek Road

Five-Falls

Shoulder Bone

Quaalude

Opossum Creek

GEORGIA

SOUTH
CAROLINA

Bull Sluice Road /
Tugaloo Lake Road

Damascus Church Road

Tugaloo
Lake   Tugaloo Lake

N

0   Kilometer   1

0   Mile   1

PADDLER'S NOTES

The US Geological Survey (USGS) gauge reads about 0.2 feet more than the bridge gauge, which local boaters use. Most paddlers enjoy Chattooga's Section IV if levels are between 1.2 and 2.0 feet on the Internet gauge. The river is run at flows over 2 feet, but the consequences increase, and rapids get close to class V. Enjoy the class III rapids full of slot moves, big slides, and ledge holes located in between the following class IV rapid descriptions.

Bull Sluice could be your first big rapid, but you can also put in just below the drop. The rapid's first successful tandem open canoe descent included the Georgia governor at the time, Jimmy Carter, and Claude Terry in 1974. Carter would go on to become President, but his actions as governor helped push the Chattooga into the Wild and Scenic system. In American River's short film *Wild President*, Carter speaks of the influence paddling had upon him. "It kind of opened my eyes to a relationship between a human being and a wild river that I had never contemplated before that."

After a few class III rapids, you'll reach Woodall Shoals. The slide on the far right here will help you avoid a very nasty hole in the center of the rapid. It is possible to take out or put in on river left here. Rapids below Woodall will increase in difficulty until you reach the pool above 7-Foot Falls. Boof to the right here to avoid the undercut on the left. After 3 miles of fun class III, you'll float around a left bend as Camp Creek flows in on the right. The whitewater party gets started just around the next right bend with the class IV Five Falls series.

Five Falls consists of five distinct drops: Entrance, Corkscrew, Crack-in-the-Rock, Jawbone, and Sock-em-Dog. The gradient increases to 100 feet per mile. These separate rapids start to merge at flows greater than 2 feet, decreasing any recovery time you had hoped to have. Know that undercut rocks (especially in Jawbone) and sieves (especially in Crack-in-the-Rock) are everywhere through Five Falls. Wood frequently clogs up Crack-in-the-Rock rapid. Scout your line or portage from either bank. A few smaller rapids lead you to the 2-mile lake paddle to reach your takeout.

"WILDERNESS IS NOT A LUXURY BUT A NECESSITY OF THE HUMAN SPIRIT, AND AS VITAL TO OUR LIVES AS WATER AND GOOD BREAD. A CIVILIZATION WHICH DESTROYS WHAT LITTLE REMAINS OF THE WILD, THE SPARE, THE ORIGINAL, IS CUTTING ITSELF OFF FROM ITS ORIGINS AND BETRAYING THE PRINCIPLE OF CIVILIZATION ITSELF."

—*Edward Abbey,* Desert Solitaire

John Abercrombie paddles Seven-Foot Falls on the Chattooga River. KATIE ABERCROMBIE

DIRECTIONS TO TAKEOUT
From Long Creek, South Carolina, take Demascus Church Road southwest off US 76 for 4 miles. Turn right onto Bull Sluice Road. This dirt road will take you to the Lake Tugaloo access in less than 4 miles.

DIRECTIONS TO PUT-IN
Drive on US 76 west from Long Creek, South Carolina, for 4.5 miles to reach the river access site, on the right before crossing the river.

NEARBY ATTRACTIONS
Spend more time paddling on the upstream sections of the Chattooga River. Sections I–III provide milder action for whitewater boaters, with class I–III rapids throughout. When the river level spikes high, many boaters head upstream to these sections rather than descending into the chaos of Section IV.

41

WILSON CREEK

Section name	Wilson Creek Gorge
Distance	2 miles
Flow range	Estimated 100–500 cfs or 8 inches—1 foot on the painted bridge gauge
Season and source of water	December through May; rainfall
Gauge location	Painted on Adako Road bridge, with Internet gauge on the way
Time required	45 minutes–2 hours; multiple laps possible
Classification	*Recreational*
Difficulty	III–IV
Managing agency	National forests in North Carolina
Permit required?	No
Shuttle type	Vehicle or hitchhike
Outstandingly Remarkable Values	Culture, fisheries, geology, history, recreation, scenery, wildlife, botany
Why paddle this section?	Smooth granite slabs; clear water even after rain; stacked with great class III–IV whitewater

RIVER DESCRIPTION

When rains pour over western North Carolina, paddlers know to load their boats. Many of those paddlers head to the whitewater of Wilson Creek, hoping that enough

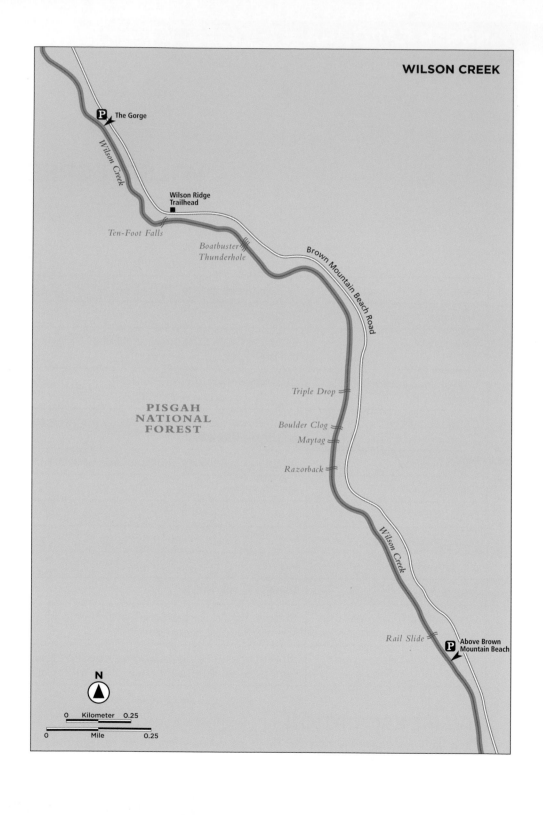

WILSON CREEK

The Gorge

Wilson Creek

Wilson Ridge Trailhead

Ten-Foot Falls

Boatbuster
Thunderhole

Brown Mountain Beach Road

PISGAH
NATIONAL
FOREST

Triple Drop

Boulder Clog

Maytag

Razorback

Wilson Creek

Rail Slide

Above Brown
Mountain Beach

N

| 0 | Kilometer | 0.25 |
| 0 | Mile | 0.25 |

Andrea Davis drops into Ten-Foot Falls on Wilson Creek. LELAND DAVIS

rain has hit the watershed. The creek is worth the gamble (no Internet gauge currently reports levels) as its clear water meanders through a rich Appalachian forest, over complicated boulder gardens, and around ancient bedrock slabs to create some of the highest quality class III–IV rapids in the state.

The steep and narrow 2-mile gorge, adored by kayakers, contains some of the oldest rock formations in the southern Appalachians. The river flows from the peaks of the Grandfather Mountains, with over 4,000 feet of elevation change from the river's source to its confluence with the Johns River. That's more relief than anywhere else on the Blue Ridge Escarpment. The smooth granite slopes throughout the gorge may remind you of California's Sierra Nevada or Idaho's Frank Church–River of No Return Wilderness.

Wilson Creek only flows a short 23 miles, all of which are protected with *Wild*, *Scenic*, and *Recreational* classifications. County governments, local community mem bers, and federal land managers all came together for the bipartisan support of the designation on August 18, 2000. Private land borders the river for 13 miles while 10 miles belong to National Forest System and a half-mile is National Park Service lands.

The creek can only be paddled when rain raises the river level. When leaves are out, more rain is necessary to make that happen. If you find blue skies and zero percent chance of precipitation in the forecast, Wilson Creek still deserves a visit. You could spend days picnicking, swimming, and fishing from the massive bedrock slabs sloping into the creek on warm days in the spring, summer, or fall.

PADDLER'S NOTES

Installation of a Wilson Creek flow gauge is planned within five years of publication of this book. In the meantime, the best gauge for this run is painted on the Adako Road bridge that you'll drive over on your way to the takeout. The gauge is read from the bottoms of the numbers (i.e., the level is 0 when the water has just reached the bottom of the painted "0"). Boaters often post the level on a Wilson Creek Facebook page. Local boaters also assume Wilson Creek is running if the Watauga River is running at least 170 cubic feet per second (cfs).

We'll describe a few of the classic class IV rapids here, but will leave some of the mystery to your own discovery. Take time to scout or meet up with a local boater. Paddlers often lap the 2-mile gorge, even if extra time is needed to show a new boater down. Many rapids have multiple names as well.

Ten Foot Falls, just a tenth of a mile downstream from the put-in, ends in a 10-foot sliding drop. Before that, you'll boof and maneuver around a class III entrance series. Know that there is a pool at the end of the whole set. Downstream, a half-mile into the run, Boatbuster and Thunderhole rapids come in quick succession, with little recovery time in between.

At 1 mile you'll encounter Triple Drop rapid, with a sticky hole at the bottom that recirculates due to a rock just downstream. Enjoy the different slot options to enter this three-tiered rapid. Slots also define the next rapid, Boulder Clog. It is a visually complex rapid that is a great one to scout, similar to most rapids on Wilson Creek. Just below is Maytag rapid, a known recirculating hazard spot. Avoid getting swept back into the undercut boulder at the left end of the ledge by aiming far right with right angle. Swims here can be nasty.

Another tenth of a mile downstream below the horizon line is Razorback rapid. Smoothly navigating it requires running a far-right line followed by a sharp left turn to avoid a piton. After a mile, you'll reach a memorable fun spot, Rail Slide. On far river left is a ridge of rock 5 feet downstream and parallel to a ledge. You can slide down this ridge like a rail—if you line up correctly. Take care not slide back into the sticky spot formed by water cascading off the ledge.

DIRECTIONS TO TAKEOUT

From I-40 near Morgantown, take exit 100 for Jamestown Road heading north. In 3.4 miles, turn left onto NC 181 northbound. In 10.7 miles turn right onto Brown

Bedrock and boulders, sunshine and friendship. Wilson Creek has it all.
Kevin Colburn / American Whitewater

Mountain Beach Road. You'll cross the river on the Adako Road bridge in 5 miles. Turn left onto Brown Mountain Beach Road / FR 1328. Just after turning, park and take the short, well-worn path to the gauge painted on the river-left bridge abutment. Then continue driving and look for the pullout on the left in about a mile, just north of the Brown Mountain Beach Resort.

DIRECTIONS TO PUT-IN
From the takeout, continue driving upstream and look for the pullout on the left in 1.7 miles. If Wilson Creek is indeed running, you will see other kayakers here.

NEARBY ATTRACTIONS
Great hiking opportunities can be found in this watershed. Try the Thorpes Creek Trail near Mortimer Campground, or look toward the Harper Creek Wilderness area. The hike to 40-foot North Harper Creek Falls is particularly rewarding. The Mortimer Campground is only open during the warmer half of the year. Dispersed camping can also be found in the valley; inquire with the Grandfather Mountain District Office.

42

DELAWARE RIVER

Section name	Upper, Middle, and Lower
Distance	198 miles
Flow range	1,000–5,000 cfs
Season and source of water	Spring, summer, and fall; rainfall
Gauge location	Port Jervis, USGS #01434000
Time required	1–8 days
Classification	*Scenic* and *Recreational*
Difficulty	I–II
Managing agency	National Park Service, Philadelphia office
Permit required?	No
Shuttle type	Vehicle
Outstandingly Remarkable Values	Recreation, scenery, geology, ecology, history
Why paddle this section?	Easy canoeing options; one-day or multiday trips for intermediate canoeists; easy access; great historical sites and towns

Tim Palmer contributed to this description.

The Delaware River slowly wears down its bedrock shoals. TIM PALMER

RIVER DESCRIPTION

The Delaware is the only major main stem river in the East that remains undammed. Its full 198 miles to tide line, from the East and West Branch confluence to Trenton, plus additional miles upstream on the East or West Branches, makes for the longest dam-free canoe trip in the Northeast. This river lies within a half-day's drive of 60 million people.

While thousands of houses, dozens of small towns, and a few cities are passed along the way, and while much of the frontage outside the Delaware Water Gap National Recreation Area is private land and none of it is truly wild, the full length of this eastern artery provides for an exceptional extended canoe voyage for experienced beginner and intermediate canoeists. With relatively easy rapids, adequate flows through autumn, many access areas, and few pesky bugs to bite or annoy boaters, this is one of the most carefree long river trips in America.

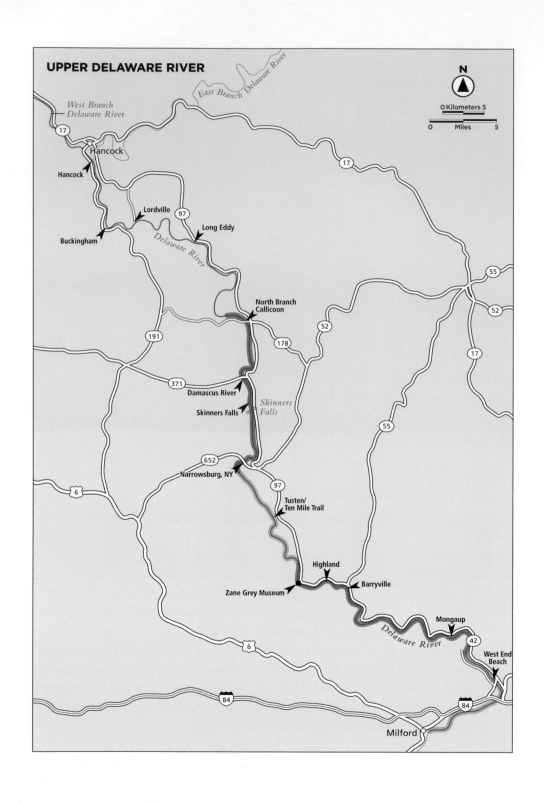

UPPER DELAWARE RIVER

N

0 Kilometers 5

0 Miles 5

East Branch Delaware River

West Branch Delaware River

17

Hancock

Hancock

Lordville

97

Long Eddy

Buckingham

Delaware River

North Branch Callicoon

191

52

178

371

Damascus River

Skinners Falls

Skinners Falls

55

652

Narrowsburg, NY

97

Tusten/ Ten Mile Trail

6

55

17

Highland

Barryville

Zane Grey Museum

Mongaup

Delaware River

42

West End Beach

6

84

84

Milford

Canoes are our favorite way to appreciate scenic flat-water rivers like the Delaware.
TIM PALMER

Delightfully relaxing, the miles, the bends, and the Delaware days blend together in a kaleidoscope of scenery: green hills, mountains, riffles that seldom stall in complete flat water, a chorus of birdlife, bass fishing, quaint small towns perched above the shores. A trove of historic landmarks can also be experienced, from author Zane Gray's home and museum to the site of George Washington's stormy Christmas Eve crossing above Trenton, which turned the tide of the Revolutionary War. The historic Roebling's Delaware Aqueduct bridge at Lackawaxen is the oldest wire cable suspension bridge in the country. Bald eagles perch on snags and eye the shallows for fish throughout the float.

At Tocks Island, 6 miles above the Water Gap, a 140-foot dam was proposed in the 1960s, but citizen activists succeeded in stopping the flooding of 37 miles of the Delaware, which were made a river-centric national recreation area instead. After heated controversy during the planning for the Upper Delaware Wild and Scenic reach, local municipalities adopted a plan that excluded significant public acquisition of riverfront open space.

Recreational use is extremely heavy at times in some reaches. Popular sections at Skinners Falls and at the national recreation area below Port Jervis are often busy, and the campgrounds filled. Crowds can be avoided on weekdays and during temperate shoulder seasons. More information on all sections of the Wild and Scenic Delaware

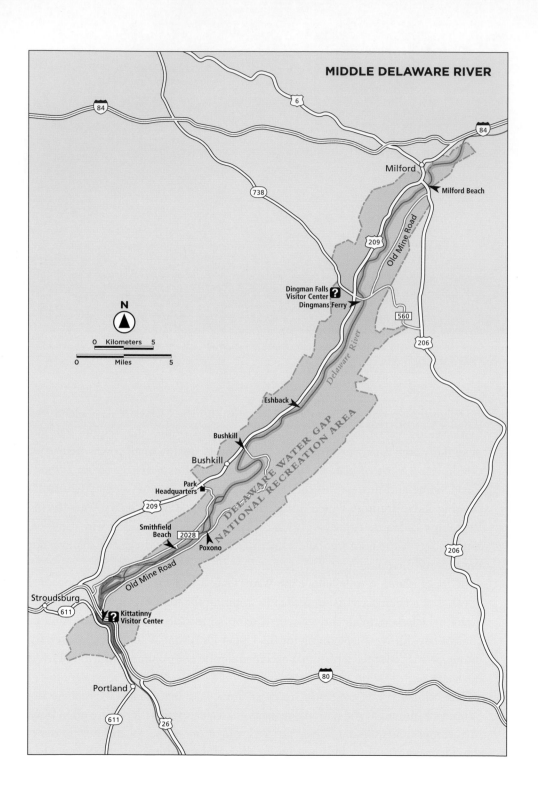

MIDDLE DELAWARE RIVER

River can be found in the *Delaware River Recreation Maps* published by the Delaware River Basin Commission or in *Canoeing the Delaware River* by Gary Letcher.

PADDLER'S NOTES

The Upper Delaware designation begins at the confluence of the East and West Branches at Hancock, and continues for 73 miles to Sparrow Bush. Along the 75-mile upper river, Hancock to Port Jervis, many cabins and summer homes occupy benches or forested slopes, yet most are screened at least somewhat by trees. Riffles are almost constant, and a few larger class II rapids come above Hankins, below Cochecton at Skinners Falls, where bedrock slabs are run on the right and deserve scouting (on the left), at swift water upstream from Lackawaxen, and elsewhere. Boaters can tie up and stroll into villages such as Callicoon.

The Delaware Water Gap National Recreation Area almost fully encompasses the designated 40 miles of the Middle Delaware. This section begins at Port Jervis, a gauge location, and ends just southeast of Stroudsburg. The Middle Delaware is maintained by the National Park Service, with free wooded campsites marked at water's edge. Most is flat water except for the Water Gap's minor class II rapids below the I-80 bridge, where the river carves 1,400 feet-deep in an S-bend through Kittatinny Mountain.

Below the Delaware Water Gap, much of the Lower Delaware's 76 miles flow through private land, but wonderfully remote sections beckon at many bends and in secluded channels behind islands. Towns along the lower river are framed in picturesque views from the water, while historic bridges are artfully latticed with iron trusses. Portland, Milford, Frenchtown, and New Hope invite travelers to step ashore, stroll historic districts, and relax in restaurants. The steep, 300-plus-foot walls of Nockamixon Cliffs have allowed rare arctic alpine plant communities to flourish, as well as provide habitat for over ninety species of birds. In the winter, ice walls that form along the cliffs taunt and lure local ice climbers. The steeples and domes of Easton rise up above the waterfront, and at Trenton the gold-painted New Jersey Capitol gleams above the river's last rapid at tide line.

You'll encounter the first of three wing dam hazards below the confluence with Tohickon Creek. Wing dams pose a hazard to boaters on the Lower Delaware. These odd rock-and-cement causeways extend from either shore toward the center and deserve caution, especially at high flows, as they channel powerful currents through a mid-river opening. Wing dams also draw out playboaters and their small, plastic playboats for surf sessions. The broken-down wing dam at Scudders Falls, just below the last designated mile, creates multiple surfing features for these "trick" kayaks at flows between 8,000–50,000 cubic feet per second (cfs) on the Trenton USGS gauge.

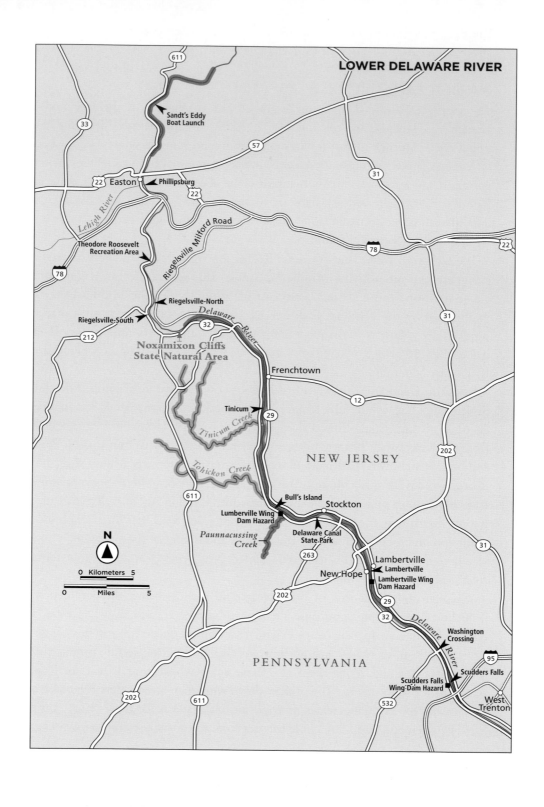

> *"WHEN WE SAVE A RIVER, WE SAVE A MAJOR PART OF AN ECOSYSTEM, AND WE SAVE OURSELVES AS WELL BECAUSE OF OUR DEPENDENCE—PHYSICAL, ECONOMIC, SPIRITUAL—ON THE WATER AND ITS COMMUNITY OF LIFE."*
>
> —*Tim Palmer,* The Wild and Scenic Rivers of America

Canoes may want to take out at the Scudders Falls access site, above these rapids, during high flows periods.

Throughout the river's length, scores of access areas and riverfront parks are open to the public. Commercial campgrounds fill on weekends. Any number of day trips, weekend outings, or longer expeditions are possible on the Delaware, and its full length offers an expedition unmatched in the East for its length of pleasant dam-free flow.

DIRECTIONS TO ACCESS SITES

With so many day and multiday trip options, there are too many access points to list here. Take a look at the Delaware River Water Trail website for a great interactive map that should help you find the perfect access location.

NEARBY ATTRACTIONS

Washington Crossing historic site; restaurants and shops; and the tourist towns of New Hope, Frenchtown, Milford, and others can easily fill your time in the region. The Delaware Canal State Park also follows the lower river and offers biking, interpretation, and more.

43

ALLEGHENY RIVER

Section name	Kinzua Dam to Emlenton
Distance	107 miles
Flow range	1,000–5,000 cfs
Season and source of water	Year-round; steady dam releases and rain
Gauge location	Kinzua Dam, USGS #03012550
Time required	1–7 days
Classification	*Recreational*
Difficulty	I–II
Managing agency	Allegheny National Forest
Permit required?	No
Shuttle type	Vehicle
Outstandingly Remarkable Values	History, recreation, scenery, ecology
Why paddle this section?	Beginner- and family-friendly for one or multiday trips; great fishing and historic connections

Author Tim Palmer contributed to this description.

Packed up and ready to go on the Allegheny River. KRISSY KASSERMAN

RIVER DESCRIPTION

The Allegheny is the largest river in volume of flow in the national Wild and Scenic Rivers system east of the Mississippi, and the fourth largest in the Wild and Scenic system nationwide, averaging 19,750 cubic feet per second (cfs) at Emlenton. The whole Allegheny runs 300 miles, and joins the Monongahela River in Pittsburgh to form the Ohio River. Contributing 60 percent of the flow there, the Allegheny is essentially the upriver extension of the Ohio, which carries twice the volume of the Mississippi where those two mega-rivers meet in Illinois.

The Wild and Scenic portion of the Allegheny lies in three sections covering most of the mileage between Kinzua Dam—upstream of Warren—to Emlenton, where I-80 spans the river. Short mileages of heavily industrialized frontage are excluded at Warren and Oil City.

The designation of the Allegheny is an anomaly in the Wild and Scenic Rivers system, not only because of this artery's enormous volume of flow and private land, but also because of its scenery and remaining amount of semiwild frontage in a developed region. The river's protected status is owed chiefly to the support of Senator John

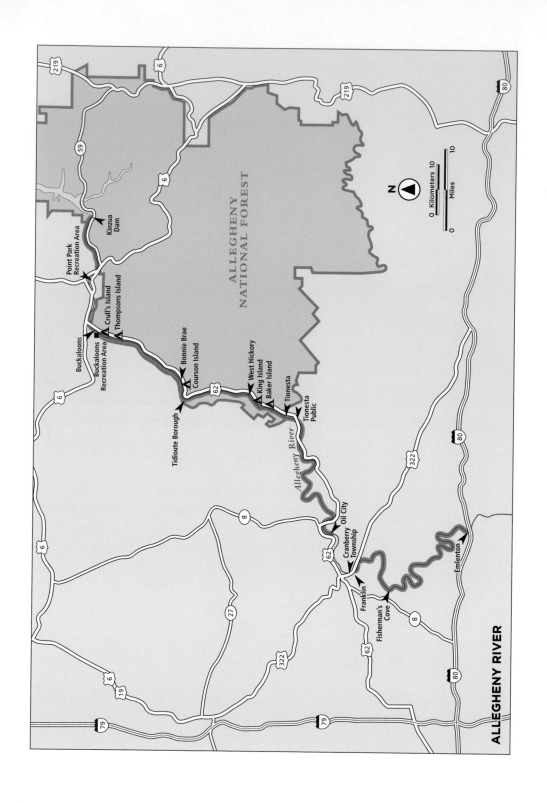

ALLEGHENY RIVER

Heinz, who courageously championed Wild and Scenic designation in 1992 before his tragic death in an airplane crash.

Flows are remarkably consistent owing to the massive Kinzua Dam, upstream, whose construction in 1965 violated a treaty with the Seneca Indians that George Washington signed. Releases never dip too low for paddling.

In addition to the river's draw as an easy but scenic canoeing river, it's an excellent sport fishery for introduced rainbow and brown trout in the tail waters of Kinzua Dam, and downstream for muskellunge, walleye, smallmouth bass, and catfish. Deep deciduous forests include excellent riparian habitat of fat, thick-limbed sycamores and arching silver maples. A varied mix of northern hardwoods such as hickories, ashes, white pines, and black cherries transition to mixed mesophytic forests common to the South.

The Allegheny may have more miles of frontage in private ownership than any other river in the Wild and Scenic system, including long reaches replete with cabins used by hunters in autumn, anglers in springtime, and vacationers throughout summer. Also uncommon in the Wild and Scenic system, the Allegheny passes through old industrial cities. The most developed of these segments are omitted from the designated mileage, but boating is continuous, and the 1-mile passage in the shadow of the United Refining Company in Warren is an amazing eyeful of heavy industry seen on few American waterways. The lower reach, from Oil City to Emlenton, is designated as the "Oil Heritage Water Trail," with recognition of the discovery of oil here and the region's role as the original oil producer of the nation. The Allegheny was heavily affected by a century of fossil fuel extraction, but has also become of model for recovery from the worst of abuses, thanks to groups like Western Rivers Conservancy, and it now flows mostly clean, with scenic views to green mountainsides.

PADDLER'S NOTES

The full length of the Allegheny from Kinzua Dam to Emlenton is easily canoed spring through autumn. Nearly all is class I, with long pools interspersed with riffles and a few nominal class II rapids—the most notable being some standing waves through Oil City under the US 62 bridge. The river is thus suitable to capable beginners and family paddling groups.

Below Buckaloons, seven islands totaling 368 acres within Allegheny National Forest are designated as one of the nation's smallest official wilderness areas. Interested in exploring these seven islands? All national forest lands, both on the islands and the shoreline, permit camping. No official sites or facilities exist, making it a wilder experience. Several hundred islands in all are found along the river—many of them public property within the Allegheny National Forest or under county or state jurisdictions.

Excellent reaches of the river await from Buckaloons to Oil City. Here gentle currents tour many islands shaded by riparian forests teeming with birdlife. Remote campsites are

Dame's rocket (*Hesperis matronalis*) adorns the banks of the Allegheny. TIM PALMER

entwined with back-channel passages isolated from roads along the shores. The Allegheny thus offers a modern view of what river travel was once like on other major eastern waterways that are now dominated by dams, railroads, highways, and urban development.

For a more detailed Allegheny river guide, see Roy Weil and Mary Shaw's *Canoeing Guide to Western Pennsylvania and Northern West Virginia*. *Middle Allegheny River Water Trail* maps can also be downloaded online from Pennsylvania Fish and Boat Commission.

DIRECTIONS TO TAKEOUT
Take the I-80 Emlenton exit, wind down to the town and PA 38 bridge, and drive upstream to a community ramp.

DIRECTIONS TO PUT-IN
Drive east from Warren on PA 59 to Kinzua Dam and its large public ramp, located just below the dam. Numerous public access areas are located along the Allegheny's full length.

NEARBY ATTRACTIONS
Consider visiting Allegheny State Park in New York, with its virgin hemlock and beech grove, as well as Oil City and oil development heritage sites. While near the river, the Tidioute Riverside Trail extends from Tidioute on river right for 4.5 miles, providing another recreation opportunity to see the Allegheny River. The Samuel Justus Recreation Trail and the Allegheny River Trails also offer riverside recreation opportunities starting in Oil City and heading downstream for 30 miles to Emlenton.

CLARION RIVER

Section name	Middle: Portland Mills to Cooksburg
Distance	34 miles
Flow range	300–5,000 cfs
Season and source of water	Spring, summer, and autumn of most years; rainfall and dam releases
Gauge location	Cooksburg, USGS #03029500
Time required	Half day–5 days
Classification	*Scenic* and *Recreational*
Difficulty	I–II
Managing agency	Allegheny National Forest; Cook Forest State Park
Permit required?	No
Shuttle type	Vehicle, bike
Outstandingly Remarkable Values	Recreation, scenery
Why paddle this section?	Easy paddling; day or multiday trip; adequate flow during most summers; woodland tour of Allegheny Plateau; old-growth forest hikes

Tim Palmer contributed to this description.

RIVER DESCRIPTION

The Northeast and greater Appalachian region spawn hundreds of rivers of boatable size and qualities, but none quite like the Clarion. Few of these other rivers offer the

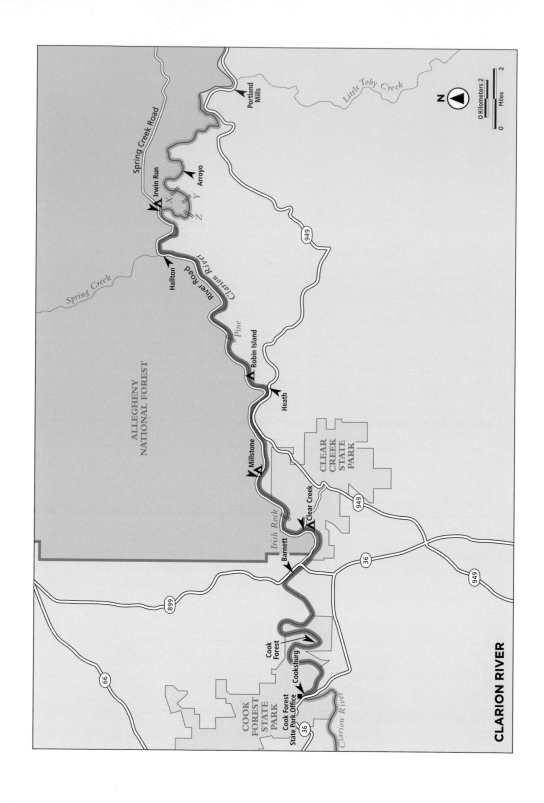

CLARION RIVER

Fall on the Clarion might be the best time to be there. WESTERN PENNSYLVANIA CONSERVANCY

combined assets of being canoeable by beginner or intermediate paddlers as a multi-day trip, runnable all summer in semiwild terrain, with public land including access areas and camping possibilities. The Clarion appeals with short runs and multiday sojourns up to five days.

Scattered islands, remote bends, gravel bars, and wooded benches above the channel all offer possibilities for camping that immerse you more fully in the wild landscape. Long pools are interspersed with hundreds of riffles and some class II rapids with occasional rocks or breaking waves to avoid.

In addition to being an outstanding easy canoe trip through a semiwild corridor of the Appalachians, the Clarion is a symbol of the effectiveness of river restoration. Once egregiously polluted with pulp mill and coal mining waste, the Clarion now runs clear. The river is a remarkable restoration success story in progress and serves as a model for improvements that can be made with long-term commitments under the Wild and Scenic and other river stewardship programs. Strip mines for coal and gas drilling have riddled the uplands above the river corridor, and remain ongoing problems as do impending threats in the age of gas fracking. But if the Clarion's recovery can be sustained, this river will continue to improve with the passage of time as a freshwater artery in its region.

Local Representative John Saylor—a powerhouse congressman of the 1960s and an original sponsor and key champion of the Wild & Scenic Rivers Act—had a special personal fondness for the Clarion, and included it in the original Wild & Scenic Act, among the prestigious 27 rivers designated under the Act for specific detailed study and possible inclusion later. It was subsequently rejected by Bureau of Outdoor Recreation planners in the 1970s because of pollution, but effective cleanup followed. With the support of Representative William Clinger, who was elected in 1979 after Saylor had been tragically killed in a plane crash, 52 miles were designated Wild and Scenic in 1996. This put to final rest a US Army Corps of Engineers' proposal to build the Saint Petersburg Dam downstream, which would have flooded the river up to Cook Forest State Park. Among the Wild & Scenic Rivers Act's original study rivers, only eighteen have subsequently been designated like the Clarion.

Cook Forest's nearby liveries attract robust business from beginning paddlers on summer weekends; serious river runners might appreciate this special stream more on weekdays or in the enticing shoulder seasons. Springtime can be cool with high flows, but the fresh greens of the Appalachian springtime in May are striking on intoxicating warm days. Autumn usually has adequate flows through a forest that rivals those of New England for its brilliant reds and oranges in maples, ashes, hickories, and oaks. A richly diverse forest community here bridges the northern hardwood community with the mixed mesophytic woodlands that extend to the southern Appalachians.

PADDLER'S NOTES

Though the Clarion is narrow and intimate in its upper reaches, flows are usually adequate all summer with nominal releases from an East Branch dam upstream. Most people limit their Clarion outings to the reaches immediately above and below the popular Cook Forest State Park. However, good class I–II paddling begins as far upstream as the mill town of Johnsonburg.

To optimize time away from roads, start at the Portland Mills access site. Here, the river quickly leaves the highway. Downstream of the Arroyo river access and your first bridge, you'll encounter three class II rapids named X, Y, and Z. These, and more class II rapids between Hallton and Belltown, all get spicier at flows above 2,000 cubic feet per second (cfs).

Some claim that the wilderness camping between Arroyo and Irwin Run access site is the best in western Pennsylvania. Below here, the riverside camping opportunities continue. A few sites in the state parks have bathrooms, cabins, launch sites, and other facilities. Clear Creek State Park offers great hiking and camping right from the river, including riverside yurts for rent. The Tobeco Trail on river left sends you upslope for a great overlook of the Clarion River's sweeping bends and deep forests.

Cook Forest State Park harbors the East's foremost old-growth grove of eastern hemlocks and white pines. The Longfellow Trail, near the ramp at PA 36, loops through the largest grove and offers one of the East's best tours of hemlock trees—a cherished keystone species that's tragically being decimated by an exotic blight promising to eliminate most groves. As of 2018, Cook Forest State Park managers are treating many of these trees with a relatively benign insecticide as a temporary measure to keep the trees alive until longer-term biological solutions hopefully become effective. However, the fate of these magnificent forests remains uncertain, so see them now!

Pennsylvania Department of Conservation and Natural Resources has maps of the *Clarion River Water Trail, Upper and Middle Sections,* available for download online. The trail maps for Clear Creek and Cook Forest State Parks are also handy.

DIRECTIONS TO TAKEOUT
From Clarion, take 5th Street north out of town. The road will turn into PA 1005 / Miola Road. Follow this for 10.5 miles before turning right on PA 36 southbound. In 3.5 miles the Cook Forest offices and access site will be on the left, just before crossing the Clarion.

DIRECTIONS TO PUT-IN
To launch your boat at Portland Mills, cross the river at Cook Forest and follow PA 36 south for 8.2 miles. Turn left on PA 949 northbound. In about 15 miles, take a sharp left to stay on PA 949 northbound for the remaining 8.6 miles to the access site on the left.

NEARBY ATTRACTIONS
The camping and hiking options in both Clear Creek State Park and Cook Forest State Park should not be overlooked during a trip to the Clarion. The nearby Allegheny River also carries a Wild and Scenic flag and offers single-day or multiday paddling options as well.

45

WESTFIELD RIVER

Section name	West Branch: Becket to Chester
Distance	8 miles
Flow range	800–9,000 cfs
Season and source of water	Early spring; rainfall
Gauge location	Near Huntington, USGS #01181000
Time required	1 day
Classification	*Scenic*
Difficulty	III–IV
Managing agency	Wild & Scenic Westfield River Committee; National Park Service
Permit required?	No
Shuttle type	Vehicle
Outstandingly Remarkable Values	Geology, recreation, scenery, biology, hydrology, history
Why paddle this section?	Tour historical Keystone Arch bridges while paddling fun whitewater rapids in a narrow, forested corridor

Supplemental description provided by Meredyth Babcock, Wild & Scenic Westfield River Committee.

The West Branch of the Westfield River has plenty of nearly continuous, challenging class III flowing through deciduous forest. Meredyth Babcock

RIVER DESCRIPTION

The Westfield River begins in the Berkshire Hills of western Massachusetts. The watershed contains one of the largest roadless wilderness areas left in the state and over 50 miles of classic Northeast paddling opportunities. It is also the longest free-flowing river segment in Massachusetts, without any water withdraws or impediments. At low to medium flows, most paddlers consider the run a class III+. As water levels increase, rapids veer toward class IV.

The first Westfield River sections were designated Wild and Scenic in 1993, with more following in 2004. The entire designation includes many smaller tributaries and sections of the East, West, and Main Westfield Branches. A total of 78 miles carry either a *Recreational*, *Wild*, or *Scenic* designation, which adds up to be an astounding amount of the watershed. The Westfield is one of the Partnership Wild and Scenic Rivers found primarily in the East. The National Park Service, the Commonwealth of Massachusetts, and the Westfield Wild & Scenic Advisory Committee all work together to manage the resource.

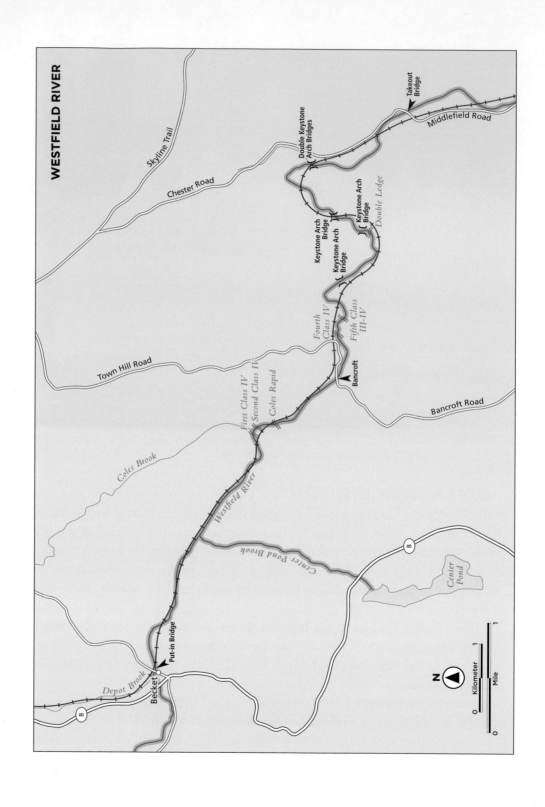

WESTFIELD RIVER

A keystone arch bridge over the West Branch Westfield River. JIM SULLIVAN

As you paddle along the West Branch, you'll navigate under historic Keystone Arch Railroad bridges, the first of their kind built in America in 1840. Originally numbering ten bridges, these early industrial age structures allowed the longest and steepest railroad when they were constructed. Only two are in use today. While floating beneath them, you'll get the best view, although a trail does meander on river left that allows foot traffic to see the bridges as well.

The Westfield River Race began in April 1954, making it one of the oldest paddling events in the country. It began with a group of braggadocious canoeists and an offering of a case of beer from a local bar owner to the fastest paddler. The Westfield Canoe Club also hosts beginner races on the main Westfield River below Huntington. The club offers beginner clinics for about a month prior to these races, helping to foster a strong and safe new boating community for the region.

Many sections of the multiple branches of the Westfield can be run. Spring rains and snowmelt draw whitewater boaters on the West and East Branches, while summertime sunshine attracts those looking for a mellower float farther downstream.

PADDLER'S NOTES

River levels rise and drop quickly on the whitewater stretches of the Westfield River. Act quickly if you're in the area and flows look good. Storms change the hazards in the river often, particularly when powerful hurricanes sweep through the region. When not paddling with locals, always scout for wood where there is a blind rapid. The length of the West Branch feels wonderfully remote, lending to its *Scenic* designation. However, the CSX railroad follows the river valley and can be used as an emergency exit. Always take precaution when walking on railroad tracks.

As you begin your paddle, start counting the railroad bridges you float beneath. After the sixth bridge the whitewater picks up to be more like class III+ or IV. The first two of these more challenging rapids will carry you to the seventh railroad bridge. Scout the next drop, Coles rapid, on the left side.

Bancroft Road will be the eighth bridge to cross the river, and offers an alternate put-in or takeout option to shorten the run, or to get out if you are in over your head. A bit of boogie water will be followed by a larger tributary entering on river left. The river splits around an island, with the left channel typically ending in wood. The right channel can be up to class IV, with larger holes on the right to navigate through and around. The river narrows and bends to the right, with more whitewater and a longer class III–IV section downstream that ends at the next railroad bridge.

The final Double Ledge rapid should keep you on your toes. This one can be hard to see before you are in it. Know that most paddlers unfamiliar with the run only scout the second ledge from an eddy on the left. The second ledge dishes out the most carnage, often from the center or the right lines.

DIRECTIONS TO TAKEOUT

From Chester, head north on US 20 for 0.2 mile and turn right on Middlefield Road. Turn right on Johnsonville Road after passing over the Westfield.

DIRECTIONS TO PUT-IN

In Becket, the river access is located at the end of Main Street, just downstream from the High Street bridge.

NEARBY ATTRACTIONS

If you happen to be near the Westfield River when flows are too low to float, grab a fishing pole or head out for a hike. The Keystone Arch Bridge hiking trail weaves for 2.5 miles, and provides interpretation of the historical structures as well as vistas of the river valley.

PARTNERSHIP RIVERS

Partnership Wild and Scenic Rivers are designated through grassroots river conservation movements of citizens, local communities, and municipalities. These groups develop a management plan before designation rather than after designation, as nonpartnership rivers do. State governments and, finally, the National Park Service are brought in as partnering managers who share the same stewardship goals. Often, a local committee forms to bring these stakeholders together, and to facilitate stewardship and management activities. All groups have a role in managing and protecting their own river.

Local citizens can engage in river stewardship activities easily on Partnership rivers. They are the protectors of the river's unique Outstandingly Remarkable Values. Often, the river's broader committee organization will provide grant funding and educational programs to empower local citizens and community groups to:

- Help maintain clean water,

- Improve passage and habitat for wildlife and fish,

- Protect and restore historic sites,

- Develop scientific data about stream and wildlife health,

- Come together for sound decision-making.

PARTNERSHIP WILD & SCENIC RIVERS AS OF 2017:

Farmington River, Connecticut

Great Egg Harbor River, New Jersey

Lamprey River, New Hampshire

Lower Delaware River, New Jersey / Pennsylvania

Maurice River and tributaries, New Jersey

Muscontcong River, New Jersey

Sudbury, Assabet, and Concord Rivers, Massachusetts

Wekiva River, Florida

Westfield River, Massachusetts

White Clay Creek, Delaware / Pennsylvania

Eightmile River, Connecticut

Taunton River, Massachusetts

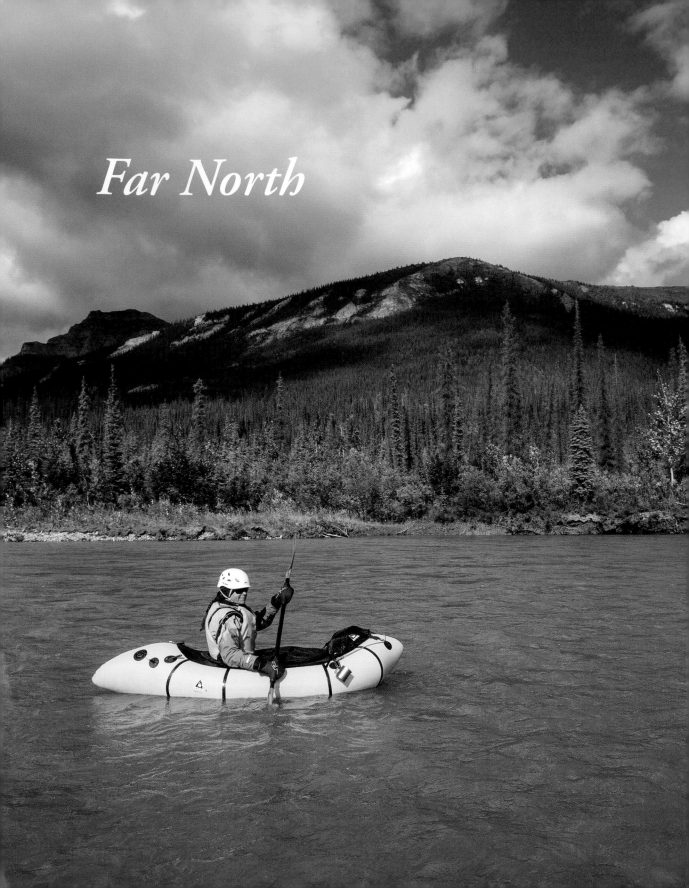

Far North

46

ALATNA RIVER

Section name	Gaedeke Lake to Lake Takahula
Distance	75 miles
Flow range	Unknown
Season and source of water	Late summer; snowmelt and rainfall
Gauge location	None
Time required	4–14 days
Classification	*Wild*
Difficulty	I–II+
Managing agency	Gates of the Arctic National Park
Permit required?	No
Shuttle type	Floatplane
Outstandingly Remarkable Values	Recreation, scenery
Why paddle this section?	Utterly pristine Arctic river; lots of wildlife including wolves, grizzly bears, lynx, caribou, and moose; option to hike to Arrigetch Peak

Supplemental description provided by Moe Witschard.

Opposite: The Alatna River near the Arrigetch Peaks is a calm float through the boreal forest. Great gravel bar camps abound. Moe Witschard

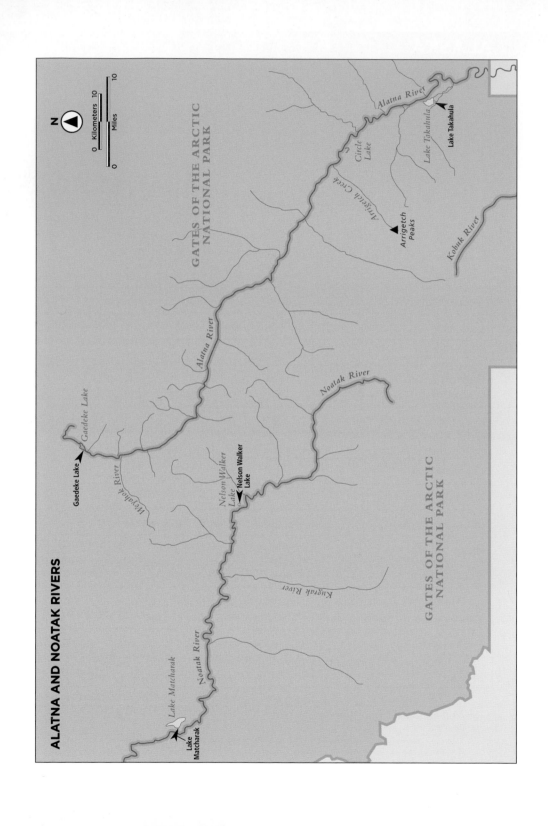

ALATNA AND NOATAK RIVERS

The Alatna River just upstream of Arrigetch Creek. MOE WITSCHARD

RIVER DESCRIPTION

The Alatna River and the backdrop of the granite Arrigetch Peaks in the Endicott Mountains combine for one of the best river expeditions in Alaska. You'll float 75 of the 83 miles of river classified as *Wild* along this stretch of the upper river, all of which are completely inside Gates of the Arctic National Park.

The upper Alatna River is infrequently floated, as a 5-mile hike is required to access it from the drop-off point at Gaedeke Lake. Packrafts are the perfect crafts for exploring this Arctic gem. The hike from Gaedeke to the start of the run is downhill over beautiful open tundra. Caribou are often seen while hiking down to where the Weyahok River joins the Alatna, the location to blow up your packrafts or assemble your skin-on-frame canoe and start floating.

Open tundra along the first day's float gives way to boreal forest about 10 miles into the run. You'll remember the great camping on gravel bars and tundra along this river. The upper Alatna has a steep gradient for a class II river. But while rapids are constant, maneuvering is generally easy. Nearby alpine ridges and deeply incised tributaries beg for exploration on foot.

The thin Arrigetch Peaks were named by the Inupiat native peoples for their likeness to outstretched fingers. These 7,000-foot granite spires have long seduced both climbers and hikers, most of whom never make the long journey to explore them in person. Floating along the Alatna is one of the best ways to explore these remote geologic monuments.

Wildlife viewing here is otherworldly. Herds of caribou numbering in the thousands migrate across hillsides, grizzlies forage along riparian zones just a stone's throw from your boat, and the song of the loon echoes across the valley floor. This bounty has supported populations of nomadic Nunamiut people for at least 11,000 years.

PADDLER'S NOTES

Be prepared for any weather condition, animal encounter, or emergency scenario in the Alaskan wilderness. These kinds of backcountry skills are essential when traveling in such a remote wonderland. You won't find signs to mark your takeout, so keep an eye on your map and compass or GPS device. Be sure you are up to speed on all of them as services are nonexistent out on the Alatna.

Most paddlers aim to paddle the Alatna in August or September. Snowmelt combines with rain to generally provide enough volume to float this time of year. However, as with any wilderness expedition, your timing could be off, and you may need to adapt your starting point accordingly. Contact the aviation company providing your drop-off for an idea of what to expect.

Potentially challenging sections of river above Arrigetch Creek may require portaging or lining depending on the water level and year. Low-water years may be better suited for putting in at Circle Lake. Below Arrigetch Creek, the river slows and winds through rugged and stunning limestone mountains.

Budget a few days for exploring this landscape on foot. An outstanding multiday side trip up Arrigetch Creek explores the mythical granite summits of the Arrigetch Peaks. Four days exploring this area on a recent trip was reported as barely enough.

A half-mile portage on river right to Takahula Lake gets you to your pickup spot.

DIRECTIONS TO TAKEOUT

Plan to end your journey at Lake Takahula. Your floatplane operator will meet you here. Alternate floatplane pickup upstream is Circle Lake.

DIRECTIONS TO PUT-IN

Begin at Gaedeke Lake after a floatplane drops you and your gear. Circle Lake can also be used as a put-in to make the trip shorter, but why would you want to do that? Brooks Range Aviation, Brooksrange.com, is the recommended operator for this run.

NEARBY ATTRACTIONS

Add a trip down the nearby Noatak River while you are in the region. Brooks Range Aviation can help you plan logistics to travel between these two Wild and Scenic rivers. For a grand multisport adventure, pack your climbing gear for a side trip up into the Arrigetch Peaks.

BALD EAGLE FACTS
Did you know . . .

- A bald eagle's vision is six to eight times better than a human's.

- Eagles typically weigh between 9 and 14 pounds, with the female eagles more than one-third heavier than males.

- Eagles are opportunistic carnivores. They will not only hunt for fish, small mammals, and other birds, but also steal food from other birds.

- We think of bald eagles as having white heads and tail feathers, but juveniles can be blotchy-brown all over.

- Many eagles live to be around thirty years old, and stay with the same mates for life.

- An eagle pair may frequent the same nest for multiple years in a row as they raise their chicks.

- Bald eagles create nests 4 to 5 feet wide and 2 to 4 feet deep in tall trees. They will add material to their nest every year, making it wider, deeper, and heavier.

An eagle sits on a branch above the Skagit River. Adam Elliott

NOATAK RIVER

Section name	Nelson Walker Lake to Lake Matcharak
Distance	45 miles
Flow range	Unknown
Season and source of water	Late summer; snowmelt
Gauge location	None
Time required	5-10 days
Classification	*Wild*
Difficulty	I
Managing agency	Gates of the Arctic National Park
Permit required?	No
Shuttle type	Floatplane
Outstandingly Remarkable Values	Culture, fisheries, recreation, scenery, wildlife
Why paddle this section?	Big, wide open valley; pristine Arctic wilderness; abundant grizzly bears in August due to salmon run

Supplemental description provided by Moe Witschard.

RIVER DESCRIPTION

Descending from Alaska's Mount Igikpak and the Schwatka Mountains of the Brooks Range, the Noatak River flows entirely north of the Arctic Circle. Alaska's pristine

Great hiking abounds on the upper Noatak River, which meanders through a wide glacial valley. MOE WITSCHARD

wilderness, abundant wildlife, and renowned scenery shine through on the upper 45 miles of the Noatak, and continue for the subsequent 327 miles of designated Wild and Scenic river.

The Noatak's claim to fame is its status as the longest mountain-ringed watershed in the United States. Perhaps for this reason, it also possesses the longest designation of continuous river mileage in the Wild and Scenic system, 372 miles total. The Alaska National Interest Lands Conservation Act of 1980 brought 3,427 miles of Alaska's rivers into the system, including the Noatak. While this seems like a lot of mileage, much of it is located in already protected parks or reserves. Many of the rivers studied for designation were left out due to potential development and controversy. Therefore, many of Alaska's rivers in need of protection did not receive it.

The upper Noatak meanders through a very large, wide-open tundra landscape. Glaciers carved the valley and sit adjacent to the river, still working their geomorphic mastery in sculpting the landscape. Very few trails extend from the river. However, in this remote and pristine wilderness, you can walk where you want, and soak in the expansive views for miles in every direction.

This slow-moving, glassy, class I river makes for a dream conveyor-belt float through this pristine Arctic wilderness. Camping is excellent on huge gravel bars and on tundra benches. The first day brings the paddler within a few hundred yards of a pingo, a periglacial feature that is cored by ice and formed by fresh water springs. Hike to the top for an unforgettable 360-degree view.

The upper Noatak is home to abundant herds of caribou, grizzly bears, Dall sheep, and moose, along with birds such as golden eagles, peregrine falcons, Arctic loons, green-winged teals, Arctic grebes, and ptarmigans. Particularly notable is the abundance of grizzlies in and around the month of August. The Kugrak River, a tributary of the upper Noatak, has a chum salmon run that draw grizzlies from many miles around. Grizzlies can be seen anywhere on the Noatak on an eight-day trip. Twenty-five were seen on an eight-day packrafting trip in 2017.

PADDLER'S NOTES

Unlike many multiday trips in the Lower 48, the Noatak and other Alaskan rivers offer paddlers a pick-your-adventure style of travel. Camp on any river bar that appeals to you or take a hike to any interesting feature. Designated camps and trails will not be found here. But even in wilderness settings, take care to not trample wildlife and to leave no trace, especially near the lakes within a short walk of the river. Hiking along this river is outstanding, and mountains rise more than 3,000 feet from the edges of the valley. Views of Mount Igikpak, the tallest mountain in the central Brooks Range at 8,276 feet, are common on the upper river.

Venturing into the Alaskan wilderness requires solid backcountry skills, including those for food storage, weather preparedness, map reading, and more. The joy of seeing absolutely no posted signs, roads, neighborhoods, or even other people is well worth the effort in obtaining the skills required to safely navigate this landscape.

Paddlers access this river via floatplanes. This makes a lightweight trip more appealing, with canoes or packrafts rather than large rafts with oar frames. Brooks Range Aviation flies trips in and out of Bettles, Alaska, to both the put-in and takeout. You can reach Bettles via a flight from Fairbanks.

DIRECTIONS TO TAKEOUT
Your chartered floatplane will pick you up at Lake Matcharak and return you to Bettles.

DIRECTIONS TO PUT-IN
From Bettles, you'll fly into Nelson Walker Lake on a floatplane to begin your trip. Brooks Range Aviation is the recommended operator for this drop-off.

Gravel bars and tundra benches provide great camping on the Noatak River. Keep an eye out for grizzly bears that migrate to the Noatak River for the August chum salmon run.
MOE WITSCHARD

NEARBY ATTRACTIONS

While "nearby" does not exactly apply in Alaska, you will be close to Gates of the Arctic National Park and Preserve, where you can find facilities for camping, hiking, and more. We also recommend adding another river trip to your Alaskan adventure itinerary because you probably traveled a long distance to get this far north.

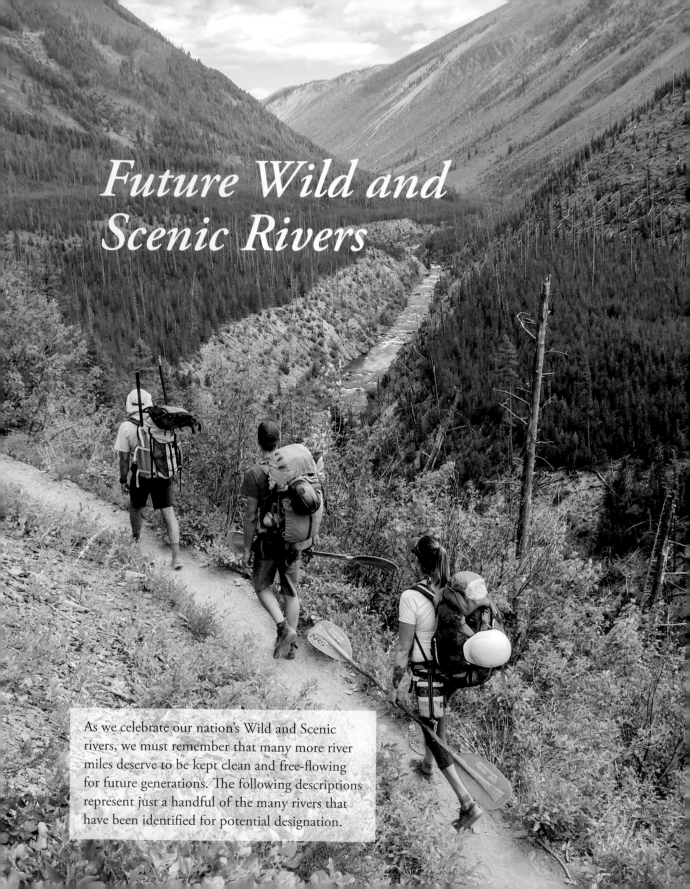

Future Wild and Scenic Rivers

As we celebrate our nation's Wild and Scenic rivers, we must remember that many more river miles deserve to be kept clean and free-flowing for future generations. The following descriptions represent just a handful of the many rivers that have been identified for potential designation.

48

NORTH FORK BLACKFOOT RIVER

Section name	Foot bridge or the flats to road bridge
Distance	5 miles
Flow range	200–2,000 cfs
Season and source of water	Late spring and early summer; snowmelt
Gauge location	Ryan Bridge, MBMG ID #76F 03500
Time required	1 day
Classification	Proposed: *Wild*
Difficulty	III–IV
Managing agency	Lolo National Forest
Permit required?	No
Shuttle type	Hike
Outstandingly Remarkable Values	Proposed: Fisheries, recreation, scenery
Why paddle this section?	Quality creeking-style paddling at many flow levels; a wilderness experience; plentiful whitewater for miles

Opposite: Hiking into the North Fork Blackfoot with packrafts. This is also known as the southern gateway to the Bob Marshall Wilderness. ADAM ELLIOTT

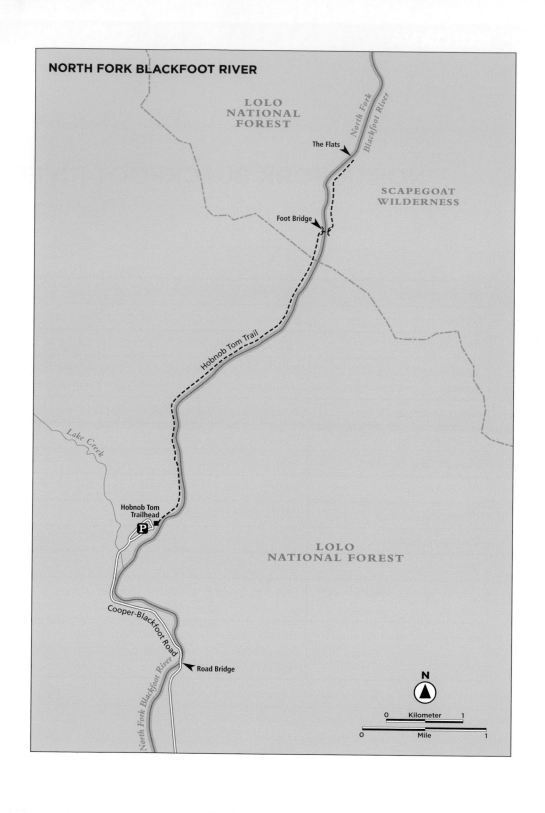

NORTH FORK BLACKFOOT RIVER

LOLO
NATIONAL
FOREST

North Fork Blackfoot River

The Flats

SCAPEGOAT
WILDERNESS

Foot Bridge

Hobnob Tom Trail

Lake Creek

Hobnob Tom
Trailhead

LOLO
NATIONAL FOREST

Cooper-Blackfoot Road

North Fork Blackfoot River

Road Bridge

N

0   Kilometer   1

0   Mile   1

We paddled the North Fork Blackfoot at low flow, around 300 cfs, which was about ideal for packrafts and fly-fishing. ADAM ELLIOTT

RIVER DESCRIPTION

Entering the wilderness on foot and leaving via the river makes a float down the North Fork Blackfoot River at the southern end of the Scapegoat Wilderness in western Montana one of the more unique days paddling anyone could want. The river itself boasts tight and technical class III action with a few steeper class IV moments at low flows, all at the base of rich and dynamic forest slopes and mountain summits. At higher flows it steps up to Class IV, with some sections approaching Class V.

You'll earn every paddle stroke by hiking the 3.5 miles into this run. The Hobnob Tom Trail follows the North Fork Blackfoot River, and continues farther into the Scapegoat Wilderness. Along the trail, you'll see evidence of the 1988 Canyon Creek Fire, with succession species such as grasses, shrubs, and small lodgepole pines filling the hillsides. Fireweed, with vibrant fuchsia petals that bloom along a taller stalk, flourishes in a disturbed ecosystem and adds beautiful color to your hike. The perspective gained from hiking high above the river fosters a deeper connection to this glacial-carved watershed, something hard to see when we only float the narrow band of blue in the valley below.

You'll be sharing this river with avid anglers. Many hike in and claim a backcountry riverside camp to search for the native westslope cutthroat trout in this stream. You may even be inspired to throw up a hammock and cast a line of your own. Read up on regulations, including those surrounding the threatened bull trout.

"EVERYBODY NEEDS BEAUTY AS WELL AS BREAD, PLACES TO PLAY IN AND PRAY IN, WHERE NATURE MAY HEAL AND CHEER AND GIVE STRENGTH TO BODY AND SOUL ALIKE."

—*John Muir*

Montanans' fondness for their rivers is indisputable. The state boasts world-class trout fishing and extraordinary paddling opportunities, not to mention high quality drinking water and water resources for irrigation and industry. These healthy headwaters may be pristine now but development threats loom ahead that could cripple these resources, both within Montana and farther downstream in other states.

It is no surprise then that a coalition of Montana citizens, sportsmen, businesses, and conservationists have come together to request Wild and Scenic protection for more of their rivers. Currently, only two rivers in the state are protected as Wild and Scenic: the Flathead (North, Middle, and South Forks) and the Missouri. Even though the fight to protect Montana's Flathead River from Spruce Park Dam catalyzed much of the initial Wild & Scenic Rivers Act momentum before 1968, the state has not seen any new designations since 1976.

Today, the Montanans for Healthy Rivers coalition has drafted a citizens' proposal to add over fifty new stretches of Montana's waterways to the system, totaling almost 700 new miles. The North Fork Blackfoot contributes nearly 23 miles of healthy and beautiful river to that total.

PADDLER'S NOTES

Hiking in provides sweeping views of the river valley not often seen by floating along a river. Rocky hillsides give way to deep-green forested faces that complement the bright blue and white hues of the river itself. If you enjoy this style of multisport day, you will be rewarded with super fun class III–IV rapids.

Calm, but short, recovery pools follow most of the characteristic tight and technical rapids. In higher flows these rest areas diminish with swift current, wave trains, and hydraulics taking the place of the tight boulder gardens.

About a quarter of the way down the run you'll find a section called Six Pin, with a slightly steeper gradient requiring more technical class IV maneuvering. Look for

Susan paddles her packraft through one of the many class III spots along the North Fork Blackfoot. ADAM ELLIOTT

really large boulders blocking your view downstream. If you are scouting what you can't see, you'll pull over above this section easily.

Always scout for wood on this run. Summer fires and winter avalanches contribute large wood to the system, a benefit for the healthy westslope cutthroat trout and bull trout populations but a hazard for paddlers. Logjams can easily span the entire river, or just hide beneath the surface. Don't forget to bring your bear spray, as there are plenty of grizzly bears in the area.

DIRECTIONS TO TAKEOUT

From Missoula, take I-90 east to exit 109 for MT 200 eastbound. In 51.7 miles, turn left onto Kleinschmidt Flat Road. Drive 2.3 miles and turn right on Dry Gulch Road. In just 2 miles take a left onto Cooper-Blackfoot Road. You'll bear to the right in 6 miles to reach the bridge over the river. This is the easiest place to take out. Leave a car here.

A few large logjams line the North Fork Blackfoot, and possibly require a portage or two.
ADAM ELLIOTT

DIRECTIONS TO PUT-IN

If you have a second vehicle, drive another mile upstream on Cooper-Blackfoot Road from the takeout. Otherwise, you'll be walking this extra mile. In a mile, bear to the right to reach the parking area for the Hobnob Tom trailhead. Hike 3 miles to a footbridge. Put in here or where the river flattens another half-mile or so upstream.

NEARBY ATTRACTIONS

Just an hour and a half away is an urban surf scene that tops the charts. Brennan's Wave, in downtown Missoula, attracts kayakers, surfers, tubers, and sunbathers alike, as does Alberton Gorge a half-hour's drive downstream.

49

NOLICHUCKY RIVER

Section name	Nolichucky Gorge
Distance	8 miles
Flow range	500–3,000 cfs
Season and source of water	Year-round; rain
Gauge location	Embreeville, USGS #03465500
Time required	1 day
Classification	Proposed: *Scenic* and *Recreational*
Difficulty	III–IV
Managing agency	Pisgah and Cherokee National Forests
Permit required?	No
Shuttle type	Vehicle
Outstandingly Remarkable Values	Proposed: Geologic, scenery, recreational
Why paddle this section?	One of the deepest river gorges and last free-flowing rivers in the region; lots of surf in and between classic whitewater rapids

RIVER DESCRIPTION

Flowing through one of the deepest gorges in the Southeast, the Nolichucky River has long attracted paddlers. The 8 miles of remote gorge between Poplar, North Carolina,

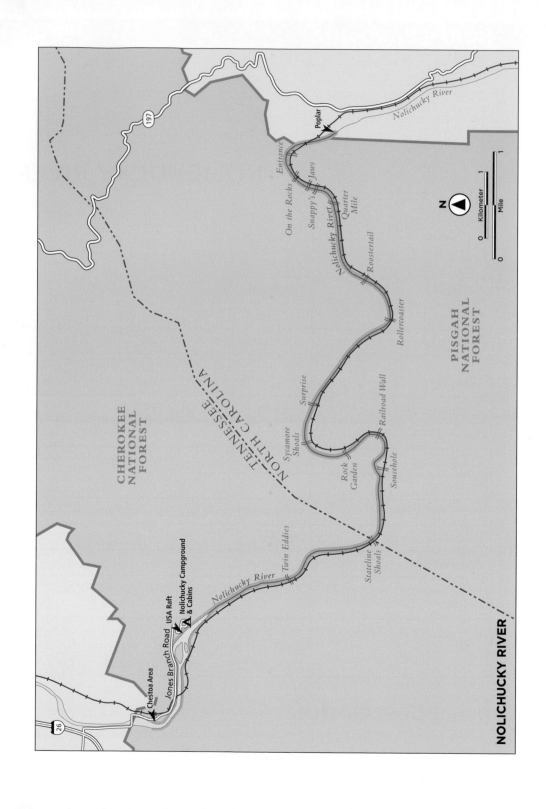

NOLICHUCKY RIVER

Adam surfs at Jaws wave on the Nolichucky in 2010. ADAM ELLIOTT

and Erwin, Tennessee, contain 2,000-foot forested slopes rising from the base of the river valley, scenery unlike anywhere in the region. Combined with fun class III–IV rapids and great recovery pools, this run is a staple of the Southeast paddler's repertoire.

Thick forests surrounding the river support many other creatures that love the river. North Carolina has designated the gorge as a black bear sanctuary. This protected area serves as an important corridor between habitats in both North Carolina and Tennessee. The fisheries have been on the mend because water quality has improved drastically in the past few decades. Today, a healthy smallmouth bass fishery thrives in the river, attracting fishermen to the access points at either end of the gorge.

Crossing the border of Tennessee and North Carolina, the Nolichucky River's free-flowing state has become somewhat of an anomaly in the region. Dams and diversions block many rivers in the Southeast. The Nolichucky, however, still responds dynamically to changes in the weather and seasons. Floods come with large storm events, while lower water flows in late summer. These natural fluctuations help sustain diverse wildlife populations, transport vital nutrients downstream, and provide a variety of habitat for fish. The variation in flows also supports a healthy recreation economy that the local communities increasingly depend upon as the railroad industry moves out of town.

A Wild and Scenic designation would mean that these benefits would remain in perpetuity. The grassroots support for the river's protection proves that local residents understand a Wild and Scenic designation simply preserves the river in its current state. It does not change or regulate what they can do with their land. If anything, it helps them protect the values that make their community special. A study conducted by the Forest Service recommended a little over 7 miles of the Nolichucky for Wild and Scenic designation in 1994. However, no bill was introduced in Congress. Today, there is a resurgence of action to call for protection. As of early 2018, the citizens' petition to designate the river has garnered nearly 20,000 signatures.

PADDLER'S NOTES

The free-flowing Nolichucky River serves up a variety of whitewater at a range of flow levels. Hurricanes bring flood flows that only the elite will attempt to paddle, while low water summer days make for great first-time flows for boaters starting to get solid in their combat rolls.

Running shuttle will add an hour to the end of your day. Avoid this and hire USA Raft at the takeout ((800) USA-RAFT) or the Noli Gorge Campground ((423) 743-8876) to run your shuttle for a small fee. Call in advance to make a reservation.

Harder rapids and plentiful play spots fill the first half of this run. Paddlers in over their heads can walk the railroad tracks back to an access site, but it could be a long and dangerous walk. Trains use the tracks too. Just below the Poplar put-in you'll pick your way through the class III Entrance rapid, looking out for holes that often form in the middle of the rapid.

On the Rocks rapid comes next, with a 4-foot ledge to kick things off. Water pouring over the ledge slams into a rock in the center, forcing boaters to be prepared to take slots to the left or right as they drop over the ledge. Scout from river left. Both of these first two rapids have decent recovery pools. Continue around the bend to find the Jaws surf wave on the right. Square up to it or avoid it on the left. Catch the eddy to relax on the rocks next to the wave and take some turns yourself.

The longest and most difficult rapid is a half-mile downstream from Jaws. Quarter Mile rapid may not have one big drop or move, but the rapid is long and without great places to break or recovery. New holes often form here following big storms. The final drop in the series, Murphy's Ledge, can hold a swimmer.

Rafters on the Nolichucky set up safety for each other at one of the more consequential rapids. CURTIS ENGLAND

The remaining class III rapids, Roostertail, Rollercoaster, Rock Garden, Railroad Wall, Sousehole (aka Maggie's Rock), and Twin Eddies are all spaced farther apart. While each is unique, you'll find good surf waves throughout and lots of maneuvering around boulders and over ledges.

DIRECTIONS TO TAKEOUT

Coming from the east on I-26, take exit 43 for US 19 westbound before you reach Erwin. Turn right at the end of the ramp and immediately left onto TN 36 north / Temple Hill Road. In 2.5 miles turn right onto Chestoa Pike. This turn is easy to miss. After you cross the river, turn right onto Jones Branch Road. The campground and outfitters are at the end of the road in 1.2 miles.

DIRECTIONS TO PUT-IN

Remember that many boaters hire a shuttle at the takeout to avoid this hour-long shuttle. Head back the way you came down Jones Branch Road, but turn right onto

A rainy afternoon on the remote-feeling Nolichucky River. CURTIS ENGLAND

Chestoa Pike instead of crossing back over the river. Get ready to meander through a lot of town streets. Stay on Chestoa as you head into Erwin, Tennessee. In 2.2 miles the road merges into Jackson Love Highway, and then turns into Ohio Avenue just 0.3 mile farther. In 0.7 mile turn right onto Love Street, and take the first left onto South Mohawk Drive. Stay right on North Mohawk Drive in 0.8 mile, and then left on East Erwin Road in 0.8 mile. At the T intersection turn right onto Rock Creek Road / 10th Street. This is also TN 395 east. In 5.2 miles, stay right at a fork to continue on NC 197. You're back in North Carolina now. You'll hit the river in 3.8 miles, where you'll take an immediate right to reach the Poplar boat launch site.

NEARBY ATTRACTIONS

It is a great idea to support the local businesses in Erwin, TN, especially those that have signed on to support the Wild and Scenic Nolichucky designation. The Appalachian Trail can be reached just downstream of the takeout, opening up an easy hiking option. Riverside camping is always recommended for a full paddling experience, and couldn't be much easier than with the Nolichucky Gorge Campground.

50

SOL DUC RIVER

Section name	Salmon Cascade to FR 2918
Distance	3.1 miles
Flow range	750–4,000 cfs
Season and source of water	Winter; rain
Gauge location	Near Fairholm, virtual American Whitewater gauge #43469
Time required	Half day
Classification	Proposed: *Scenic*
Difficulty	III–IV
Managing agency	Olympic National Park and Olympic National Forest
Permit required?	No
Shuttle type	Vehicle or hitchhiking
Outstandingly Remarkable Values	Proposed: Scenery, recreation, geology, fisheries, wildlife
Why paddle this section?	Migrating salmon; clear water; easy access; rich temperate rainforest ecosystem characteristic of the Olympic Peninsula

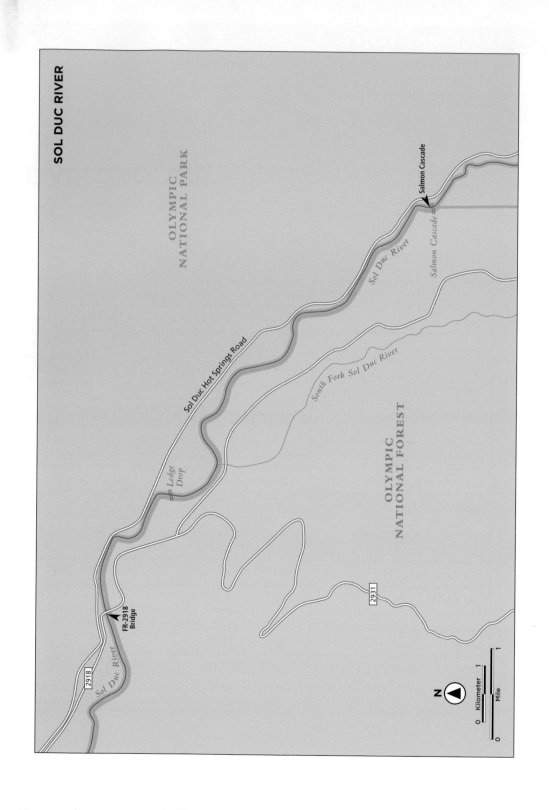

Adam paddles the right line boof at Salmon Cascade on the Sol Duc River.
THOMAS O'KEEFE / AMERICAN WHITEWATER

RIVER DESCRIPTION

Capturing the clear water from the subalpine lake basin of the Olympic Peninsula's High Divide, the Sol Duc River serves as a popular paddling destination in this remote corner of Washington. With easy access and quality class III–IV boulder gardens and ledge drops, intermediate boaters will quickly learn that the river may be the best way to experience this diverse temperate rainforest ecosystem.

Flows on the Sol Duc River respond quickly to winter storms or approaching cold fronts, but the old-growth forests filter the water, leaving the river itself beautifully clear most days. With easy access, this run is a great first stop on a peninsula paddling tour.

Many rivers on the Olympic Peninsula are famous for their healthy salmon runs, and the Sol Duc is no exception. Sit at Salmon Cascade rapid for a while and you will likely see a coho salmon leaping from the pool to migrate toward spawning grounds in the headwaters. The Sol Duc is one of the only rivers on the peninsula to support all five major species of salmon.

While the Olympic Peninsula may be one of the most iconic outdoor recreation destinations on the West Coast, and much of this pristine landscape is now protected in the national park and national forest, the rivers remain vulnerable. Seeing the steady increase in the recreation economy and the benefits of wild rivers as an important life amenity, locals began to organize around conserving these valuable and vulnerable natural features. The Wild Olympics Campaign proposes Wild and Scenic designation for nineteen rivers and their major tributaries, all radiating out from the peninsula's high-elevation core. The proposal also includes the addition of 122,661 acres of protected land. These efforts would permanently protect the world-class outdoor recreation, the peninsula's ancient forested watersheds, and the healthy rivers feeding this wild and wonderful place. Perhaps by the time you float beneath the old-growth giants that line the banks, this river will be Wild and Scenic.

PADDLER'S NOTES

Flows on the Sol Duc are correlated from nearby gauges on Americanwhitewater.org, based on flow data from the historic USGS gauge that reported flows for this river. While the run begins at the Salmon Cascade, most boaters put in below this rapid, or portage around it if starting upstream. Considered a class V drop, the falls can be a bit chunky at times and a flip could hurt.

Most of the whitewater on this run consists of fun boulder gardens that likely don't need a scout for a confident class III paddler. Catch surf on the fly and play in those eddies to your heart's content. Ledge Drop, near the end of the run, can feel more like a class IV, with a large hydraulic just right of center. Scout or portage on the left as this one is tricky to see from your boat.

For more river beta head over to AmericanWhitewater.org for a digital copy of the out-of-print *A Paddler's Guide to the Olympic Peninsula* by Gary Korb.

DIRECTIONS TO TAKEOUT

To reach the FR 2918 bridge takeout, turn on Sol Duc Hot Springs Road off US 101 at milepost 219.2. Park at mile 4.2. The river can be reached by first walking across the vegetated strip in between FR 2918 and Sol Duc Hot Springs Road, then proceeding a short distance up the forest road to the bridge.

"THE FIRST RIVER YOU PADDLE RUNS THROUGH THE REST OF YOUR LIFE. IT BUBBLES UP IN POOLS AND EDDIES TO REMIND YOU WHO YOU ARE."

—*Lynn Noel*

A kayaker cruises down the Sol Duc on a rare sunny afternoon on the Olympic Peninsula.
THOMAS O'KEEFE / AMERICAN WHITEWATER

DIRECTIONS TO PUT-IN

The put-in can be reached by driving another 3.1 miles up Sol Duc Hot Springs Road (to mile 7.3) to park at the Salmon Cascade viewing area. Check with Olympic National Park for road conditions as the road can close due to snow.

NEARBY ATTRACTIONS

Turn your Olympic Peninsula trip into a grand paddling adventure. The Elwha River recently became free flowing with the removal of two large dams. On the west side of the peninsula you'll find the Calawah, Bogachiel, Hoh, Queets, and more for paddling options on rivers and their tributaries. All these runs are proposed for Wild and Scenic designation.

Acknowledgments

Our gratitude goes out to Tim Palmer for inspiration and a legacy of river storytelling; Todd and Jaco at Wet Planet Whitewater Center for warm places to land and a steady river family; Zach with Northwest Rafting Company; the Canyons Inc. family; Dick and Wilma Shedd; Duncan Storlie and Diane Tessari; Kerr Duson; the American Packrafting Association; and American River Touring Association (ARTA). Our deepest gratitude goes to all of our family for their support, encouragement, and babysitting.

Special thanks to the incredible staff at American Whitewater: Thomas O'Keefe for fact-checking and accompanying us on the water; Kevin Colburn for the Montana connections and explorations; and Mark Singleton for his leadership of this powerhouse river conservation nonprofit.

Thanks to our contributors:
Tim Palmer, Moe Witchard, Thomas O'Keefe, Kevin Colburn, Nate Wilson, Matt Curry, Lori Turbes, Anna Wagner, Sam Swanson, Michelle Francesco, Rob Elliott, Northwest Rafting Company, Dave Fusilli, Dave Hoffman, Michael Hughes, Zach Collier, Danielle Keil, Krissy Kasserman, Kathy Lampman, Brendan Wells, Dave Gardner, Leland Davis, Curtis England, Western Rivers Conservancy, Meredyth Babcock, Jim Sullivan, Priscilla Macy, Jacob Cruser, Leif Embertson, Will Taggert, Aaron Pruzan, Kylee Allen, Katie Abercrombie, and Andrea Cracchiolo.

Flat-water paddling on the Clarion is great for people of all skill levels. WESTERN PENNSYLVANIA CONSERVANCY